4
Grün

Logo!

Teacher's Guide

Oliver Gray • Sarah Provan

Heinemann

Heinemann Educational,
Halley Court, Jordan Hill, Oxford OX2 8EJ

Heinemann is a registered trademark of Reed Educational & Professional Publishing Ltd.

OXFORD   MELBOURNE   AUCKLAND
JOHANNESBURG   BLANTYRE   GABORONE
IBADAN   PORTSMOUTH (NH) USA   CHICAGO

All rights reserved. No part of this publication may be reproduced in any material form (including photocopying or storing it in any medium by electronic means and whether or not transiently or incidentally to some other use of this publication) without the written permission of the copyright owner, except in accordance with the provisions of the Copyright, Designs and Patents Act 1998 or under the terms of a licence issued by the Copyright Licensing Agency, 90 Tottenham Court Road, London W1P 9HE. Applications for the copyright owner's written permission to reproduce any part of this publication should be addressed to the publisher.

© Oliver Gray and Sarah Provan

First published 2001

01 02 03 04 05 06 10 9 8 7 6 5 4 3 2 1

A catalogue record is available for this book from the British Library on request.

ISBN 0 435 36723 4

Produced by **AMR** Ltd.

Cover photo provided by Arcaid (Richard Bryant).

Printed in Great Britain by Thomson Litho Ltd, Scotland

Tel: 01865 888058   www.heinemann.co.uk

Contents

	page
Introduction	iv
Coverage of AQA themes and topics in *Logo! 4 Grün*	vii
Coverage of Edexcel topic areas in *Logo! 4 Grün*	viii
Coverage of OCR contexts in *Logo! 4 Grün*	ix
Coverage of WJEC topic areas in *Logo! 4 Grün*	x
Logo! 4 Grün for Scotland	xi

1 Hallo! Ich bin's! ... 12
Workbook: solutions ... 25

2 Schulstress ... 27
Kursarbeit: Die Schule ... 37
Workbook: solutions ... 38

3 Wir haben frei! ... 40
Workbook: solutions ... 49

4 Urlaub ... 51
Kursarbeit: Die Ferien ... 59
Workbook: solutions ... 60

5 Meine Stadt ... 62
Kursarbeit: Stadt/Umgebung ... 71
Workbook: solutions ... 72

6 Einkaufen ... 75
Workbook: solutions ... 84

7 Freizeit und Urlaub ... 86
Kursarbeit: Freizeit ... 95
Workbook: solutions ... 96

8 Mein Leben zu Hause ... 98
Workbook: solutions ... 106

9 Die Arbeit ... 108
Kursarbeit: Betriebspraktikum ... 118
Workbook: solutions ... 119

10 Teenies! ... 121
Workbook: solutions ... 128

Lesen/Schreiben ... 130
Solutions to Grammatik exercises ... 137
Photocopiable grids ... 138

Introduction

Logo! offers a lively, communicative approach, underpinned by clear grammatical progression.

The course is suitable for a wide ability range and includes differentiated materials in the Pupil's Books and differentiated workbooks in *Logo! 1* and *Logo! 2*. *Logo! 3* offers differentiated Pupil's Books and workbooks.

In *Logo! 4*, the Student's Books are differentiated to cater for the two examination tiers: *Logo! 4 Rot* is for the Higher level and *Logo! 4 Grün* is for the Foundation level. The workbooks also reflect the examination tiers. *Logo! 4* is specifically designed to continue from *Logo! 1, 2* and *3*, but is also suitable for students who have followed a different introductory course prior to opting to study German at GCSE or Standard Grade level.

The components

Logo! 4 Grün consists of:
Student's Book
Cassettes or CDs
Teacher's Guide
Foundation Workbook

Three different assessment packs are available to accompany *Logo! 4 Grün* and *Logo! 4 Rot* (AQA, OCR, Edexcel).

Student's Book
The Student's Book is designed to last for two years (Years 10 and 11 in England and Wales and S3 and S4 in Scotland) and contains all the language required for the preparation of the GCSE or Standard Grade examination. There are ten chapters or *Kapitel*, and it is expected that the first six will be completed in the first year of the course and four in the second.

At the end of each chapter is a summary of the vocabulary covered, arranged into subject groups. These pages, entitled *Wörter*, will serve as a valuable examination revision tool. At the end of alternate chapters there is a double-page spread entitled *Sprechen*. This page is designed to help the student prepare for the Speaking Examination, and contains example role-plays and conversations from the two preceding chapters.

At the back of the Student's Book there are four sections of further practice and reference. The *Kursarbeit* sections contain guidelines for students preparing coursework or extended pieces of writing, the *Lesen/Schreiben* pages provide further reading and writing practice and the *Grammatik* explains and practises grammar points introduced in *Logo! 4 Grün* – see separate section of this introduction for further information. Finally, there is a comprehensive German–English word list and a shorter English–German word list (*Wortschatz*).

Recorded material
There are three cassettes or CDs for *Logo! 4 Grün*. They contain listening material for both presentation and practice. The material includes passages, dialogues and interviews recorded by native speakers.

Workbooks
There are two parallel workbooks to accompany *Logo! 4*, one for Foundation level and one for Higher level. The Foundation Workbook is designed to be used alongside *Logo! 4 Grün*, while the Higher Workbook accompanies *Logo! 4 Rot*. The workbooks provide self-access reading and writing tasks and are ideal for homework. The pages of activities are cross-referenced to the units of the Student's Book that they accompany. At the end of each chapter there is a page of Grammar revision and a page for Speaking preparation. All workbook pages are referred to at the appropriate place in the Teacher's Guide, with a miniature version of the page and solutions to the activities provided at the end of the chapter.

Teacher's Guide
The *Teacher's Guide* contains:
- general overview of *Logo! 4 Grün*
- overview grids for each chapter or *Kapitel*
- clear teaching notes for all activities
- solutions for activities
- full transcripts of recorded material
- mapping charts for UK examinations
- photocopiable grids for selected listening activities in the Student's Book.

Coursework sections (*Kursarbeit*)

The coursework section in *Logo! 4 Grün* gives regular, guided practice in preparing for the coursework element of the GCSE examination. It is cross-referenced to relevant sections in the core units. Each double-page spread is linked to a GCSE theme, and always starts with a model text on that theme (at a higher level than that expected by the student). This text acts as a stimulus to give students ideas about what they might include in their own piece of work. Students are encouraged to look at the detail of the text through the structured reading activities. They are gradually guided to produce good German sentences in the various activities, through to the final task in which they are asked to produce an extended piece of writing.

The *Hilfe* column is a feature on all the spreads. It shows students language they might include and particular structures that will raise the level of their writing. It is important to remind students who are capable of achieving a grade at the upper end of the Foundation level that they should always include examples of two or three tenses in their writing.

Reading/Writing pages (*Lesen/Schreiben*)

These pages are designed to give students extra practice in reading and structured writing. There are two pages for each chapter. They are differentiated, with the *Lesen/Schreiben A* page being simpler and *Lesen/Schreiben B* a little more challenging. The intention is to give students a variety of types of authentic texts to work on. Sometimes these relate closely to the relevant chapter of the Student's Book, sometimes the link is more general. This is deliberate, to avoid the impression of all the language tasks being too tightly controlled and over-prescriptive.

Teachers may feel it is useful to work with the class on the activities, but it should also be possible for most students to work independently. They are not designed as GCSE tests, but rather as ways of developing the skills of Reading and Writing. With that in mind, teachers might allow some judicious use of dictionaries. The writing tasks are based on the language of the reading texts and the reading tasks. It is important that students understand this – once they have done all the reading tasks, they should be able to re-use much of the language they have encountered in the writing activities.

Grammar (*Grammatik*)

The key structures being introduced in a unit are presented in a Grammar box (*Grammatik*) on the Student's Book page, providing support for the speaking and writing activities. Structures that have already been introduced in *Logo! 4 Grün* sometimes need further revision – in these instances a similar box is used but with the title *Wiederholung*. Both types of boxes contain page references for the comprehensive Grammar Section at the end of the Student's Book, where all the grammar points introduced in the core units are explained fully. Grammar practice is given within the Grammar Section and in the Workbooks.

Skills and strategies

Many of the pages of *Logo! 4 Grün* have boxes giving students tips to improve their language-learning skills or to equip them with strategies that will enhance their performance in the forthcoming examination. These are highlighted by a symbol to make them easily recognisable. If the tip box is related to the pronunciation of German, the icon also shows a speech bubble symbol.

Tip box   Pronunciation box

Skills and strategies taught in the core units are listed in the Teacher's Guide, in the planning summary at the beginning of each chapter.

There is also a double-page spread devoted to examination strategies for Listening, Speaking, Reading and Writing on pp. 148–149 of the Student's Book.

Progression

The first two double-page spreads or units (*Rückblick*) of each chapter are devoted to language that will already be familiar to students; the rest of the units continue to revise earlier material but new grammar and structures are built in to the activities to ensure steady progression.

As well as the clear progression within each chapter, language is constantly recycled through all chapters in a systematic spiral of revision and extension. Clear objectives are given in the Teacher's Guide, in the planning summary at the beginning of each chapter, to help teachers plan a programme of work appropriate for the ability groups that they teach.

Assessment

There are three separate Assessment Packs available to accompany *Logo! 4*. Each pack has been written by an experienced examiner from the appropriate examination bodies (AQA, Edexcel, OCR). The design and type of questions follow the examination bodies' own papers and give much-needed regular practice in developing examination techniques.

Each pack contains assessment material at three levels, making it suitable for use with *Logo! 4 Grün* and *Logo! 4 Rot*:
- Foundation level
- Foundation/Higher level
- Higher level.

Each of the main assessment blocks represents two chapters. It is suggested that one assessment block is used at the end of each term of the two-year course, and that the final assessment be used at the end of the course as a pre-examination test.

The Logo! 4 Assessment Packs include the following important features:
- Assessments have clear and concise mark schemes for Listening, Speaking, Reading and Writing.
- Each assessment contains several tasks at each level for both Listening and Reading
- Listening assessments are accompanied by cassettes with transcripts.
- Speaking assessments contain pages for students and for teachers.
- Bilingual lists of rubrics are given, for familiarising students with the instructions used by the examination body.

For information about how the specification of each of the above examining bodies is covered in *Logo! 4 Grün*, please refer to pages vii–ix of this introduction. Information about coverage of the Welsh GCSE specification is given on page x. Information about coverage for Scottish Standard Grade examinations is on page xi. For the Northern Ireland GCSE examinations, please refer to the Heinemann website or contact the publishers by telephone to arrange for a copy to be sent to your school.

Tel: 01865 888058 www.heinemann.co.uk

The teaching sequence

Core language can be presented using the cassettes or CDs, ensuring that students have authentic pronunciation models. Often, the text is also given in the Student's Book so that students can read the new language and check the pronunciation at the same time. Next, students usually engage in a simple comprehension activity, such as a matching or true and false task, to consolidate the language taught.

Students then move on to a variety of activities in which they practise the language that has been introduced, through Speaking and Writing tasks. Some of the practice activities are open-ended, allowing students to work at their own pace and level. Ideas for additional practice are presented in the teaching notes for each unit.

Using the target language in the classroom
Instructions are usually given in German throughout. A page summarising these instructions is supplied for handy reference on p. 147 of the Student's Book. They have been kept as simple and as uniform as possible. In the Foundation Workbook, the instructions are also translated into English, so that students will not be in any doubt about what to do if they are working on their own. Classroom language is also recycled and extended in Chapter 2, which focuses on school. In the Assessment Packs, the instructions are in line with those used by the appropriate examination body, and reference pages in each pack give a bilingual list of question forms that teachers may like to photocopy and give to their students for reference purposes.

Incorporating ICT
Appropriate use of Information and Communication Technology (ICT) to support Modern Foreign Language learning is a requirement of the National Curriculum. It is an entitlement for all students.

Word-processing and desktop-publishing skills will be particularly useful for students who are preparing for the coursework option for the Writing part of the GCSE examination. References to e-mail and websites occur throughout the course, as they do in the GCSE examination papers. Students should be encouraged to e-mail contemporaries in German-speaking countries and to research authentic information in German on the internet.

A selection of useful websites is given below, but please refer to the Heinemann website (www.Heinemann.co.uk/secondary/languages) for the most up-to-date information.

Information and organisations for teachers of German:
www.linguanet.org
www.cilt.org.uk
www.all-languages.org.uk
www.goethe.de/london
www.centralbureau.org.uk

On-line services for teachers in England, with Modern Languages sections:
www.standards.dfee.gov.uk
www.becta.org.uk
www.qca.org.uk

German search engines:
www.de.yahoo.com
www.web.de
www.hurra.de
www.lycos.de

Examining bodies:
www.ocr.org.uk
www.aqa.org.uk
www.edexcel.org.uk
www.wjec.co.uk
www.ccea.org.uk

Examination revision:
www.bbc.co.uk/education/gcsebitesize/ask/german

An interactive CD-ROM giving additional reading practice for GCSE is available from REVILO. This has been written by the same author as the *Logo! 4* Students' Books, and teachers and students will find it forms a useful way to complement the reading tasks in the *Logo! 4* materials, and to practise ICT skills at the same time. The CD-ROM contains 100 Foundation level pages and 50 Higher level pages. A free demonstration pack can be ordered from REVILO – www.revilolang.co.uk.

Coverage of AQA themes and topics in *Logo! 4 Grün*

For the German modular (specification B syllabus), please use the chapters and page numbers to access the material in the order of the chapters you are covering.

My world

1A Self, family and friends
Self, family and friends: Chapter 1, pp. 6–11
Greetings and introductions: Chapter 1, pp. 14–15

1B Interests and hobbies
Activities: Chapter 3, pp. 34–37
Invitations: Chapter 3, pp. 38–41

1C Home environment
House/flat and rooms: Chapter 1, pp. 12–13
Town and region: Chapters 5 and 10, pp. 64–67 and pp. 138–139
Comparison of Germany and home country: Chapter 5, pp. 74–75

1D Daily routine
Daily routine: Chapter 8, pp. 110–111
Meals at home: Chapter 8, pp. 108–109

1E School and future plans (up to age 18)
Classroom language: Chapter 2, pp. 22–23
School routine: Chapter 2, pp. 24–25
School building: Chapter 2, pp. 26–27
School subjects: Chapter 2, pp. 20–21
Future plans: Chapter 2, pp. 28–29

Holiday time and travel

2A Travel, transport and finding the way
Travel and transport: Chapter 5, pp. 70–71
Finding the way: Chapter 5, pp. 68–69
Buying tickets: Chapter 5, pp. 72–73
Journey: Chapters 4 and 5, pp. 52–53 and pp. 70–71

2B Tourism
Weather: Chapter 4, pp. 50–51
Holidays: Chapter 4, pp. 48–49 and pp. 52–55

2C Accommodation
Accommodation: Chapter 4, pp. 56–57
Problems with accommodation: Chapter 4, pp. 58–59

2D Holidayn activities
Eating out: Chapter 7, pp. 94–97
Holiday activities: Chapter 4, pp. 54–55

2E Services
Postal services: Chapter 6, pp. 86–87
Money transactions: Chapter 7, pp. 100–101
Lost property: Chapter 1, pp. 16–17
Illness: Chapter 8, pp. 114–115
Breakdown and accident: Chapter 7, pp. 104–105

Work and lifestyle

3A Home life
Meals at home: Chapter 8, pp. 108–109
Household chores: Chapter 8, pp. 112–13
Important festivals: Chapter 8, pp. 116–117

3B Healthy living
Eating healthily: Chapter 8, pp. 118–119
Healthy/unhealthy lifestyles: Chapters 9 and 10, pp. 118–119, pp. 140–141

3C Part-time jobs and work experience
Weekend jobs and work experience: Chapter 9, pp. 126–127 and pp. 130–131
Telephone calls: Chapter 9, pp. 128–129

3D Leisure
TV programmes, etc: Chapter 3, pp. 42–43
Leisure facilities: Chapter 7, pp. 98–99 and pp. 102–103
Arrangements to go out: Chapter 3, pp. 38–39
Sporting activities: Chapter 3, pp. 34–35
Main features of book, film, etc: Chapter 3, pp. 42–43

3E Shopping
Shops, signs, facilities: Chapter 6, pp. 78–79
Buying things: Chapter 6, pp. 80–85
Complaints: Chapter 6, pp. 88–89

The young person in society

4A Character and personal relationships
Character: Chapter 10, pp. 136–137
Relationships: Chapter 3, pp. 44–45

4B The environment
Environmental issues: Chapter 10, pp. 142–143

4C Education
Issues at school: Chapter 2, pp. 28–29 and pp. 132–133

4D Careers and future plans (post age 18)
Career and future plans: Chapter 9, pp. 132–133

4E Social issues, choices and responsibilities
Teenage problems: Chapter 10, pp. 144–145
Issues concerning smoking, alcohol and drugs: Chapter 10, pp. 140–141

Coverage of Edexcel topic areas in *Logo! 4 Grün*

At home and abroad

- **Things to see and do:** Chapter 5, pp. 64–67
- **Life in the town, countryside, seaside:** Chapters 5 and 10, pp. 74–75 and pp. 138–139
- **Weather and climate:** Chapter 4, pp. 50–51
- **Travel, transport and directions:** Chapter 5, pp. 66–73
- **Holidays, tourist information and accomodation:** Chapter 4, pp. 48–59
- **Services and shopping abroad**
  Shopping: Chapter 6, pp. 75–85
  Post office: Chapter 6, pp. 86–87
  Money transactions: Chapter 7, pp. 100–101
- **Customs, everyday life and traditions in target-language counties and communities:** throughout *Logo! 4*

Education, training and employment

- **School life and routine**
  School subjects, opinions, school routine and school building: Chapter 2, pp. 20–27
- **Different types of jobs:** Chapter 9, pp. 124–127
- **Job advertisements, applications and interviews:** Chapter 9, pp. 124–133
- **Future plans and work experience**
  Work experience: Chapter 9, pp. 130–131
  Future plans: Chapters 2 and 9, pp. 28–29 and 132–133

House, home and daily routine

- **Types of home, rooms, furniture and garden:** Chapters 1 and 10, pp. 12–13 and pp. 138–139
- **Information about self, family and friends:** Chapters 1, 3 and 10, pp. 6–11, pp. 44–45 and pp. 136–137
- **Helping around the house:** Chapter 8, pp. 112–113
- **Food and drink**
  Eating at home: Chapter 8, pp. 108–109
  Eating out: Chapter 7, pp. 94–97

Media, entertainment and youth culture

- **Sport, fashion and entertainment**
  Sport: Chapter 3, pp. 34–35
  Entertainment: Chapter 7, pp. 98–99
- **Famous personalities**
- **The media:** Chapter 3, pp. 42–43
- **Current affairs, social and environmental issues:** Chapter 10, pp. 141–145

Social activities, fitness and health

- **Free time (evenings, weekends, meeting people):**
  Chapters 3 and 7, pp. 34–41 and pp. 102–103
- **Special occasions:** Chapter 8, pp. 116–117
- **Hobbies, interests, sports and exercise:** Chapters 3 and 8, pp. 34–37 and pp. 118–119
- **Shopping and money matters:** Chapter 6, pp. 78–89
- **Accidents, injuries, common ailments and health issues (smoking, drugs)**
  Ailments: Chapter 8, pp. 114–115
  Health issues: Chapters 8 and 10, pp. 118–119 and pp. 140–141

Coverage of OCR contexts in *Logo! 4 Grün*

1 Everyday activities

(a) **Home life**
House and rooms: Chapters 1 and 10. pp. 12–13 and pp. 138–139
Daily routine: Chapter 8, pp. 110–111

(b) **School life**
School routine, subjects and opinions: Chapter 2, pp. 20–21 and pp. 24–27

(c) **Eating and drinking**
General likes/dislikes: Chapter 8, pp. 108–109
Eating out: Chapter 7, pp. 94–97
Problems at a restaurant: Chapter 7, pp. 96–97

(d) **Health and fitness**
Illness: Chapter 8, pp. 114–115
Healthy living: Chapter 8, pp. 118–119
Health matters: Chapters 8 and 10, pp. 118–119 and pp. 140–141

2 Personal and social life

(a) **People – the family and new contacts**
Family and descriptions: Chapters 1 and 10, pp. 8–11 and pp. 136–137
Greeting people: Chapter 1, pp. 14–15
Invitations: Chapter 3, pp. 38–41
Good and bad points of family life: Chapters 3 and 10, pp. 44–45 and 144–145

(b) **Free time**
School activities: Chapters 3 and 7, pp. 36–37 and pp. 102–103
Sports: Chapter 3, pp. 34–35
Personal interests: Chapter 3, pp. 36–37
Weekends: Chapters 3 and 7, pp. 38–39 and pp. 102–103
Entertainment: Chapter 7, pp. 98–99

(c) **Making appointments**
Making arrangements: Chapter 3, pp. 38–41

(d) **Special occasions**
Festivals: Chapter 8, pp. 116–117

3 The world around us

(a) **Local and other areas**
Local town and region: Chapter 5, pp. 64–67

(b) **Shopping and public services**
Shopping: Chapter 6, pp. 78–79
Buying items: Chapter 6, pp. 80–85
Complaints: Chapter 6, pp. 88–89
Post office: Chapter 6, pp. 86–87
Money transactions: Chapter 7, pp. 100–101
Telephone: Chapter 9, pp. 128–129
Lost property: Chapter 1, pp. 16–17

(c) **Environment**
Weather: Chapter 4, pp. 50–51
Environmental issues: Chapter 10, pp. 142–143

(d) **Going places**
Finding the way: Chapter 5, pp. 68–69
Transport: Chapter 5, pp. 66–67 and pp. 70–71
Travel: Chapter 5, pp. 70–71
Buying tickets: Chapter 5, pp. 72–73
Accidents and car breakdown: Chapter 7, pp. 104–105

4 The world of work

(a) **Jobs and work experience**
General jobs: Chapter 9, pp. 124–127
Pocket money: Chapter 6, pp. 84–85
Work experience: Chapter 9, pp. 130–131

(b) **Careers and life-long learning**
Work and further study: Chapter 2, pp. 28–29
Future careers: Chapter 9, pp. 132–133

5 The international world

(a) **The media**
TV: Chapter 3, pp. 42–43
Other media: Chapter 3, pp. 42–43

(b) **World issues, events and people**

(c) **Tourism and holidays**
Tourist area: Chapters 4 and 5, pp. 48–49 and pp. 74–75
Holidays: Chapter 4, pp. 52–55

(d) **Tourist and holiday accommodation**
Accommodation and facilities: Chapter 4, pp. 56–57
Problems with accommodation: Chapter 4, pp. 58–59

Coverage of WJEC topics areas in *Logo! 4 Grün*

Home life

Daily routine: Chapter 8, pp. 110–113
Meals: Chapter 8, pp. 108–109
Description of house and garden: Chapter 1, pp.12–13
Members of the family: Chapters 1 and 3, pp. 8–11 and pp. 44–45

Home town and region

Local facilities: Chapters 5 and 10, pp. 64–67 and pp. 138–139
Comparisons with other towns: Chapter 5, pp.74–75

Education

School life: Chapter 2, pp. 20–27
Future plans: Chapter 2, pp. 28–29

Environmental issues

Weather and seasons: Chapter 4, pp. 50–51
Pollution and recycling: Chapter 10, pp. 142–143

Social issues

Homelessness, crime, drugs: Chapter 10, pp. 140–141
Healthy living: Chapters 8 and 10, pp. 118–119 and pp. 140–141
Injuries and accidents: Chapters 7 and 8, pp. 104–105 and pp. 114–115
Religion and politics: –

Life in other countries

People and personalities abroad: –
Global issues and events: Chapter 10, pp. 140–145
Leisure time: Chapters 3 and 7, pp.36–41 and pp. 94–99
Travel: Chapter 5, pp. 68–73
Tourism: Chapter 4, pp. 48–49 and pp. 52–59

Youth culture

Fashion and music: Chapter 6, pp. 82–83
Shopping: Chapter 6, pp. 78–89
Sport: Chapter 3, pp. 34–35
Holidays: Chapter 4, pp. 52–59

New technologies

Sending messages, accessing information: Chapter 6, pp. 86–87

The world of work

Work experience: Chapter 9, pp. 126–131
Future careers: Chapter 9, pp. 132–133

The media

Newspapers, television, film and radio: Chapters 3 and 7, pp. 42–43 and pp. 98–99
Reviews: Chapter 3, pp. 42–43

Logo! 4 Grün for Scotland

Personal information in polite/vocational context: Chapter 1, pp. 6–7 and pp. 14–15	**Simple and complex directions:** Chapter 5, pp. 68–69
Members of family: Chapter 1, pp. 8–9	**Tourist information:** Chapter 5, pp. 64–67 and pp. 74–75
Friends and friendship: Chapters 1 and 10, pp. 10–11 and pp. 144–145	**Comparisons town/country:** Chapter 5, pp. 64–67 and pp. 74–75
Physical and character description: Chapters 1 and 10, pp. 10–11 and pp. 136–137	**Helping the environment:** Chapter 10, pp. 142–143
Interpersonal problems and relationships: Chapters 3 and 10, pp. 44–45 and pp. 144–145	**Changing money:** Chapter 7, pp. 100–101
Parts of body, accidents and illnesses: Chapters 7 and 8, pp. 104–105 and pp. 114–115	**Negotiating transactional problems:** Chapters 4, 5 and 6, pp. 56–59, pp. 72–73 and pp. 80–89
Making appointments: – **Houses/rooms:** Chapters 1 and 10, pp. 12–13 and pp. 138–139	**Jobs/working and studying:** Chapters 9, pp. 124–127
Ideal house: – **Daily routine and lifestyles (comp. with countries of TL):** Chapter 8, pp. 108–113 and pp. 116–117	**Relative merits of jobs:** Chapter 9, pp. 124–133
	Work experience: Chapter 9, pp. 130–131
Life in present, past and future routines: Chapter 7, pp. 102–103	**Future employment:** Chapter 9, pp. 132–133
School (comp. with countries of TL): Chapter 2, pp. 20–29	**Travel information:** Chapter 5, pp. 70–71
	Travel plans: Chapter 5, pp. 72–73
Leisure and sports: Chapter 3, pp. 34–43	**Relative merits of different means of transport:** –
Health issues – healthy eating, exercise, drugs: Chapters 8 and 10, pp. 118–119 and pp. 140–141	**Comparisons between different countries:** Chapter 5, pp. 74–75
TV, film and music: Chapters 3 and 7, pp. 42–43 and pp. 98–99	**Weather:** Chapter 4, pp. 50–51
Food issues: Chapter 8, pp. 108–109	**Future holidays:** Chapter 4, pp. 56–57
	Ideal holidays: –
Restaurants/menus, making arrangements: Chapter 7, pp. 94–99	**Past holidays:** Chapter 4, pp. 52–59

1 Hallo! Ich bin's! (pp. 6–19)

Topic area	Key language	Grammar	Language skills
1.1 Hallo! Ich bin's! (pp. 6-7) Use the German alphabet Spell words out Use numbers 1-100 Give personal details	Revision: personal details Questions and answers: names, ages, birthdays	*sein*, (*ich*, *du*, *er/sie* and *wir* forms) Ordinal numbers in dates (*ersten ... zwanzigsten*)	German alphabet
1.2 Das Familienspiel (pp. 8-9) Talk about family members (names, ages and siblings)	Ich/Er/Sie heiße/heißt ... Ich/Er/Sie bin/ist ...Jahre alt Ich habe einen Bruder / eine Schwester / ... Geschwister / ... Brüder / ...Schwester Ich bin ein Einzelkind Mein Vater/Stiefvater Meine Mutter/Stiefmutter [+ other family memebers]	Practice of *haben*, *sein* and *heißen* (*ich*, *er*, *sie* and *Sie* plural forms)	
1.3 So sehe ich aus (pp. 10-11) Describe people's appearance (hair and eye colour, size)	Er/Sie hat blaue/braune/grüne/graue Augen Er/Sie hat graue/rote/schwarze/blonde/braune/kurze/lange Haare Er/Sie hat eine Glatze / einen Bart / einen Schnurrbart Er/Sie ist groß/mittelgroß/klein/dick/schlank/dünn	Adjective endings: freestanding and with nouns Practice of *haben*	Qualifying words with adjectives: *sehr*, *ziemlich*
1.4 Mein Zuhause (pp. 12-13) Describe a home and its furnishings	Unser/Mein Haus / Unser/Meine Wohnung hat eine Küche / eine Toilette / eine Treppe / ein Wohnzimmer / ein Esszimmer / zwei Schlafzimmer / einen Flur Es gibt einen Herd / eine Waschmaschine / ein Bett and other furniture	*Es gibt* plus the accusative *im* / *in der* used to describe location	
1.5 Guten Tag! (pp. 14-15) Greet people Use simple commands	Komm / Kommen Sie herein Darf ich vorstellen Guten Tag / Grüß Gott / Servus Wie geht es dir/Ihnen? Setz dich / Setzen Sie sich Auf Wiedersehen / Danke gut, und dir / Ihnen? / Auf Wiederhören / Tschüs	Common imperatives (*sich setzen*, *kommen herein*) Use of *dir/Ihnen* (*wie geht es dir/Ihnen?*)	Using greetings (formal and informal) *Herzlich willkommen*
1.6 Ich habe meine Tasche verloren (pp. 16-17) Describe things you have lost	Ich habe mein Handy/Geld/Portemonnaie / meine Uhr / meine Tasche / Kette / meinen Schlüssel/Pass/Ring verloren. Ich habe ... gefunden. (Die Tasche) ist klein/rot/neu/aus Gold ... ist nebem dem Computer / unter dem Stuhl / in der Tasche / auf dem Tisch / vor dem Fernseher / hinter dem Sofa	Prepositions used to indicate place: *auf*, *in*, *unter*, *hinter*, *neben*, *vor* with the dative Possessives (*mein/dein*) in the accusative	Writing a formal letter
Lesen/Schreiben (pp. 162–163)			Reading and Writing skills

- The vocabulary and structures taught in Chapter 1 are summarised on the **Wörter** pages of the Student's Book, 18-19.
- Further Speaking practice of the language of the chapter is provided on **Sprechen** p.32.
- For a selection of assessment tasks for Chapters 1 and 2, please refer to the separate Assessment Pack for your chosen examination board: AQA, OCR or Edexcel.

Logo! 4 1 Hallo! Ich bin's!

1 Wie schreibt man das? (pp. 6–7)

Students will learn how to:
- use the German alphabet
- use numbers 1-100

Key language	Juni
Zahlen 1-100	Juli
Wie heißt du?	August
Ich heiße ...	September
Wie alt bist du / sind Sie?	October
	November
Ich bin ...	Dezember
Wie schreibt man ... ?	
Mein Geburtstag ist am ...	**Grammar points**
ersten/zweiten/ dritten/vierten ... zwanzigsten/ einundzwanzigsten ...	• *sein*
	• ordinal numbers in dates
Januar	**Language skills**
Februar	• alphabet A-Z
März	
April	**Resources**
Mai	• Cassette A, Side A
	• Workbook p. 1

This spread allows students to revise and practise spelling, numbers and dates.

Remind students of the necessity both to understand someone spelling something out to them (e.g. a name, address, e-mail or website address of someone they have just met) and to be able to dictate their own details (name, address, etc., in a formal or informal situation).

Point out the letters which cause particular confusion, i.e. those which don't sound like their English equivalents. These are the letters highlighted in the text. The alphabet is recorded.

1 Hör zu und schreib die Wörter auf. (1-5) (Listening)

Students listen to the words being dictated and write them down.

Answers

1 Bonn, 2 Kronberg, 3 Liverpool, 4 Paris, 5 Ramsey Street

1 B-O-N-N
2 K-R-O-N-B-E-R-G
3 L-I-V-E-R-P-O-O-L
4 P-A-R-I-S
5 R-A-M-S-A-Y S-T-R-E-E-T

2 Partnerarbeit. Partner(in) A buchstabiert. Partner(in) B schreibt auf. (Speaking)

Pairwork dictation activity. Partner A dictates the words while Partner B writes them down. Partner B should cover his/her book. The exercise can be divided in two, with each partner doing half the words. The exercise can then continue with each partner simply choosing their own words to dictate (writing them down first so that they can be checked afterwards).

3 Hör zu und schreib die Zahlen auf. (1-10) (Listening)

Students listen to the tape and note down the numbers. As a follow-up, they can work in pairs, dictating numbers, sums, phone numbers, etc. to each other. They should write them down before dictating them, so there are no disputes about whether it is the speaker or the listener who has made the mistake!

Students may be confident that they are already capable of understanding numbers. Remind them how important it is to recognise phone numbers, bus numbers, etc., often spoken at speed.

Answers

1 5, 2 15, 3 50, 4 11, 5 41, 6 17, 7 38, 8 8, 9 76, 10 4

1 fünf
2 fünfzehn
3 fünfzig
4 elf
5 einundvierzig
6 siebzehn
7 dreiundachtzig
8 acht
9 sechsundsiebzig
10 vier

4 Schreib diese Zahlen auf. (Writing)

Students write out the numbers with the help of the printed words on this page.

Answers

1 zwölf, 2 dreiunddreißig, 3 neun, 4 neunzehn, 5 neunzig, 6 elf, 7 sechsundzwanzig, 8 sechzehn, 9 acht, 10 vierzig

5 Hör zu. Schreib das Formular ab und füll es aus. (Listening)

The scene is a quiz in the style of *Family Fortunes*. Students copy the table from the book and fill in the information. The first one is done for them. The script is not printed, so the tape may need to be played a couple of times.

Answers

Frank, 25; **Vater:** Olaf, 51; **Mutter:** Brigitte, 46; **Tante:** Heike, 39

- Zuerst die Familie Richter. Guten Abend, Frank.
- 'Abend, Christoph!
- Wie alt sind Sie, Frank?
- Ich bin fünfundzwanzig.
- Wie alt?
- Fünfundzwanzig. Hier ist mein Vater, Olaf ...
- Wie schreibt man Olaf?
- O-L-A-F.
- Und wie alt sind Sie, Olaf?
- Naja ... ich bin einundfünfzig, ja, einundfünfzig. Das hier ist meine Frau, Brigitte ...
- Wie schreibt man Brigitte?
- B-R-I-G-I-T-T-E. Ich bin sechsundvierzig ... sechsundvierzig Jahre alt. Und meine Schwester, Heike ...
- ... Heike ...?
- H-E-I-K-E. Ich bin neununddreißig.
- Neunundzwanzig?
- Nein, neununddreißig!

Grammatik: *sein*
A reminder for students of the most useful parts of *sein*. Go over useful expressions which use *sein* and stress the importance of learning this vocabulary.

6 Partnerarbeit. Mach Interviews mit *du*.
(Speaking)
Students practise their spelling and numbers in pairs with the help of the photos, based on the model dialogue provided. As a follow-up, they can make up further personalities and, if they wish, make up their own *Family Fortunes* quiz for recording on tape or video.

7a Hör zu und schreib die Geburtstage auf.
(1-8) (Listening)
Revision of months and ordinal numbers. Students listen to some dates and note them down.

Answers
1 12.4, **2** 20.3, **3** 8.5, **4** 21.9, **5** 14.7, **6** 1.1, **7** 22.6, **8** 3.8

1 Mein Geburtstag ist am zwölften April.
2 Mein Geburtstag ist am zwanzigsten März.
3 Mein Geburtstag ist am achten Mai.
4 Mein Geburtstag ist am einundzwanzigsten September.
5 Mein Geburtstag ist am vierzehnten Juli.
6 Mein Geburtstag ist am ersten Januar.
7 Mein Geburtstag ist am zweiundzwanzigsten Juni.
8 Mein Geburtstag ist am dritten August.

7b Schreib die Sätze auf. (Writing)
Students write out the answers to the previous exercise in German. The Grammar Box will help them with spelling.

Answers
1 Mein Geburtstag ist am zwölften April. **2** Mein Geburtstag ist am zwanzigsten März. **3** Mein Geburtstag ist am achten Mai. **4** Mein Geburtstag ist am einundzwanzigsten September. **5** Mein Geburtstag ist am vierzehnten Juli. **6** Mein Geburtstag ist am ersten Januar. **7** Mein Geburtstag ist am zweiundzwanzigsten Juni. **8** Mein Geburtstag ist am dritten August.

7c Partnerarbeit. (Speaking)
Students practise asking and answering questions about birthdays, finishing with their own. They should then have the opportunity to make up lots more similar little dialogues of their own.

Answers
1 am sechsten März, **2** am vierzehnten September, **3** am sechsundzwanzigsten Juni, **4** am dritten April, **5** am siebten Dezember

Further practice of the language and vocabulary of this unit is given on the following pages:
Workbook: p. 1

Logo! 4 I Hallo! Ich bin's!

2 Das Familienspiel (pp. 8–9)

Students will learn how to:
- talk about family members and themselves, giving names and ages and listing siblings

Key language	Meine Mutter/Stiefmutter/Tante/Cousine/Oma
Ich heiße ...	
Er/Sie heißt ...	**Grammar points**
Ich bin ... Jahre alt	• Practice of *haben, sein, heißen*
Er/Sie ist ... Jahre alt	
Ich habe einen Bruder / ... Brüder	**Resources**
Ich habe eine Schwester / ... Schwestern	• Cassette A, Side A
Ich habe ... Geschwister	• Workbook p. 2
Ich bin ein Einzelkind	• Sprechen p. 32, Gespräch 1
Mein Vater/Stiefvater/Onkel/Cousin/Opa	

Introduce the spread by talking about your own family (which can be done as a listening comprehension) and then inviting contributions from students about their own families, based on what they remember from earlier in the course.

1 Hör zu und lies. Was passt zusammen?
(Listening, Reading)
Students link sentences to pictures with the help of the tape. As this is revision, the tape can be played first without students looking at the book, while they note down in English what they think the sentences mean. They should then listen to the tape while looking at the sentences, to reinforce correct pronunciation.

Answers
1 c, 2 e, 3 b, 4 d, 5 a, 6 f

1 Ich habe einen Bruder.
2 Ich habe zwei Schwestern.
3 Ich habe einen Bruder und eine Schwester.
4 Ich bin ein Einzelkind.
5 Ich habe zwei Brüder.
6 Ich habe einen Bruder und zwei Schwestern.

2a Hör zu. Schreib Formulare für Peter und Sylvia und füll sie aus. (Listening)
Students fill in forms for two people, based on what they hear. Play the tape while students look at Anja's completed form on the page. Then allow time for them to draw out two more forms. Play the tape as often as necessary for the forms to be filled in. The format is a radio phone-in, with callers providing personal information.

A photocopiable grid is available for this exercise. (p.138)

Answers
Peter: Dornhausen; nein, Einzelkind; Karl, 45; Stiefmutter – Anita, 39
Sylvia: Memmingen; Bruder – Manfred, 12; Mutter – Klara, 36; Vater – Hans, 37

Beispiel
– Hallo, wer ist da?
– Hier spricht Anja aus Woltmershausen.
– Bitte?
– Woltmershausen! W-O-L-T-M-E-R-S-H-A-U-S-E-N.
– Hast du eine große Familie?
– Oh ja, ich habe fünf Geschwister, also drei Brüder und zwei Schwestern.
– Oha!
– Mein Vater heißt Rolf und er ist vierzig. Meine Stiefmutter heißt Petra und sie ist sechsunddreißig.

1
– Und nun?
– Hallo, hier ist Peter aus Dornhausen.
– Woher?
– Dornhausen. D-O-R-N-H-A-U-S-E-N.
– Hast du Geschwister?
– Nein, ich bin ein Einzelkind. Mein Vater heißt Karl und er ist fünfundvierzig.
– Fünfundvierzig?
– Ja.
– Und deine Mutter?
– Meine Stiefmutter ... Sie heißt Anita und sie ist ... Moment ... neununddreißig? ... Ja, neununddreißig.

2
– Und wer ist jetzt dran?
– Hier spricht die Sylvia aus Memmingen.
– Bitte?
– Memmingen, das schreibt man M-E-M-M-I-N-G-E-N.
– Okay, Sylvia. Hast du Geschwister?
– Ich habe einen Bruder, er heißt Manfred und er ist 12.
– Und deine Eltern?
– Meine Mutter heißt Klara und sie ist sechsunddreißig.
– Und dein Vater? Ist er auch sechsunddreißig?
– Nein, mein Vater heißt Hans und er ist siebenunddreißig.

2b Partnerarbeit. Mach Interviews mit Peter und Sylvia. (Speaking)
Students try to re-create the interviews with Peter and Sylvia based on the information they have noted down.

As a follow-up, in small groups, students can make up their own phone-in shows with people calling in. They can be famous people, friends and, most importantly, themselves, since this is very much the type of material required in Speaking Tests.

Answers

Peter: Dornhausen; D-O-R-N-H-A-U-S-E-N; Nein, ich bin ein Einzelkind; Vater heißt Karl und er ist fünfundvierzig; Stiefmutter heißt Anita und sie ist neununddreißig.

Sylvia: Memmingen; M-E-M-M-I-N-G-E-N; einen Bruder, er heißt Manfred und er ist 12; Vater heißt Hans und ist siebenunddreißig; Mutter heißt Klara und ist sechsunddreißig.

3a Lies die E-Mail und beantworte die Fragen.
(Reading)
Students read the passage and answer questions in German. Brief answers are fine but the more able can be asked to write sentences. Numbers don't need to be written out but the more able can be asked to do so.

Answers

1 Manja, 2 vierzehn Jahre alt, 3 Ültjen, 4 Dirk, 5 vierzig Jahre alt, 6 Paula, 7 achtunddreißig, 8 Kevin, 9 drei Jahre alt, 10 am ersten Oktober

3b Schreib eine E-Mail an Manja. (Writing)
Students write an e-mail back to Manja. This should be based on the e-mail printed on this page. Emphasise that this is the sort of writing task frequently featured in Writing Tests.

Further practice of the language and vocabulary of this unit is given on the following pages:
Sprechen: p. 32
Workbook: p. 2

Logo! 4 1 Hallo! Ich bin's!

3 So sehe ich aus (pp. 10–11)

Students will learn how to:
- describe people's appearance (hair and eye colour, size)

Key language
... habe/hat blaue/braune/grüne/graue Augen
graue/rote/schwarze/blonde/braune
kurze/lange Haare
eine Glatze / einen Bart / einen Schnurrbart
Er/Sie ist groß/mittelgroß/klein/dick/schlank/dunn

Grammar points
- adjective endings
- practice of *haben*

Language skills
- qualifying words (*sehr, ziemlich*)

Resources
- Cassette A, Side A
- Workbook pp. 3–4
- Sprechen p. 32, Gespräch 2
- Lesen/Schreiben B p. 163

Start the spread by describing various people the students will know well, such as staff members, TV personalities, etc. Bring in photos from magazines and describe them. Students can join in and reveal how well they remember this topic by describing friends and asking you to identify who they are talking about.

1 Hör zu und lies. Was passt zusammen? (Listening, Reading)
Students link the sentences to the pictures. First, do it as a pure listening activity in which students listen to the tape without looking at the book and note down in English (or draw) what they think the people should look like. Then they can compare them with the real pictures. Make sure they also have the opportunity to hone their pronunciation by listening to the tape while reading the sentences. The sentences can also be read out loud.

Answers
1 Mike, 2 Udo, 3 Angela, 4 Ulrike

> 1 Ich habe braune Augen und kurze, rote Haare.
> 2 Ich habe grüne Augen und blonde Haare.
> 3 Ich habe blaue Augen und lange, braune Haare.
> 4 Ich habe braune Augen und kurze, schwarze Haare.

2 Hör zu und schreib die richtigen Buchstaben auf. (Listening)
Students listen to descriptions without the help of the printed word and match the descriptions to the right pictures.

Answers
1 b, 2 d, 3 e, 4 a, 5 f, 6 c

> 1 Ich habe braune Augen und braune Haare.
> 2 Ich habe blonde Haare und blaue Augen.
> 3 Ich habe lange, schwarze Haare und grüne Augen.
> 4 Ich habe graue Augen und kurze, dunkelbraune Haare.
> 5 Ich habe lange, hellbraune Haare und blaue Augen.
> 6 Ich habe graue Haare und einen Schnurrbart.

3a Partnerarbeit. (Speaking)
Students communicate descriptions of the people pictured on the page. Partner B must prove that he or she has understood by identifying who is being described. This work can then be extended by both students drawing faces and describing them to the partner. They then compare the results.

3b Beschreib jetzt die Personen aus Übung 3a. (Writing)
Students write out their descriptions of the people in Exercise 3a. There is plenty of spelling support on the page, so demand as accurate work as possible.

Grammatik: *Adjektive*
Adjectives standing on their own do not take endings but adjectives with a noun do take endings. Ask for further examples of adjectives in both situations, e.g. *Meine Augen sind blau. Ich habe blaue Augen.*

Tip box: How to use qualifying words with adjectives
Point out to students how much more natural they will sound just by using these qualifying words.

4 Wer ist wer? Schreib die Namen auf. (Reading)
Students write down the names of the people being described, practising the topic of shape and size. Help is available in the Key Language box above.

Answers
1 Sven, 2 Kai, 3 Angelika, 4 Claudia, 5 Harry

5 Lies den Text und wähle die richtige Antwort. (Reading)
Students complete a multiple-choice task in this extended reading activity on the material from this spread. This is suitable for students to work on individually or for homework.

If students complain about having to read German handwriting (which they have to do on a number of occasions in this book), point out that this is something they will have to do both in real life and in the exam, so they will have to get used to it!

Answers

1 Sonja ist mittelgroß. 2 Sonja ist ziemlich schlank. 3 Sonja hat braune Haare. 4 Bettina ist sehr schlank. 5 Bettina hat schwarze Haare. 6 Bettina hat braune Augen. 7 Freddi ist ziemlich dick. 8 Freddi hat blaue Augen.

Grammatik: *haben*

A reminder for the students of the most useful parts of *haben*.

6 Jetzt du! (Writing)

Students write out information about themselves, based on the material on this spread. This work is suitable for homework and needs to be marked and kept for reference.

Further practice of the language and vocabulary of this unit is given on the following pages:
Sprechen: p. 32
Lesen/Schreiben B: p. 163
Workbook: pp. 3–4

Logo! 4 1 Hallo! Ich bin's!

4 Mein Zuhause (pp. 12–13)

Students will learn how to:
- describe a house or flat
- describe the furnishings in a room

Key language	Badewanne/
Mein/Unser Haus / Meine/	Dusche/
Unsere Wohnung hat	Spülmaschine/
...	Lampe/Heizung
eine Küche	ein Bett/Poster/Sofa
eine Toilette	
eine Treppe	**Grammar points**
ein Wohnzimmer	• *es gibt*
ein Esszimmer	• *im, in der* used to
ein/zwei Schlafzimmer	describe location
einen Flur	
Es gibt ...	**Resources**
einen Herd/	• Cassette A, Side A
Kühlschrank/	• Workbook p. 5
Kleiderschrank/	• Sprechen p. 32,
Tisch/Stuhl/Sessel/	Gespräch 3
Fernseher/Teppich	• Lesen/Schreiben A
eine Waschmaschine	p. 162

1a Wo ist Ludo? Hör zu und schreib das Zimmer auf. (1–7) (Listening)

Students listen and note down where Ludo is. The format is a TV show along the lines of *Through The Keyhole*. Give students a few minutes to study the illustration and revise the vocabulary before listening to the tape as many times as necessary to identify which room Ludo Kleinmann is in, in each case. Full sentences are not necessary.

Answers

> 1 im Wohnzimmer, 2 in der Küche, 3 im Badezimmer, 4 im Schafzimmer, 5 im Esszimmer, 6 in der Toilette, 7 in der Garage

```
1 – Hallo Ludo! Wo bist du?
  – In diesem Zimmer gibt es einen Fernseher und einen
    Sessel.
2 – Aha! Und wo bist du jetzt?
  – Hier gibt es eine Spülmaschine und einen Kühlschrank.
3 – Ludo, wo bist du?
  – In diesem Zimmer gibt es eine Badewanne und eine Dusche.
4 – So! Und wo bist du nun?
  – Hier haben wir eine Lampe und ein Bett.
5 – Ach, so! Wo bist du jetzt, Ludo?
  – Hier gibt es einen Tisch und Stühle.
6 – Wo bist du jetzt?
  – Äääh ... hier gibt's ein Klo!
7 – Und zum Schluss, Ludo, ... Wo bist du?
  – Hier gibt's ein Auto! Also, wer wohnt in diesem Haus?
```

Grammatik: Prepositions (*in + article*)

Emphasise that this is an area where it really is necessary either to know the genders of the nouns or to learn a good selection of correct prepositional phrases, because it is something which has no English equivalent and will lose marks if done wrongly.

1b Partnerarbeit. (Speaking)

Students replicate the TV show in pairs. They should choose which room to be in and copy the formula presented in the example. Useful language is provided in the Key Language box on page 13.

2 Schreib Sätze. (Writing)

Students write sentences describing various rooms along the lines of the example given.

Answers

> 1 Mein Haus hat eine Küche. Es gibt eine Waschmaschine und einen Herd. 2 Mein Haus hat ein Wohnzimmer. Es gibt einen Sessel und einen Fernseher. 3 Mein Haus hat ein Badezimmer. Es gibt eine Dusche und eine Badewanne. 4 Mein Haus hat ein Schlafzimmer. Es gibt ein Bett und einen Schrank.

3 Lies die Anzeigen. Was passt zusammen? (Reading)

Students match the advertisements to the German sentences. A follow-up activity can be to ask them to make a similar advert for their own house or flat, or that of a friend. More able students can produce UK-style estate agents' "particulars", using full sentences.

Answers

> 1 a, 2 d, 3 e, 4 c, 5 b

Grammatik: *Es gibt ...*

Es gibt takes the accusative (*einen, eine, ein*). *Es gibt* is inverted if something else starts the sentence. Practise this by giving sentences and the different beginnings:
Teacher: Es gibt einen Stuhl in der Küche.
In der Küche ...
Student: In der Küche gibt es einen Stuhl.
Teacher: Richtig!

4a Lies den Brief. Richtig oder falsch? (Reading)

Students read the text and the sentences and answer *Richtig* or *Falsch*. This is a reading task which should be done individually or for homework. Encourage more able students to elaborate on the answers if they can.

Answers

> 1 Falsch (drei Schlafzimmer), 2 Falsch (In der Küche gibt es eine Spülmaschine), 3 Falsch (Im Wohnzimmer gibt es einen Fernseher), 4 Richtig, 5 Richtig, 6 Falsch (In der Küche gibt es einen Kühlschrank)

4b Jetzt du! Schreib einen Brief an Olivia. Beschreib dein Haus und dein Schlafzimmer.
(Writing).
Students put what they have learnt in this spread into practice by describing their own houses. They should follow the format of Olivia's letter, paying attention to the layout. They can add in any extra details they are confident about. This work should be corrected and retained for revision reference.

Further practice of the language and vocabulary of this unit is given on the following pages:
Sprechen: p. 32
Lesen/Schreiben A: p. 162
Workbook: p. 5

Logo! 4 1 Hallo! Ich bin's!

5 Guten Tag! (pp 14–15)

Students will learn how to:
- greet people
- give simple commands

Key language	Grammar points
Komm / Kommen Sie herein	• Common imperatives (*du* and *Sie* forms)
Darf ich vorstellen ...	• *dich/sich* and *dir/Ihnen*
Guten Tag / Grüß Gott / Servus	
Setz dich / Setzen Sie sich	**Language skills**
Herzlich willkommen	• Useful expressions (*du* and *Sie* forms)
Wie geht es dir/Ihnen?	• Hello and goodbye (formal and informal)
Danke gut, und dir/Ihnen?	
Auf Wiedersehen / Auf Wiederhören / Tschüs / Nichts zu danken	**Resources**
	• Cassette A, Side A
	• Sprechen p. 32, Rollenspiel

This spread contains a selection of useful material for initial communication with a German partner or family. Start the spread by eliciting, in English, what things might be said on arriving at an exchange partner's house. Find out how many the students remember.

1a Hör zu und lies den Dialog.
(Listening, Reading)
Students listen to a dialogue which contains expressions useful for an initial meeting. Let them hear the tape once before seeing the text. They should note down in English anything they understand.

Then play the tape while they read the script. As these are such vital pieces of oral communication, the dialogue also needs to be read aloud in pairs. Make sure students realise that this dialogue is not very realistic, in that it contains both North and South German expressions. They are included for the student's information.

- Komm herein, Susan. Also, Mama, Papa, darf ich vorstellen? Das ist Susan aus England.
- Guten Tag, Frau Dresch! Guten Tag, Herr Dresch!
- Grüß Gott, Susan. Herzlich willkommen!
- Servus, Susan! Wie geht's?
- Danke, gut, und Ihnen?
- Auch gut. Setz dich bitte!

1b Schreib auf Deutsch. (Writing)
Students pick out and copy down the German equivalents of the English expressions, all of which need to be learnt.

Answers
1 Komm herein. 2 Guten Tag / Grüß Gott / Servus. 3 Darf ich vorstellen? 4 Herzlich willkommen! 5 Wie geht's? 6 Setz dich bitte!

Tip box: *Du* and *Sie* forms (greetings)
Students need to understand that it really is important not to inadvertently use the *du* form to an adult, as it could easily be seen as impolite. Give them a few examples of people and ask them to say *Du* or *Sie*: *Herr Frank / Olaf / der Lehrer / Tante Marlies*

2a Partnerarbeit. (Speaking)
This is a guided pairwork activity to be carried out in the *du* form, following the English prompts provided.

2b Wiederhole das Gespräch, aber mit *Sie/Ihnen* statt *dich/dir*. (Speaking)
The same activity as 2a, this time using the *Sie* form. For reinforcement, it would be a good idea for both dialogues to be written out.

3a Hör zu und lies den Dialog.
(Listening, Reading)
Students listen to the dialogue, which contains expressions useful for taking one's leave. Let the students hear the tape once before seeing the text. They should note down in English anything they understand. Then play the tape while they read the script. As these are such vital pieces of oral communication, the dialogue also needs to be read aloud in pairs.

- Tschüs, Susan!
- Auf Wiedersehen, Herr Dresch. Vielen Dank für Ihre Gastfreundschaft!
- Nichts zu danken, Susan.
- Tschüs, Susan!

3b Wie sagt man auf Deutsch ...? (Writing)
Students identify and copy out the German equivalents of these English expressions.

Answers
1 Auf Wiedersehen, 2 Tschüs, 3 Vielen Dank für Ihre Gastfreundschaft, 4 Nichts zu danken.

Tip Box: The use of *Auf Wiedersehen, Auf Wiederhören* and *Tschüs*.
This reinforces Exercise 3b. Make sure students understand when each of these expressions is appropriate.

4 Was passt zusammen? (Reading)
Students link the expressions to the appropriate illustrations. Make sure they look carefully at the pictures and are certain which characters are adults and which are children. It would be very helpful to note down all these expressions.

Answers
1 i, 2 g, 3 d, 4 a, 5 c, 6 f, 7 h, 8 b, 9 j, 10 e

Further practice of the language and vocabulary of this unit is given on the following pages:
Sprechen: p. 32

Logo! 4 I Hallo! Ich bin's!

6 Ich habe meine Tasche verloren (pp. 16–17)

Students will learn how to:
- describe items they have lost

Key language	Grammar points
Ich habe mein Handy/ Geld/Portemonnaie / meine Uhr/Kette/ Tasche / meinen Schlüssel/Pass/ Ring verloren Hast du … gefunden? Ich habe … gefunden (Die Tasche) ist klein/rot/ groß/neu/aus Gold … ist neben dem Computer / unter dem Stuhl / in der Tasche / auf dem Tisch / vor dem Fernseher / hinter dem Sofa	• *auf, in, unter, hinter, neben, vor* with the dative to indicate position • Possessives (*mein/ dein*) in the accusative **Resources** • Cassette A, Side A **Language skills** Writing a formal letter

Introduce the spread by seeing how much students remember about the use of prepositions of place by placing various classroom objects around the room and asking where they are.

1 Hör zu. Was ist wo? (Listening)
Students note down where the lost items are. After the exercise has been done (play the tape as many times as necessary), oral work can be carried out by asking students various questions about the illustration. For example, the teacher can make false assertions about where things are and get the students to contradict.

The descriptions of place need to be written down. One good way to arrange this would be to get students to draw labelled illustrations of their own chaotic bedrooms!

Answers
1 unter dem Stuhl, 2 in der Tasche, 3 neben dem Computer, 4 auf dem Tisch

- Mutti, ich habe meine Uhr verloren.
- Deine Uhr ist da, auf dem Tisch.
- Oh ja, danke. Aber ich habe auch meinen Schlüssel verloren!
- Ist okay. Ich habe deinen Schlüssel gefunden. Er ist in der Tasche.
- Aber ich habe meine Tasche verloren!
- Kein Problem. Die Tasche ist unter dem Stuhl.
- Aber … Wo ist mein Handy? Ich habe mein Handy verloren.
- Nein, ich habe dein Handy gefunden. Es ist da, neben dem Computer.

2 Partnerarbeit. (Speaking)
Students follow the example to create lost property conversations. The kind official has found all the items, so the answer is always going to be *Ja, …* . Point out that the child is saying *Sie* to the adult but the adult is saying *du* to the child.

3a Lies den Brief und wähle die richtige Antwort. (Reading)
Students should do this multiple-choice activity individually. It prepares them for the writing task which is to follow.

Answers
1 am Freitag, 2 ein Portemonnaie, 3 braun, 4 eine Kreditkarte

3b Schreib einen Brief an ein Restaurant. Benutze den Brief in Übung 3a und ersetze die Wörter. (Writing)
Students get practice in writing a formal letter by following the format of Oliver Bauer's original letter.

Answer
Sehr geehrter Herr,
Ich war am letzten Samstag in Ihrem Restaurant. Ich habe ein Problem. Ich habe meine Tasche verloren! Sie ist schwarz. In der Tasche ist mein Geld. Haben Sie meine Tasche gefunden?
Mit freundlichen Grüßen

4a Partnerarbeit. (Speaking)
This pairwork activity gives practice in adjectives and the rest of the language on this page. The Key Language box can be used (and added to, e.g. with more colours) to give further practice with these structures.

4b Schreib die Antworten aus Übung 4a auf. (Writing)
Students write down the descriptions. This will help them with accuracy and to retain the language. Remind them that they might well have to write down a description of something they have lost.

Answers
1 Der Pass ist klein und rot. 2 Die Tasche ist groß und grün. 3 Die Uhr ist neu und aus Gold.

Grammatik: Prepositions (*auf, in, unter, hinter, neben, vor* + dative)
Students can gain further practice by drawing their own annotated picture of obscure objects in strange places. The sillier the better!

5 Wo sind die Sachen? (Writing)

Students write down where the illustrated objects are. More able students should be encouraged to write full sentences.

Answers

1 auf dem Tisch, 2 neben dem Telefon, 3 unter dem Bett, 4 hinter der Mauer, 5 in dem Schrank, 6 vor dem Fernseher, 7 neben der Vase, 8 unter dem Sofa, 9 hinter dem Vorhang, 10 in der Tasche

---

All the vocabulary and structures from this chapter are listed on the **Wörter** pages 18–19. These can be used for revision by covering up either the English or the German. Students can check here to see how much they remember from the chapter.

Assessment materials for Chapters 1 and 2 are available after Chapter 2.

Further speaking and grammar practice on the whole chapter is provided on Workbook pp. 6–7.

Workbook

Logo! 4 1 Hallo! Ich bin's!

p. 1

1 **1** sechzehn, **2** neunundzwanzig, **3** elf, **4** sieben, **5** einundzwanzig, **6** dreizehn
2 **1** Angela, **2** Markus, **3** Barbara **4** Eva, **5** Dennis, **6** Kai
3 **1** Mein Geburtstag ist am dritten Juni. **2** Mein Geburtstag ist am zwölften September. **3** Mein Geburtstag ist am siebenundzwanzigsten Januar. **4** Mein Geburtstag ist am vierzehnten März. **5** Mein Geburtstag ist am vierten Oktober. **6** Mein Geburtstag ist am fünfundzwanzigsten Februar.

p. 2

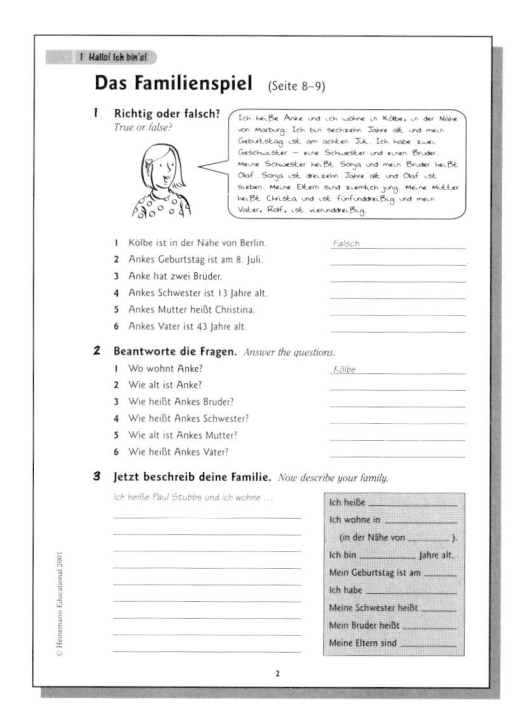

1 **1** falsch, **2** richtig, **3** falsch, **4** richtig, **5** falsch, **6** falsch
2 **1** Kölbe, **2** 16, **3** Olaf, **4** Sonja, **5** 35, **6** Rolf
3 Open-ended. 1 mark per correct sentence. Overlook minor errors.

p. 3

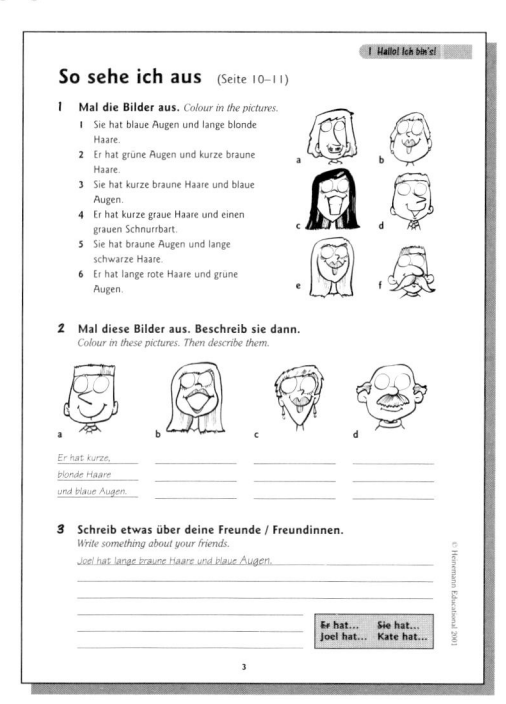

1 Pictures coloured in as follows: **1** e: blue eyes and long, blonde hair, **2** d: green eyes and short, brown hair, **3** b: short, brown hair, blue eyes, **4** f: short, grey hair and grey moustache, **5** c: brown eyes, long, black hair, **6** a: long, auburn hair and green eyes
2 Open-ended
3 Open-ended. 1 mark per correct sentence. Overlook minor errors.

p. 4

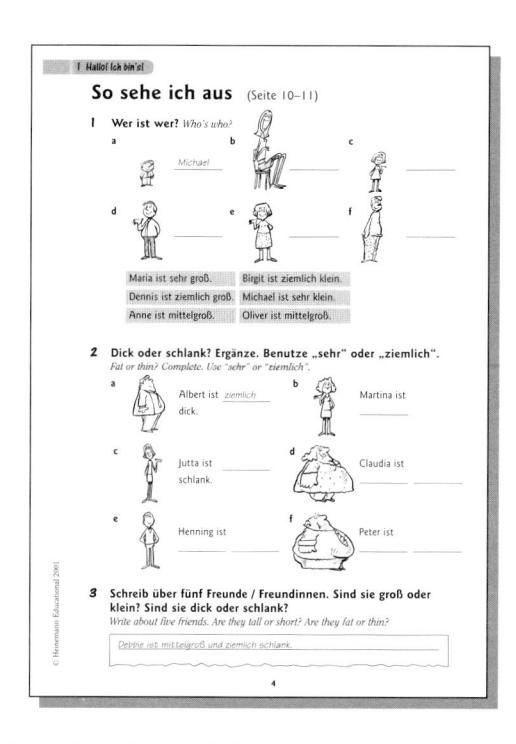

1 **a** Michael, **b** Maria, **c** Birgit, **d** Oliver, **e** Anne, **f** Dennis
2 **a** ziemlich, **b** ziemlich schlank, **c** sehr, **d** sehr dick, **e** ziemlich schlank, **f** sehr dick
3 Open-ended. 1 mark per correct sentence. Overlook minor errors.

25

p. 5

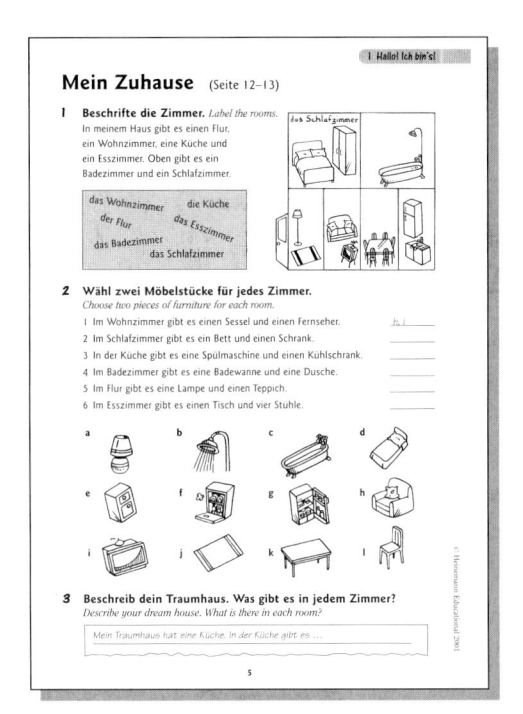

1

- das Schlafzimmer
- das Badezimmer
- der Flur
- die Küche
- das Wohnzimmer
- das Esszimmer

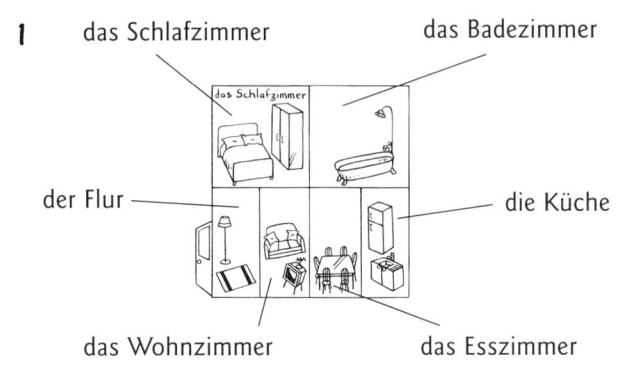

2 1 h, i 2 d, e 3 f, g 4 b, c 5 a, j 6 k, l
3 Open-ended. 1 mark per correct sentence. Overlook minor errors.

p. 6

p. 7

1 1 bin, 2 ist, 3 ist, 4 sind, 5 Bist
2 1 Mein Geburtstag ist am vierzehnten Mai. 2 Mein Geburtstag ist am dreiunzwanzigsten September. 3 Mein Geburtstag ist am siebten November. 4 Mein Geburtstag ist am dreizehnten Dezember. 5 Mein Geburtstag ist am zwölften Januar.
3 1 blaue, 2 braun, 3 blonde, 4 grün, 5 lange, schwarze
4 du bist; ich habe; er/sie/es hat; wir haben

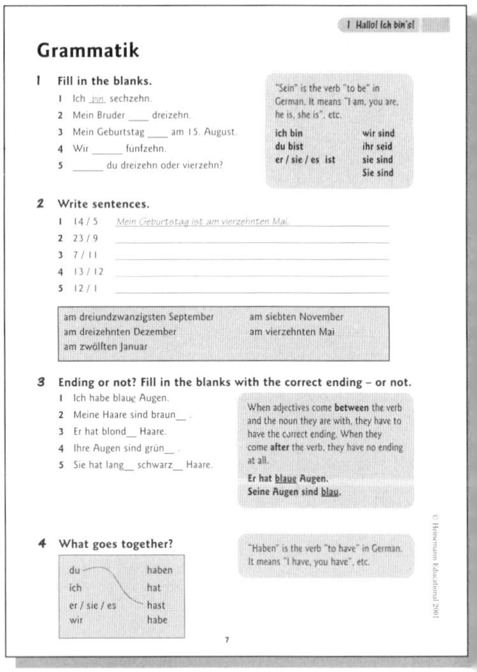

26

2 Schulstress (pp. 20–31)

Topic area	Key language	Grammar	Language skills
2.1 Was lernst du? (pp. 20–21) Talk about school subjects Give opinions	School subjects *Meine erste/zweite/dritte/vierte/fünfte/sechste Stunde ist …* *Was hast du am Montag/Dienstag/Mittwoch/Donnerstag/Freitag? Ich finde (Englisch) furchtbar/gut/interessant/langweilig/nicht gut/okay/schlecht/schwer/super.* *Mein Lieblingsfach ist …*	First and second person of *haben* Ordinal numbers Possessives: *mein + dein*	
2.2 Im Klassenzimmer (pp. 22–23) Communicate in the classroom	*Wie sagt man … auf Englisch/Deutsch? Wie schreibt man …? Was bedeutet … auf Englisch?* *Kann ich / Darf ich das Fenster aufmachen / auf Toilette gehen / mein Heft haben? Können Sie die Frage wiederholen? Ich verstehe nicht. Ich weiß nicht.*	*Darf ich / Kann ich …?* (followed by infinitive at end of sentence)	Pronunciation: *Wie sagt man …? Kann ich … sprechen? Können Sie …?* Learning set expressions by heart
2.3 Der Schultag (pp. 24–25) Talk about daily life at school	*Die Schule / große Pause / Mittagspause beginnt/ist um … Uhr. Die Schule ist um … Uhr aus.* *Es gibt … Stunden / große Pausen. Eine Stunde dauert … Minuten. Ich komme/fahre mit dem Auto/Bus/Rad/Zug/zu Fuß zur Schule. Ich gehe um … Uhr nach Hause.*	Times (*… Uhr, Viertel vor …*) Time-manner-place (*komme mit … zur Schule*)	Two meanings of *eine Stunde* Question words: asking and answering questions
2.4 Meine Schule (pp. 26–27) Describe your school Give opinions	*Meine Schule heißt/ ist in … / ist ein Gymnasium / eine Gesamtschule / eine Privatschule. Die Schule hat [numbers of pupils and teachers]. Sie ist (sehr/ziemlich) groß/klein/alt/modern. Es gibt / Wir haben [names of rooms in school]. Ich finde die Schule/Uniform/Hausaufgaben/Lehrer/den Schuldirektor gut/interessant/langweilig/nett/schwer/streng/super/toll.*	*Er/Sie/Es ist …* *Es gibt … / Wir haben einen/eine/ein …*	Qualifying words: *sehr/ziemlich* Types of school in Germany
2.5 Pläne (pp. 28–29) Talk about future plans	*Ich gehe auf die Oberschule / in die Oberstufe. Ich gehe arbeiten. Ich mache (kein) Abitur / eine Lehre. Ich verlasse die Schule. Ich mache Urlaub. Ich suche mir einen Job.*	Using present tense to express future plans	Post-16 education *Abitur, Oberschule, Oberstufe, Lehre*
Lesen/Schreiben (pp. 164–165)			Reading and Writing skills

- The vocabulary and structures taught in Chapter 2 are summarised on the **Wörter** pages of the Student's Book, 30–31.
- Further Speaking practice on the language of the chapter is provided on **Sprechen** p.33.
- Cousework pages relating to this chapter can be found on pp. 152–153 of the Student's Book.
- For a selection of assessment tasks for Chapters 1 and 2, please refer to the separate Assessment Pack for your chosen examination board: AQA, OCR or Edexcel.

1 Was lernst du? (pp. 20–21)

Students will learn how to:
- talk about school subjects
- give opinions

Key language	Ich habe …
Meine erste/zweite/ dritte/vierte/fünfte/ sechste Stunde ist …	Was ist am … deine … Stunde?
Chemie	Ich finde … furchtbar/ gut/interessant/ langweilig/nicht gut/ okay/schlecht/schwer/ super
Deutsch	
DSP	
Englisch	
Erdkunde	Mein Lieblingsfach ist …
Französisch	
Geschichte	**Grammar points**
Informatik	• first and second person of *haben*
Kunst	• possessives: *mein* and *dein*
Mathe	• ordinal numbers
Musik	
Natur	**Resources**
Physik	• Cassette A, Side A
Religion	• Workbook p. 8
Spanisch	• Sprechen p. 33, Gespräch 2 + Rollenspiel
Sport	
Werken	• Lesen/Schreiben A p. 164
Was hast du am Montag/Dienstag/ Mittwoch/Donnerstag/ Freitag?	

Before starting this spread, brainstorm all the school subjects which students remember from earlier in the course.

1 Hör zu und lies. Schreib die Tabelle ab und füll sie aus. (Listening, Reading)

Students copy the table and complete the information, based on what they hear. This can first be used as a pure listening, in which students listen to the tape without seeing the script. They can note down in English all that they understand.

As a follow-up, the script can be read aloud for pronunciation practice and also adapted with different times and different lessons.

Answers
Felix: 1 Mathematik 2 Deutsch 3 Französisch
Fatima: 1 Biologie 2 Französisch 3 Englisch

– Meine erste Stunde ist Mathematik.
– So? Meine erste Stunde ist Biologie.
– Mein bestes Fach ist Deutsch. Ich habe in der zweiten Stunde Deutsch.
– Ja? Ich habe in der zweiten Stunde Französisch.
– Ich habe in der dritten Stunde Französisch.
– Ich habe in der dritten Stunde Englisch.

2a Um wie viel Uhr beginnt die Stunde? (Reading)

Students note down the times when the illustrated lessons begin. Most will be familiar with German school timetables, but it is worth pointing out again the difference between the German and the English school day (elaborated on later in the chapter). Certain schools also have occasional Saturday lessons, although this is far less common than it used to be.

When doing this reading exercise, students should make sure they take note of which day is mentioned next to each picture. They can answer just using figures (telling the time is revised later in the chapter).

Answers
1 9.20, 2 11.20, 3 8.20, 4 10.15, 5 11.20, 6 11.20,
7 9.20, 8 9.20

2b Partnerarbeit. Schau dir den Stundenplan an und stell Fragen. (Speaking)

Pair work exercise based on the same timetable.
Format 1: Students list the subjects they have each day.
Format 2. Students ask and answer questions about what subjects they have in particular lessons.

As an extension, students should then describe their OWN timetable in a similar way. This can be done as an information gap activity, with one student dictating the information and the other filling in a blank timetable.

Another enjoyable approach is a "Battleships" idea, with students inventing a timetable and asking questions about their opponent's school day, e.g.
– Hast du Mathe in der dritten Stunde am Mittwoch?
– Nein. Hast du Deutsch in der vierten Stunde am Freitag?
– Ja!

3a Hör zu. Schreib die Tabelle ab und füll sie aus. Finden Felix und Fatima diese Fächer gut ✔ oder nicht gut ✘? (Listening)

Students copy out the form and write in a tick if the person they hear likes the subject and a cross if they don't.

A photocopiable grid is available for this exercise. (p.138)

Answers
Felix: Mathe ✘, Biologie ✘, Deutsch ✔, Französisch ✔, Englisch ✔
Fatima: Mathe ✔, Biologie ✔, Deutsch ✔, Französisch ✔, Englisch ✘

– Magst du Mathe, Felix?
– Nein! Igitt! Herr Brinkman! Ich finde Mathe nicht gut.
– Ich finde Mathe okay, aber mein Lieblingsfach ist Biologie.
– So? Ich finde Biologie nicht gut. Mein bestes Fach ist Deutsch.
– Ja? Deutsch ist okay. Ich liebe Französisch.
– Ich finde Französich auch gut. Die Lehrerin ist toll!

Logo! 4 2 Schulstress

- Ich hasse Englisch. Ich finde Englisch langweilig.
- Ich finde Englisch gut.

3b Lies den Brief und wähle die richtige Antwort. (Reading)
Students read this handwritten letter and choose from multiple-choice answers about what they have read.

Answers
1 b, 2 c, 3 b, 4 b, 5 a

3c Partnerarbeit. (Speaking)
Students ask each other what they think about subjects. Make sure they appreciate the importance of *Ich finde ...* and use it. Emphasise the likelihood that in real life and in the Speaking Test they are very likely to need to say *Mein Lieblingsfach ist ...*

Grammatik: *mein und dein*
Explain the importance of the correct ending and elicit as many examples as students can think of, e.g. *mein Haus, mein Vater, meine Schwester, meine Katze*.

4 Schreib einen Brief an Kai. (Writing)
Students write a letter to Kai using the prompts given.

Further practice of the language and vocabulary of this unit is given on the following pages:
Sprechen: p.33
Lesen/Schreiben A: p. 164
Workbook: p. 8

2 Im Klassenzimmer (pp. 22–23)

Students will learn how to:
- communicate in the classroom

Key language	Grammar points

Wie sagt man ... auf Englisch/Deutsch?
Wie schreibt man ...?
Was bedeutet ... auf Englisch?
Kann ich / Darf ich ...
  Englisch sprechen?
  das Fenster aufmachen?
  auf Toilette gehen?
  mein Heft haben?
Können Sie die Frage wiederholen?
Ich verstehe nicht
Ich weiß nicht
	• *Darf ich / Kann ich ...?*
	
	Language skills
	• Pronunciation: *Wie sagt man ...? Kann ich ... sprechen? Können Sie ...?*
	• Learning set expressions by heart
	
	Resources
	• Cassette A Side A
	• Workbook p. 9

Before starting work on this spread, invite students to ask as many classroom questions in German as they can remember. Prompts can be provided by mimes. They can then compare their ideas with those on the first page of the spread.

1 Hör zu. Wer fragt was? (Listening)
First, allow students to read and practise pronouncing the expressions in the speech bubbles. Students then identify who is asking which question by listening to the tape as often as necessary in order to write down the names of the speakers.

Answers
Kevin d, Isabell c, Björn b, Sina e, Jasmin f, Florian a

> – Herr Schultz!
> – Ja, Kevin?
> – Darf ich bitte auf Toilette gehen?
> – Okay, Kevin.
> – Herr Schultz!
> – Ja, Isabell?
> – Kann ich bitte das Fenster aufmachen?
> – Ja, Isabell.
> – Herr Schultz!
> – Ja, Björn?
> – Wie sagt man „doof" auf Englisch?
> – „Stupid", Björn.
> – Herr Schultz!
> – Ja, Sina?
> – Sina: Wie schreibt man „stupid"?
> – S-T-U-P-I-D.
> – Herr Schultz!
> – Ja, Jasmin?
> – Kann ich bitte mein Heft haben?
> – Hier, bitte schön, Jasmin.
> – Herr Schultz!

> – Ja, Florian?
> – Kann ich bitte Englisch sprechen?
> – Ja, natürlich, Florian, das ist eine Englischstunde!

Tip box: Pronunciation help for useful classroom phrases
Students need to practise sounding as "un-English" as possible when using these expressions in their Speaking Test.

> Wie sagt man "stupid" auf Englisch?
> Was bedeutet "Fenster" auf Englisch?
> Darf ich bitte Deutsch sprechen?
> Kann ich bitte Englisch sprechen?
> Können Sie bitte die Frage wiederholen?
> Ich verstehe nicht.
> Ich weiß nicht.

Grammatik: the difference between *Kann ich ...?* and *Darf ich ...?*
Remind students of just how common and useful sentences beginning *Kann ich ...* are. Make sure they understand how to use the slightly more polite *Darf ich ...?* .

2 Du bist in der mündlichen Prüfung. Was sagst du? (Speaking)
Students look at the English descriptions of situations they may encounter and decide what to say. These items should also be written down for future reference.

Answers
1 Was bedeutet „Jugendherberge" auf Englisch?
2 Können Sie bitte die Frage wiederholen? 3 Ich verstehe nicht. 4 Wie sagt man „computer" auf Deutsch? 5 Ich weiß nicht. 6 Darf ich bitte auf Toilette gehen?

Further practice of the language and vocabulary of this unit is given on the following pages:
Workbook: p. 9

Logo! 4 2 Schulstress

3 Der Schultag (pp. 24–25)

Students will learn how to:
- talk about daily life at school

Key language
Die Schule / große Pause / Mittagspause beginnt/ ist um … Uhr
Die Schule ist um … Uhr aus
Es gibt … Stunden / große Pausen
Eine Stunde dauert … Minuten
Ich komme / fahre mit dem Auto/Bus/Rad/Zug/zu Fuß zur Schule
Ich gehe um … Uhr nach Hause

Grammar points
- times (… *Uhr*, *Viertel vor* …)
- time-manner-place (*komme mit … zur Schule*)

Language skills
- two meanings of *eine Stunde*
- question words and asking and answering questions

Resources
- Cassette A Side A
- Workbook pp. 10–11
- Sprechen p. 33, Gespräch 3

The clocks at the top of the page illustrate various times, not necessarily particular references to German or English school days. Before starting this spread, take the opportunity to revise telling the time.

1 Hör zu und lies den Dialog. Ordne die Sätze unter *England* oder *Deutschland*. (Listening, Reading)

Students listen to a comparison of a German and English school day. They copy the grid and write in the phrases under the headings *England* and *Deutschland*. The script of this listening task is also printed on the page.

Depending on the ability level of the students, it can be used as a "pure" listening task or they can be allowed to see the page at the same time as listening.

In Germany, as in England, exact timings of the school day vary from school to school. The ones presented here are fairly typical. The word *Vollversammlung* is provided as a near equivalent to the English daily Assembly (which German schools do not have). Such vocabulary is occasionally provided in this book because it is necessary for students to describe their OWN experiences.

Answers
England: Beginnt um 9.00; Vollversammlung – ja; 8 Stunden pro Tag; Stunde = 35 Minuten
Deutschland: Beginnt um 7.45; Vollversammlung – nein; 5 oder 6 Stunden pro Tag; Stunde = 45 Minuten

---

– Carolin, du warst in Bristol. Wie ist die Schule in England?
– Bei uns in Hamburg beginnt die Schule um Viertel vor acht, aber in England beginnt sie um neun Uhr. Dann gibt's eine Vollversammlung, das heißt „assembly" auf Englisch. Bei uns in Deutschland gibt es keine Vollversammlung.
– Wie viele Stunden gibt es in Bristol pro Tag in der Schule?
– Es gibt acht Stunden. Aber eine Stunde dauert nur 35 Minuten. In Deutschland dauert eine Stunde 45 Minuten. Und in Deutschland haben wir nur 5 oder 6 Stunden pro Tag. In der Schule in Bristol haben sie 8 Stunden!

2 Wähle die richtige Antwort. (Reading)

Students read four extracts from a letter which Carolin has written during her stay in Bristol. They answer the questions by selecting from the German answers provided. More able students should be asked to try and write full sentences.

Answers
1 um 11 Uhr, 2 um 12.45, 3 in der Schule, 4 zu Hause, 5 um 16 Uhr, 6 um 1 Uhr

Tip box: The two different meanings for *eine Stunde*
Make sure that students understand this apparent anomaly.

3a Partnerarbeit. Lies das Gespräch vor.
(Speaking, Reading)

Working in pairs, students construct a dialogue about their school day based on the material provided. Make sure that both partners do both the asking and the answering.

Wiederholung: *wie, wann, wie viele, wie lange, was*

Students need both to use and understand these words. Explain that if they mistake, for example, *Wie kommst du zur Schule?* with *Wann kommst du zur Schule?*, they will lose vital marks.

3b Jetzt beantworte die Fragen für DEINE Schule. (Speaking)

Further pair work based on 3a. This time, the students must alter the variables in the brackets, in order to give a truthful account. They can learn the responses by heart for possible use in the Speaking Test.

4 Schreib einen Artikel über deinen Schultag. Beantworte die Fragen in Übung 3a.
(Writing)

Students construct a written record of what they have learnt in this spread by writing down their answers to the questions in Exercise 3 in a paragraph. This must then be learnt by heart.

> Further practice of the language and vocabulary of this unit is given on the following pages:
> Sprechen: p. 33
> Workbook: pp. 10–11

Logo! 4 2 Schulstress

4 Meine Schule (pp. 26–27)

Students will learn how to:
- describe their school
- give opinions

Key language
Meine Schule heißt …
Die Schule ist ein
  Gymnasium /
  eine Gesamtschule /
  eine Privatschule
Die Schule hat … Schüler
  und Schülerinnen /
  Lehrer und
  Lehrerinnen
Die Schule ist in …
Sie ist sehr/ziemlich …
groß/klein
modern/alt
Es gibt / Wir haben …
… Klassenzimmer,
ein Lehrerzimmer
eine Aula/Bibliothek/
  Turnhalle
einen Schulhof/
  Informatikraum
zwei/mehrere Labors
Ich finde die Schule /
  die Uniform /
  die Hausaufgaben /
  den Schuldirektor /
die Lehrer gut/
interessant/langweilig/
nett/schwer/streng
super/toll

Grammar points
- Er/Sie/Es ist …
- Es gibt / Wir haben einen/eine/ein …

Language skills
- qualifying words: *sehr, ziemlich*
- Types of school in Germany

Resources
- Cassette A Side A
- Workbook p. 12
- Sprechen p. 33, Gespräch 1
- Lesen/Schreiben B p. 165
- Kursarbeit pp. 152–153

Before starting work on this spread, elicit as many vocabulary items as possible for physically describing a school. Then compare them with those provided in the illustration.

Tip box: Types of school plus the word *Turnhalle*.
As in the UK, there are many regional variations within the German school system, providing different structures and titles for types of school The most common ones are provided here, along with the prominent "false friend", *Gymnasium*. Make sure students know the term for their own school and point out that other types of school are very likely to be asked about in Listening and Reading Tests.

1 Hör zu und lies den Text. Wähle die richtige Antwort. (Listening, Reading)
Students read the school description and select the correct answer from two alternatives. Answers should be written down.

Answers
1 Die Schule ist ein Gymnasium. 2 Die Schule hat 900 Schüler und Schülerinnen. 3 Die Schule hat 60 Lehrer und Lehrerinnen. 4 Die Schule ist in Koblenz. 5 Man kann auf dem Schulhof Fußball spielen. 6 Die Turnhalle ist klein. 7 Die Aula ist groß. 8 Es gibt mehrere Labors.

> Meine Schule heißt Frank-Meyer-Schule und ist ein Gymnasium in Koblenz. Die Schule ist ziemlich groß und ganz modern. Wir haben 900 Schüler und Schülerinnen und 60 Lehrer und Lehrerinnen. Wir haben viele Klassenzimmer, eine Bibliothek, eine große Aula, eine kleine Turnhalle, mehrere Labors und natürlich einen Schulhof. Da spielen wir Fußball. Ich mag meine Schule sehr.

2a Partnerarbeit. Mach ein Interview und beschreib diese Schule. (Speaking)
Students use the information about the Frank-Meyer-Schule to construct an interview. The information is taken from the reading and listening text in Exercise 1 but is also provided alongside. Make sure that both partners have the opportunity to ask and answer the questions.

Tip box: A reminder to use *sehr* and *ziemlich*
It cannot be emphasised too often the immediate and beneficial effect that using such qualifying words has on making the language sound more natural.

2b Partnerarbeit. Mach mit den Fragen aus Übung 2a ein Interview über DEINE Schule. (Speaking)
Students repeat the pairwork exercise from 2a but this time insert the true information about their own school.

Grammatik: Using *Er, Sie* or *Es ist* … depending on the gender of the noun
Explain that it is tempting to use *es* each time we want to say "it", because of the influence of English. Remind students that there are three German words for "it" and that care must be exercised. The example given in the Key Language box is *Sie ist* … meaning "It is …" (referring to *die Schule*).

3 Partnerarbeit. (Speaking)
Students should now express opinions about their own school, using the language provided in the Key Language box. They must understand that giving opinions is a vital element in gaining a high grade.

When the conversation has been conducted both ways round, students write down the information provided in the answers.

4 Beschreib deine Schule. (Writing)
Students now write a paragraph describing their school, using the Key Language box and the answers to the questions in Exercise 2. The work should be done for homework, preferably well-presented using a computer, and must also be learnt by heart.

Further practice of the language and vocabulary of this unit is given on the following pages:
Sprechen: p. 33
Lesen/Schreiben B: p. 165
Workbook: p. 12

The activities of this unit form an ideal introduction to coursework preparation. For further information and guidelines about the preparation of coursework on this topic, please refer to the **Coursework** spread pp. 152–153.

Logo! 4 2 Schulstress

5 Pläne (pp. 28–29)

Students will learn how to:
- talk about future plans

Key language	Language skills
Ich gehe auf die Oberschule / in die Oberstufe	• useful sixth-form vocabulary: *Abitur, Oberschule, Oberstufe, Lehre*
Ich gehe arbeiten	
Ich mache (kein) Abitur / eine Lehre	**Resources**
Ich verlasse die Schule	• Cassette A Side A
Ich mache Urlaub	• Workbook p. 13
Ich suche mir einen Job	• Sprechen p. 33, Gespräch 4

Grammar points
- using present tense to express future plans

This spread is likely to contain much new material. Explain to the students that this is an area of the syllabus which they will need for talking or writing about their future education plans.

1 Hör zu und lies. Finde die Ausdrücke im Text. (Listening, Reading)

Students first listen to the tape and note down in English as much as they can understand. They then listen again to identify and write down the German equivalents of some English expressions. In order to do this, they will probably need to have the text in front of them.

Answers
1 Ich suche mir einen Job. 2 Ich gehe in die Oberstufe.
3 Ich mache Urlaub. 4 Ich gehe auf die Oberschule.
5 Ich verlasse die Schule. 6 Ich mache Abitur. 7 Ich mache eine Lehre. 8 Ich mache kein Abitur.

– Was machst du nächstes Jahr, Dennis?
– Ich gehe auf die Oberschule und mache Abitur.
– Gut. Und du, Lars?
– Ich mache kein Abitur. Ich verlasse die Schule und mache eine Lehre.
– Und du, Fiona? Was machst du nächstes Jahr?
– Ich mache Urlaub in der Türkei, dann gehe ich in die Oberstufe und lerne für mein Abitur.
– Und du, Ines?
– Ich suche mir einen Job.

Tip box: Vocabulary help for discussing plans after GCSEs

Because the school systems vary so much, there is no exact equivalent of the British Sixth Form College. In this book, we have called it the *Oberschule*. Apprenticeships are now rare in the UK but very much alive in Germany.

The word *Lehre* needs to be recognised and can be used to convey any type of training scheme.

Grammatik: Using the present tense to talk about the future

The syllabus requires students to demonstrate use of the future tense. Explain that the most common way to do this in German is to use the present. To show the examiner that they mean the future, they should include expressions like *Nächstes Jahr, Wenn ich die Schule verlasse*, etc. Explain that they will be learning another way to talk about the future later.

2a Was passt zusammen? (Reading)

Students match each quote to the correct picture.

Answers
1 e, 2 b, 3 c, 4 f, 5 d, 6 a

2b Partnerarbeit. Schau die Bilder in Übung 2a an und mach Dialoge. (Speaking)

This is an information gap activity. One student chooses a sentence from Exercise 2a and the other identifies which picture is being referred to. They can swap roles.

3 Lies die Pläne. Sind die Sätze falsch oder richtig? (Reading)

Students read the notes made by a German teacher about the destinations of her students. They then note down whether the sentences are true or false. More able students can insert the correct answers to the false sentences.

Answers
1 falsch, 2 falsch, 3 richtig, 4 falsch, 5 richtig, 6 falsch, 7 falsch, 8 richtig

4 Jetzt du! Was machst du nächstes Jahr? Schreib es auf. (Writing)

Students note down a simple sentence about what they themselves plan to do next year. Encourage the more able to elaborate with more information (e.g. which college in which town, what subjects they will take, etc.).

Further practice of the language and vocabulary of this unit is given on the following pages:
Sprechen: p. 33
Workbook: p. 13

All the vocabulary and structures from this unit are listed on the **Wörter** pages 30–31. These can be used for revision by covering up either the English or the German. Students can check here to see how much they remember from the chapter.

Assessment materials for Chapters 1 and 2 are available after Chapter 2.

For further speaking and grammar practice for the whole chapter, see pp. 14–15 of the **Workbook**.

Kursarbeit

Logo! 4 2 Schulstress

2 Die Schule (pp. 152–153)

The coursework section in *Logo! 4 Grün* gives regular, guided practice in preparing for the coursework element of the GCSE examination. It is cross-referenced to relevant sections in the core units. Each double-page spread is linked to a GCSE theme, and always starts with a model text on that theme (at a higher level than that expected by the student). This text acts as a stimulus to give students ideas about what they might include in their own piece of work. Students are encouraged to look at the detail of the text through the structured reading activities. They are gradually guided to produce good German sentences in the various activities, through to the final task in which they are asked to produce an extended piece of writing.

The *Hilfe* column is a feature on all the spreads. It shows students language they might include and particular structures that will raise the level of their writing. It is important to remind students who are capable of achieving a grade at the upper end of the Foundation level that they should always include examples of two or three tenses in their writing.

This spread guides students to produce an extended piece of writing on the topic of school.

1 Schreib die unterstrichenen Wörter auf Deutsch und Englisch hin.
Students write out the underlined words both in German and English, using a dictionary or the glossary if necessary.

Answers

Fragen = answer; beantworten = to answer;
Es gibt = There is/are; ungefähr = about;
Wie = How; Lieblingsfächer = favourite subjects;
Erdkunde = grography; Kunst = art; Informatik = IT;
früher = earlier; erste Stunde = first lesson;
Frühstück = breakfast; verlasse = leave;
Hausaufgaben = homework; jeden Tag = every day;
anderthalb = one and a half; fertig = ready (finished);
oder = or; Schulmannschaft = school team

2 Du bist Tobias. Beantworte die Fragen. Die Antworten sind braun.
Students answer the questions as if they are Tobias. The answers are all in brown in the text.

Answers

1 Meine Schule ist eine große Realschule in Hamburg. 2 Es gibt ungefähr 900 Schüler. 3 Die Schule liegt in der Stadtmitte in der Nähe vom Krankenhaus. 4 Ich fahre mit dem Rad zur Schule. 5 Ich fahre mit dem Bus, wenn es regnet. 6 Kunst ist interessant. 7 Meine Lieblingsfächer sind Sport und Informatik. 8 Die erste Stunde beginnt um Viertel vor acht. 9 Ich verlasse das Haus um 7.30 Uhr. 10 Ich komme um 7.30 Uhr in der Schule an. 11 Wir haben sechs Stunden pro Tag. 12 Die Schule ist um 1.20 Uhr aus. 13 Ich bekomme jeden Tag in zwei Fächern Hausaufgaben. 14 Ich sehe fern oder ich höre Musik.

3 Jetzt beantworte die Fragen für dich.
Now students answer the questions for themselves.

4 Schreib eine E-Mail an deinen Brieffreund/deine Brieffreundin. Beschreib deine Schule.
Students should now be ready to write their own e-mail to a penfriend using the *Hilfe* column as support.

Hilfe

Tips for students to use when writing an e-mail:
- use answers from Activity 3
- starting and finishing an e-mail
- using link words
- saying you like something
- expressing opinions

Workbook

p. 8

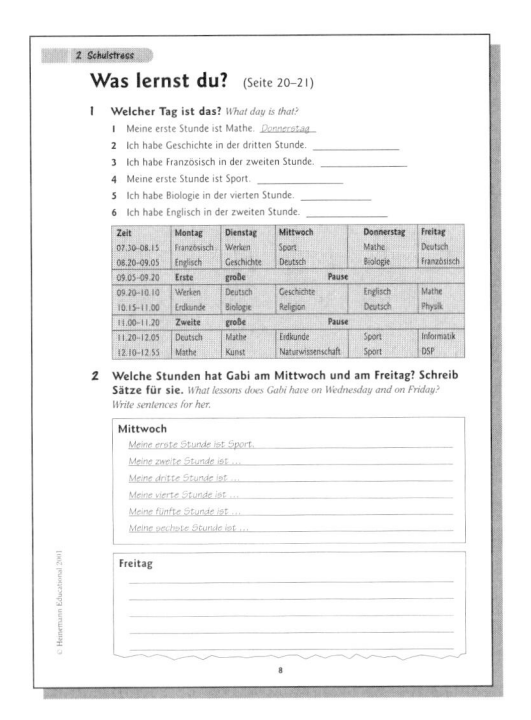

1 1 Donnerstag, **2** Mittwoch, **3** Freitag, **4** Mittwoch, **5** Dienstag, **6** Montag
2 Meine erste Stunde ist Sport. Meine zweite Stunde ist Deutsch. Meine dritte Stunde ist Geschichte. Meine vierte Stunde ist Religion. Meine fünfte Stunde ist Erdkunde. Meine sechste Stunde ist Naturwissenschaft

p. 9

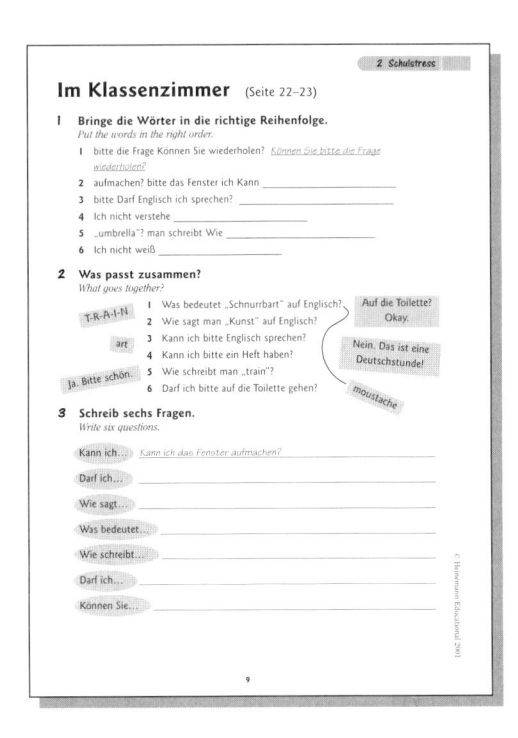

1 1 Können Sie bitte die Frage wiederholen? **2** Kann ich bitte das Fenster aumachen? **3** Darf ich bitte Englisch sprechen? **4** Ich verstehe nicht. **5** Wie schreibt man „umbrella"? **6** Ich weiß nicht.
2 1 moustache, **2** art, **3** Nein. Das ist eine Deutschstunde! **4** Ja. Bitte schön. **5** T-R-A-I-N, **6** Auf die Toilette? Okay
3 Open-ended.

p. 10

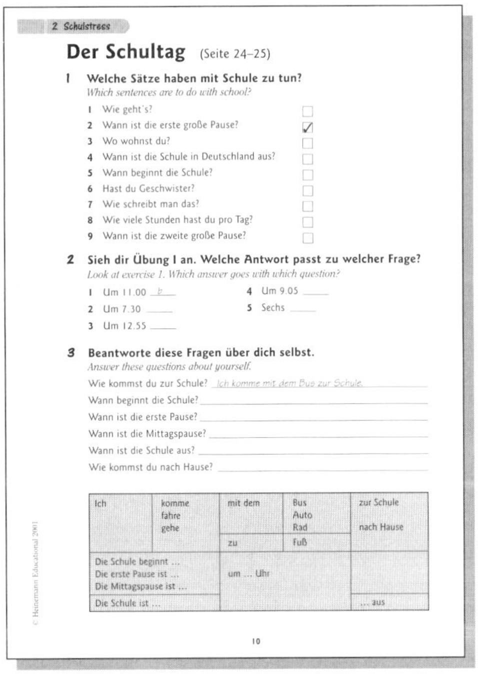

1 2, 4, 5, 8, 9
2 1 i, **2** e, **3** d, **4** b, **5** h
3 Open-ended

p. 11

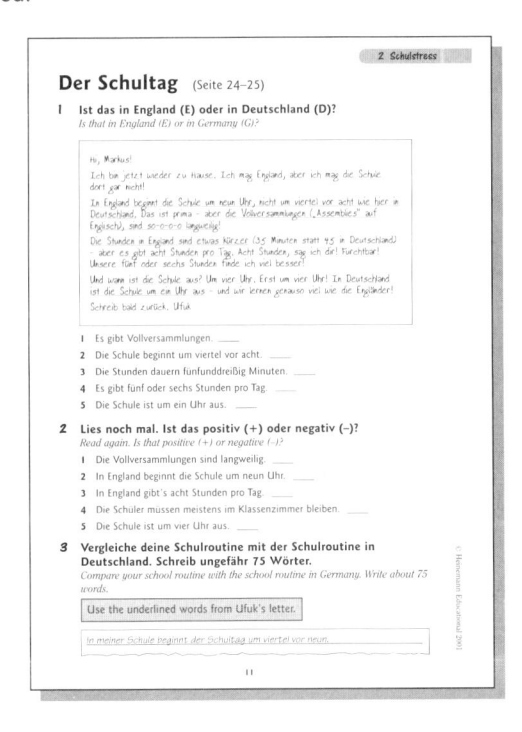

1 1 E, **2** G, **3** E, **4** G, **5** G,
2 1 –, **2** +, **3** –, **4** +, **5** –,
3 Open-ended. Overlook minor errors.

38

p. 12

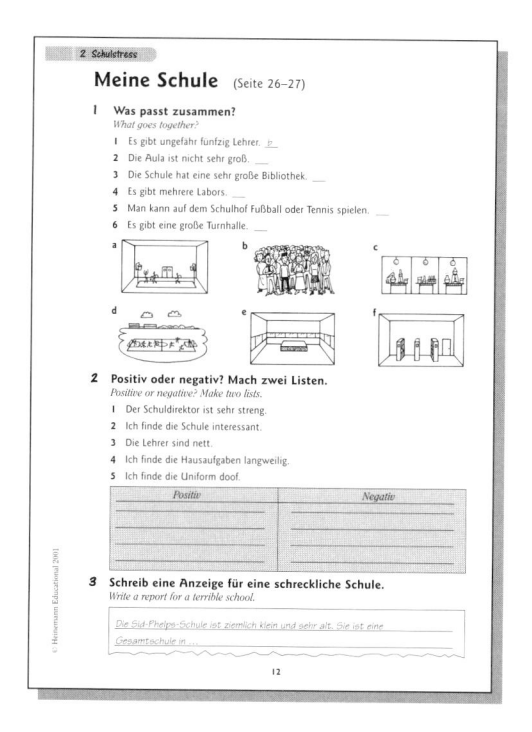

1 1 b, 2 e, 3 f, 4 c, 5 d, 6 a
2 Positiv: 2, 3, Negativ: 1, 4, 5
3 Open-ended. 1 mark per correct sentence. Overlook minor errors.

p. 13

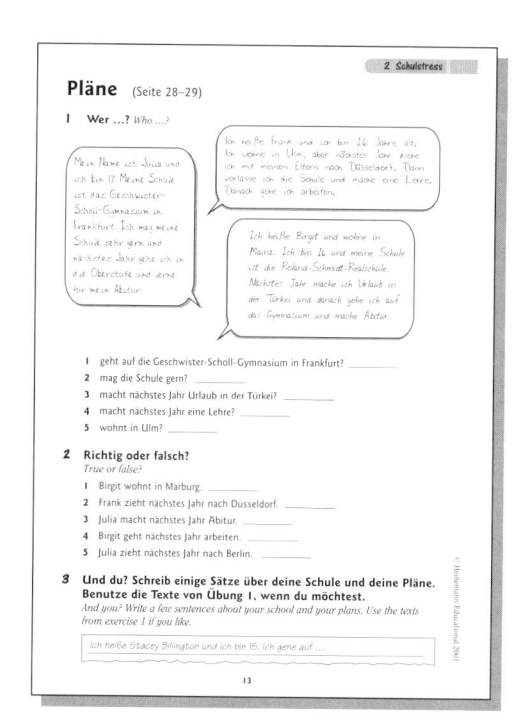

1 1 Julia, 2 Julia, 3 Birgit, 4 Frank, 5 Frank
2 1 falsch, 2 richtig, 3 richtig, 4 falsch, 5 falsch
3 Open-ended. 1 mark per correct sentence. Overlook minor errors.

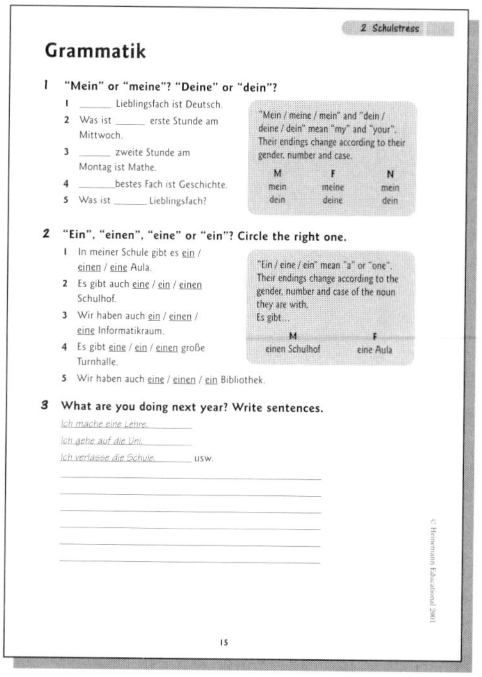

p. 14

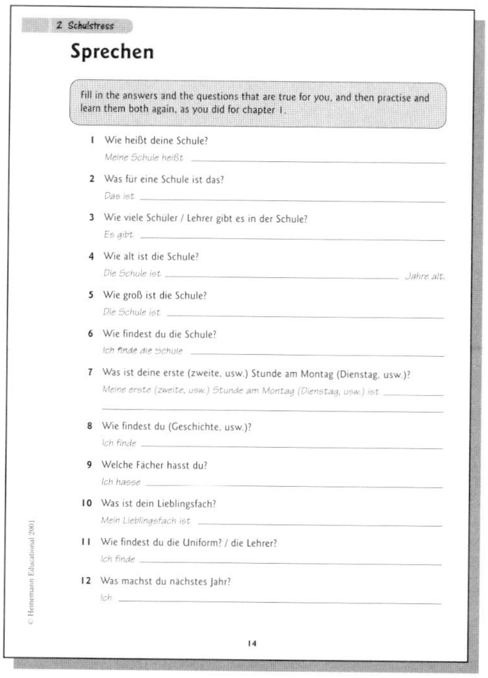

p. 15

1 1 Mein, 2 deine, 3 Meine, 4 Mein, 5 dein
2 1 eine, 2 einen, 3 einen, 4 eine, 5 eine
3 Open-ended

3 Wir haben frei! (pp. 34–47)

Topic area	Key language	Grammar	Language skills
3.1 Sport (pp. 34–35) Describe your sporting activities	Ich spiele Basketball/Federball/Fußball/Tischtennis/Rugby/Volleyball. Ich gehe angeln / ins Fitnesszentrum. Ich fahre Rad/Ski. Ich reite/schwimme/segele. Manchmal / jeden Tag / am Wochenende / am Samstag / einmal/zweimal in der Woche / oft / im Winter	First person of *spielen, gehen, fahren, reiten, schwimmen, segeln*	Tips on sports vocabulary Pronunciation of *s*
3.2 Hobbys (pp. 36–37) Talk about other hobbies	Ich lese gern Bücher/Zeitschriften. Ich höre gern Musik. Ich spiele gern Gitarre/Klavier/Computer usw. Ich sehe gern fern. Ich sammle gern Briefmarken. Ich gehe gern ins Kino/Theatre / in die Disco. Ich mache gern Fotos.	Use of *gern* and *nicht gern*	
3.3 Einladungen (p. 38–39) Give and respond to invitations	Möchtest du [places] gehen? Möchtest du schwimmen/tanzen gehen / zu meiner Party kommen? Wann treffen wir uns? Um ... Uhr. Wo treffen wir uns? Vor dem / Im Bahnhof/Kino/Theater/Rathaus/Sportzentrum/Schwimmbad. Vor der / In der Disco/Stadt.	*in den, in die, ins* used to invite someone somewhere *im, in der, vor dem, vor der* used to indicate place	
3.4 Ausreden (p. 40–41) Explain and make excuses	Möchtest du heute Abend / morgen / am Samstag / am Wochenende ...? Nein, ich kann nicht, weil ich müde bin / krank bin / kein Geld habe / zu viele Hausaufgaben habe. Ja, ich komme gern mit.	*Ich kann (nicht) ...* with verb to end *Weil* used in answering questions, verb to end plus comma if necessary	Advice to learn a set of excuses and reasons
3.5 Wir sehen fern (pp. 42–43) Talk about TV and radio	Ich sehe (nicht) gern ... Das ist ein Krimi / eine Serie / ein Film / eine Quizsendung / eine Musiksendung / die Nachrichten. Meine Lieblingssendung heißt ... (Serien) finde ich toll/interessant/langweilig/doof usw.	Inversion (*Serien finde ich toll*)	*das Programm, die Sendung gucken*
3.6 Wir verstehen uns gut (pp. 44–45) Talk about getting on with people	Was ist los? Ich bin sauer. Ich habe Ärger mit meiner Mutter. Meine Eltern sind geschieden. Ich verstehe mich (nicht) gut mit meiner Mutter / meinem Vater. Das ist unfair! Du hast Pech/Glück! Es ist mir egal.	The dative after *Ich verstehe mich (nicht) gut mit ...* Recognising common verbs in the imperfect	Answers must match the tense of questions Useful expressions
Lesen/Schreiben (pp. 166–167)			Reading and Writing skills

- The vocabulary and structures taught in Chapter 3 are summarised on the **Wörter** pages of the Student's Book, 46–47.
- Further Speaking practice on the language of the chapter is provided on **Sprechen** p. 62.
- For a selection of assessment tasks for Chapters 3 and 4, please refer to the separate Assessment Pack for your chosen examination board: AQA, OCR or Edexcel.

Logo! 4 3 Wir haben frei!

1 Sport (pp. 34–35)

Students will learn how to:
- describe their sporting activities

Key language
Ich spiele Basketball/ Federball/Tischtennis/ Fußball/Rugby/ Volleyball
Ich gehe angeln / ins Fitnesszentrum
Ich fahre Rad/Ski
Ich reite/schwimme/ segele
oft/manchmal/jeden Tag/am Wochenende/ am Samstag/einmal in der Woche/zweimal in der Woche/im Winter

Grammar points
- First person of *spielen, gehen, fahren, reiten, schwimmen, segeln*

Language skills
- German sports vocabulary
- Pronunciations of *s*

Resources
- Cassette A Side B
- Workbook p. 16

Introduce this spread by asking students to brainstorm in German all the types of sport they can remember, preferably in the form of sentences rather than just words.

1a Hör zu und wiederhole. (Listening, Speaking)
Students practise the pronunciation of these sporting expressions, using the tape as a model.

a – Ich spiele Basketball.
b – Ich spiele Fußball.
c – Ich fahre Ski.
d – Ich schwimme.
e – Ich fahre Rad.
f – Ich gehe ins Fitnesszentrum.

Tip box: Practice in pronouncing *s*
Write various words on the board or OHP and get students to practise the pronunciation of *s* until they are confident.

1b Hör zu. Wer sagt was? Antworte für Olaf, Ingrid, Jessica, Mehmet und Martha. (Listening)
Students listen to the interviews and identify which type of sport each person does. The answer for Jan (the first person interviewed) is provided. They write down the person's name and the appropriate letter from the illustrations.

Draw their attention to the format of the listening activity. It features a studio talk show along the lines of *Kilroy* or *Trisha*. Certain German TV stations (notably RTL and SAT 1) run these programmes back-to-back all day because they are so popular.

Answers
Jan d, **Olaf** a, **Ingrid** e, **Jessica** f, **Mehmet** c, **Martha** b

– Herzlich willkommen bei „Jugend heute". Die Frage heute ist „Bist du sportlich?" Hallo! Wie heißt du?
– Ich bin der Jan.
– Und bist du sportlich, Jan?
– Jawohl! Sehr sportlich! Ich schwimme im Hallenbad.
– Und du, Olaf?
– Ich spiele Basketball.
– Magst du Sport, Ingrid?
– Ich fahre gern Rad.
– Super! Vielen Dank. Und du?
– Ich bin Jessica. Ich gehe ins Fitnesszentrum.
– Danke, Jessica. Hallo!
– Hallo! Mein Name ist Mehmet. Ich fahre gern Ski.
– Und du, Martha?
– Ich spiele Fußball, aber nicht sehr gut!

1c Wer sagt was? (Writing)
Now students write out in simple form the answers to Exercise 1b. Again, Jan is done for them as an example.

Answers
1 Jan: Ich schwimme. **2** Olaf: Ich spiele Basketball. **3** Ingrid: Ich fahre Rad. **4** Jessica: Ich gehe ins Fitnesszentrum. **5** Mehmet: Ich fahre Ski. **6** Martha: Ich spiele Fußball.

2 Hör zu. Wann macht man das? (1–6) (Listening)
Students listen to the tape and write down when the activities take place. The expressions of time are provided and illustrated below.

Answers
1 jeden Dienstag, **2** einmal in der Woche, **3** jeden Tag, **4** am Wochenende, **5** im Winter, **6** am Samstag

1 Ich schwimme jeden Dienstag im Hallenbad.
2 Ich spiele einmal in der Woche Basketball.
3 Ich fahre gern Rad. Ich fahre jeden Tag in die Schule.
4 Ich gehe am Wochenende ins Fitnesszentrum.
5 Ich fahre gern im Winter Ski.
6 Ich spiele am Samstag Fußball.

Explain that there isn't enough space to include all the unusual sports that students might be interested in. They can use a dictionary or ask the teacher.

3 Partnerarbeit. (Speaking)
Students use the picture prompts to make brief dialogues about what sports are carried out and how often. Make sure the students change roles.

Tip box
This contains advice for students on sports vocabulary not included in the language grid on the page.

4 Lies die Anzeigen. Wer ist ein guter Brieffreund/eine gute Brieffreundin? (Reading)

Students read the penfriend adverts carefully and identify suitable penfriends for each from the illustrations below. Make sure they understand exactly what they have to do before they start; it may not be immediately obvious just from looking at the page.

Answers
Peter: Mike und Frank, **Sabine:** Anne, **Otto:** Adrian und Paul, **Sigrid:** Sandra und Mary, **Marcel:** Sean

5 Schreib eine Anzeige für einen Brieffreund/eine Brieffreundin für DICH! (Writing)

Students write a similar advert to those in Exercise 4, this time for themselves. This will enable them to have a short paragraph about their sporting activities, which must be learnt for later use. Encourage the more able to go into as much detail as they can.

Further practice of the language and vocabulary of this unit is given on the following pages:
Workbook: p. 16

Logo! 4 3 Wir haben frei!

2 Hobbys (pp. 36–37)

Students will learn how to:
- talk about other hobbies

Key language	Ich mache gern Fotos
Ich lese gern Bücher/ Zeitschriften	**Grammar points**
Ich höre gern Rockmusik/klassische Musik/Popmusik	• *gern* and *nicht gern*
Ich spiele gern Gitarre/ Klavier/Computer/ Geige/Schlagzeug	**Resources**
Ich sehe gern fern	• Cassette A Side B
Ich sammle gern Briefmarken	• Workbook p. 17
Ich gehen gern ins Theater/Kino / in die Disco	• Sprechen p. 62, Gespräch 1
	• Lesen/Schreiben A p. 166

Start work on this spread by asking students to contribute in German as many pastimes and hobbies as they can remember, whether they are actually true for themselves or not. Ask for short sentences in the *ich* form in preference to just single words.

1a Wer ist wer? (Reading)
Students read the speech bubbles and work out who is speaking on the basis of the illustrations below. They write down the names.

Answers
1 Robert, 2 Angela, 3 Udo, 4 Morten, 5 Adrian, 6 Ben, 7 Wiebke, 8 Vincent, 9 Jana, 10 Silke

1b Hör zu. Wer spricht? (1–10) (Listening)
Now that they know who is who, students listen to the tape as often as they need in order to note down the name of who is speaking in each case.

Answers
1 Silke, 2 Udo, 3 Robert, 4 Ben, 5 Morten, 6 Jana, 7 Wiebke, 8 Vincent, 9 Angela, 10 Adrian

> 1 Ich gehe gern ins Kino.
> 2 Ich lese gern Bücher und Zeitschriften.
> 3 Ich sammle gern Briefmarken.
> 4 Ich spiele gern Computer.
> 5 Ich spiele Gitarre in einer Band.
> 6 Ich sehe gern fern.
> 7 Ich mache gern Fotos von meiner Familie.
> 8 Ich spiele gern Klavier.
> 9 Ich gehe gern in die Disco.
> 10 Ich höre gern Musik, meistens Rockmusik.

2 Gruppenarbeit. Stell die Frage an fünf Klassenkamaraden. Jede Person muss ZWEI Antworten geben. (Speaking)
There are no prompts. Each student must simply ask the question about free time to five others in the class and receive genuine answers. If any students claim not to have any hobbies (this happens!), insist that they make some up.

Grammatik: Using *gern* and *nicht* gern
Emphasise how useful this small and simple word is for expressing opinions, an aspect of the syllabus which attracts high marks!

3 Was machst du gern? Was machst du nicht gern? (Writing)
Students practise writing the *Ich* forms of the various activities depicted in the illustrations, using gern and nicht gern.

Answers
1 Ich sehe nicht gern fern. 2 Ich spiele gern Klavier. 3 Ich lese nicht gern. 4 Ich gehe gern ins Kino. 5 Ich höre nicht gern klassische Musik. 6 Ich spiele gern Computer.

4 Beantworte Vanessas Brief. (Writing)
Following the template of Vanessa's letter, students write a reply in which they give as much information as they can about what they do and don't like doing. Make sure the more able write as much detail as they can and include some questions as well.

Further practice of the language and vocabulary of this unit is given on the following pages:
Sprechen: p. 62
Lesen/Schreiben A: p. 166
Workbook p. 17

3 Einladungen (pp. 38–39)

Students will learn how to:
- give and respond to invitations

Key language	Grammar points
Möchtest du ... in die Disco/Stadt/ins Kino/Theater/ Schwimmbad/ schwimmen/tanzen gehen? zu meiner Party kommen? Wann treffen wir uns? Um ... Uhr / Viertel vor (nach) / halb ... Wo treffen wir uns? Vor dem / In dem Bahnhof/Kino/Theater/ Rathaus/ Sportzentrum/ Schwimmbad Vor der / In der Disco/Stadt	• *in den, in die, ins* to invite someone somewhere • *im, in der* and *vor dem, vor der* used to indicate a meeting place **Resources** • Cassette A Side B • Workbook pp. 18–19 • Sprechen p. 62, Rollenspiel 1a + 1b • Lesen/Schreiben B p. 167

Before starting this spread, elicit *Möchtest du ...?* and ask students to invite each other to as many activities as they can think of.

1 Hör zu und lies. Wähle die richtige Antwort.
(Listening, Reading)
Students should first listen to the tape without referring to the book and note down in English what they understand of it. Then, following the text as they listen, they should complete the multiple-choice questions. If you wish, they can read the dialogue aloud to familiarise themselves with the expressions.

Answers
1 a, 2 c, 3 b, 4 c

- Müller!
- Hallo, Birgit. Sag mal, möchtest du heute Abend ins Kino gehen?
- Was läuft?
- Ich glaube, ein Krimi.
- Und um wie viel Uhr?
- Um acht.
- Okay. Wo treffen wir uns?
- Vor dem Kino?
- Ist gut. Bis dann!

2 Wann treffen wir uns? Schreib die Antwort auf. (Writing)
Make sure students remember telling the time in German. They write down the arrangements for meeting, following the example provided.

Answers
1 Treffen wir uns um sechs Uhr. 2 Treffen wir uns um Viertel nach sechs. 3 Treffen wir uns um halb sieben. 4 Treffen wir uns um Viertel vor sieben. 5 Treffen wir uns um sieben Uhr. 6 Treffen wir uns um Viertel nach sieben. 7 Treffen wir uns um halb acht.

3a Hör zu. Wohin möchtest du gehen? (1–6)
(Listening)
Students listen to the tape and match the invitations to the appropriate pictures.

Answers
1 d, 2 b, 3 e, 4 a, 5 c, 6 f

1 Möchtest du ins Schwimmbad gehen?
2 Möchtest du in die Stadt gehen?
3 Möchtest du am Freitag mit mir in die Disco gehen?
4 Möchtest du zu meiner Party kommen?
5 Möchtest du ins Kino gehen?
6 Möchtest du mit ins Theater kommen?

Grammatik: Using *in* + accusative to invite someone somewhere (*in den/in die/ins*)
This explains the "motion" use of the accusative with prepositions, complementing the previous explanation of prepositions with the dative. Teachers may like to use this opportunity to go into this grammatical point in more depth. Further practice is provided in the grammar section (page 193).

3b Partnerarbeit. Lade deinen Partner / deine Partnerin ein. (Speaking)
Students invite each other out, using the picture prompts from Exercise 3a.

4 Wo treffen wir uns? Was passt zusammen?
(Reading)
Students match pictures to locations.

Answers
1 f, 2 e, 3 a, 4 d, 5 b, 6 c

Grammatik: Using *in* + dative (*im/in der*) and *vor* + dative (*vor dem/vor der*) to indicate place
This offers further revision of prepositions with the dative. There are endless possibilities to practise this with various classroom objects.

5 Partnerarbeit. (Speaking)
Students practise complete "asking out" dialogues with four further prompts, following the template provided. Make sure that the dialogues are practised both ways round.

6 Schreib drei Einladungen an deine Klassenkameraden. (Writing)
Students produce three written invitations, following the example provided.

Further practice of the language and vocabulary of this unit is given on the following pages:
Sprechen: p. 62
Lesen/Schreiben B: p. 167
Workbook pp. 18–19

4 Ausreden (pp. 40–41)

Students will learn how to:
- explain and make excuses

Key language	Grammar points
Möchtest du heute Abend / morgen / am Samstag / am Wochenende …?	• *Ich kann nicht*
Nein, ich kann nicht, weil ich …	• *weil* used in giving Answers
müde bin	
krank bin	**Language skills**
kein Geld habe	• advice to learn some excuses and reasons
zu viele Hausaufgaben habe	
Ja, ich komme gern mit	**Resources**
	• Cassette A Side B
	• Workbook p. 20
	• Sprechen p. 62, Rollenspiel 2

Before starting this spread, ask students to brainstorm (in both English and German) reasons they might give for being late, failing to do homework, etc.

1a Hör zu und lies. Was möchten sie machen? Warum geht es nicht? Schreib a, b, c, UND 1, 2, 3, usw. (Listening, Reading)
Students should first listen to the tape and make notes in English to show how much they have understood. Then they complete the task (either referring to the text or not, according to the teacher's preference). Make sure they understand that for each question they need to write both a letter and a number, indicating both the activity and the excuse.

Answers
1 e, 3, 2 d, 2, 3 b, 4, 4 c, 1, 5 a, 5

1 – Möchtest du schwimmen gehen?
  – Nein, ich kann nicht schwimmen gehen, weil ich müde bin.
2 – Möchtest du ins Kino gehen?
  – Nein, ich kann nicht ins Kino gehen, weil ich kein Geld habe.
3 – Möchtest du morgen in die Stadt kommen?
  – Nein, ich kann nicht in die Stadt kommen, weil ich zu viele Hausaufgaben habe.
4 – Möchtest du am Sonnabend zum Fußballspiel gehen?
  – Nein, ich kann nicht zum Fußballspiel gehen, weil ich krank bin.
5 – Möchtest du am Freitag in die Disco kommen?
  – Ja, ich komme gern mit!

1b Hör zu. Was möchten sie machen? Warum geht es nicht? Schreib a, b, c, UND 1, 2, 3, usw. (1–5) (Listening)
Students complete a similar exercise which is a "true" listening activity, i.e. only on tape, not printed in the book.

Answers
1 a, 3, 2 b, 2, 3 d, 1, 4 c, 5, 5 e, 4

1 – Möchtest du heute Abend in die Disco gehen?
  – Nein, ich kann es nicht, weil ich müde bin.
2 – Möchtest du am Wochenende in die Stadt kommen?
  – Nein, ich kann nicht in die Stadt, weil ich kein Geld habe.
3 – Möchtest du morgen ins Kino gehen?
  – Nein, ich kann es nicht, weil ich krank bin.
4 – Möchtest du am Sonntag zum Fußballspiel gehen?
  – Ja, ich komme gern mit.
5 – Möchtest du am Freitag schwimmen gehen?
  – Nein, das geht nicht, weil ich zu viele Hausaufgaben habe

Grammatik: Using *Ich kann* to say you can or can't do something, with infinitive at end
Point out the usefulness and simplicity of the *ich* form of *können*. Get students to provide answers to the questions *Was kannst du machen?* and *Was kannst du nicht machen?*.

Grammatik: Using *weil* in answers, with a comma where necessary, and verb at end
Emphasise that students will gain marks for giving reasons and explanations, using the word *weil*, both in the Speaking and the Writing Tests. Make sure they learn a few useful phrases using this structure. The more able should refer to the grammar section (page 195) for a fuller explanation and more practice.

Tip box
Advice to students to learn some excuses and reasons.

2 Partnerarbeit. (Speaking)
With the help of the prompts provided, students practise conversations using excuses and explanations. Make sure they do the dialogues both ways round.

3 Schreib die Antworten auf. (Writing, Reading)
Students practise writing excuses, using the *weil* construction, based on written invitations and visual prompts.

Answers
1 Lieber Jan, ich kann am Samstag nicht in die Disco gehen, weil ich kein Geld habe. 2 Liebe Stefanie, ich kann heute Abend nicht ins Kino gehen, weil ich müde bin. 3 Liebe Kirsten, ich kann morgen nicht Tennis spielen, weil ich krank bin. 4 Lieber Dieter, ja, ich komme gern mit OR ich kann am Mittwoch schwimmen gehen.

Further practice of the language and vocabulary of this unit is given on the following pages:
Sprechen: p. 62
Workbook: p. 20

Logo! 4 3 Wir haben frei!

5 Wir sehen fern (pp. 42–43)

Students will learn how to:
- talk about TV and radio habits

Key language	Grammar points
Das ist …	Inversion (*Serien finde ich …*)
ein Krimi	
eine Serie	**Language skills**
ein Film	• *das Programm* and *eine Sendung*
eine Musiksendung	• *gucken*
eine Quizsendung	
die Nachrichten	**Resources**
Ich sehe (nicht) gern …	• Cassette A Side B
Meine Lieblingssendung heißt …	• Workbook p. 21
(Serien) finde ich …	• Sprechen p. 62, Gespräch 2
toll/interessant/langweilig/ doof, usw.	

Start this spread by asking students to come up with as many types of TV programme as they can (in English). How many do they know in German? Which programmes do they think are probably on German TV as well as UK TV?

1a Was läuft wann? Schreib die Zeit auf. (Reading)
Students look at the TV listing and note down what time each programme starts.

Answers
a 18.30, b 19.00, c 20.00, d 20.00, e 18.30

1b Hör zu. Wer will was sehen? Schreib die Tabelle ab und füll sie aus. (Listening)
Based on the same TV listing as in Exercise 1a, students listen to the tape as often as they need to in order to complete the grid, which they first copy out. They must fill in the programme title, the type of programme and the time it starts.

A photocopiable grid is available for this exercise. (p.138)

Answers
Gabi: Liebe im Krankenhaus, Serie, 18.30, **Hans:** Wer wird Millionär?, Quizsendung, 19.00, **Mutti:** Tatort, Krimi, 20.00, **Vati:** Tagesschau, Nachrichten, 20.00

– Also, was gucken wir heute Abend? Was meinst du, Gabi?
– Im zweiten Programm läuft heute um 18.30 Uhr eine neue Serie, „Liebe im Krankenhaus".
– Ach nee, ich hasse Serien.
– Was willst du denn gucken, Hans?
– Schau mal: Wer wird Millionär? Das ist eine neue Quizsendung mit Günther Jauch. Da kannst du eine Million Euro gewinnen! Toll, nicht, Mutti?
– Nein, Hans, ich möchte einen Krimi sehen. Hier, im zweiten Programm gibt es um acht Uhr „Tatort" mit Ulrich Meyer. Was meinst du, Vati?
– Nein, um acht Uhr will ich die Nachrichten sehen.

Tip box
1 An explanation of the difference between *das Programm* and *eine Sendung*.
2 The commonly-used verb *gucken*.
Mention also that the word *Seifenoper* is actually used in German for Soap Opera, as well as just *Soap*.

2 Partnerarbeit. Was siehst du gern im Fernsehen? (Speaking)
In pairs, students construct dialogues about what they like watching, their favourite programmes and their opinions about programmes.

3 Was siehst du gern im Fernsehen? Schreib deine Antworten auf. (Writing)
Students write a paragraph on their viewing habits and their opinions about TV programmes. This must be marked and kept for reference. Point out that this topic is very likely to come up in Speaking or Writing tests.

Further practice of the language and vocabulary of this unit is given on the following pages:
Sprechen: p. 62
Workbook: p. 21

6 Wir verstehen uns gut
(pp. 44–45)

Students will learn how to:
- talk about their relationships with others

Key language	Grammar points
Was ist los?	• recognising common verbs in the imperfect
Ich bin sauer	• dative after *Ich verstehe mich gut mit ...*
Ich habe Ärger mit meiner Mutter	
Meine Eltern sind geschieden	**Language skills**
Ich verstehe mich (nicht) gut mit ... meiner (Stief)Mutter/ Schwester mit meinem (Stief)Vater/ Bruder	• answers must match the tense of questions
Das ist mir egal	**Resources**
Du hast Pech/Glück	• Cassette A Side B
	• Lesen/Schreiben pp. 166–167

1 Hör zu und lies. Finde die Ausdrücke im Text.
(Reading, Listening)
Students should listen to the tape while reading the story, which is based on an imaginary German TV soap. They identify the German equivalents of the English expressions and write them down.

Answers
1 Was ist los? 2 Du hast Pech. 3 Es ist mir egal. 4 Meine Eltern sind geschieden. 5 Ich habe Ärger mit meiner Mutter. 6 Ich bin sauer. 7 Ich verstehe mich nicht gut mit Olaf. 8 Das ist unfair.

> – Was ist los, Peter?
> – Ach, ich bin sauer. Ich habe Ärger mit meiner Mutter.
> – Wieso denn?
> – Du weißt, meine Eltern sind geschieden. Aber jetzt hat meine Mutter einen neuen Freund, Olaf.
> – Ist das ein Problem?
> – Ja. Ich verstehe mich nicht gut mit Olaf. Olaf sagt, ich darf nicht zum Rockfestival gehen. Er sagt, Rockfestivals sind gefährlich. Aber das ist unfair. Er ist nicht mein Vater.
> – Was sagt deine Mutter dazu?
> – Sie sagt, Olaf hat Recht.
> – Du hast Pech! Ich verstehe mich gut mit meinem Stiefvater. Was machst du denn?
> – Es ist mir egal. Olaf ist doof. Ich gehe sowieso zum Festival ... [*door opens and Olaf comes in*] Ach, hallo Olaf ...

2 Partnerarbeit. (Speaking)
Students use visual prompts to practise saying how they get on with people.

Tip box
Some useful expressions for students to learn.

3 Was ist in der Meyerstraße passiert? Schreib drei oder vier Sätze auf Englisch. (Reading)
Students write a brief English summary of the story.

Answer
Suggested answer: Peter's stepfather Olaf had said Peter was not allowed to go the a rock festival. Just as Peter was telling his girlfriend about this, Olaf came in. Peter lied and said he had been telling her that he wanted a new moped. Olaf surprised Peter by telling him that he had bought him a moped and also that he could go to the festival.

Tip box
A reminder to students to make sure that their answer is in the same tense as the question (vital for exam success).

Grammatik: Help in recognising some common verbs in the imperfect
Students need to recognise the odd imperfect tense form which may crop up in Reading tasks. They don't need to use them at Foundation level (apart from *war* and *hatte*).

4 Was passt zusammen? Verbinde die englischen Wörter mit den deutschen Wörtern.
(Reading)
Students match the English and German equivalents of some key verbs.

Answers
1 h, 2 a, 3 g, 4 b, 5 f, 6 d, 7 c, 8 e

5 Schreib die Sätze richtig aus. (Writing)
Students put words in the right order to make sentences showing they have understood the story.

Answers
1 Olaf findet Festivals gefährlich. 2 Peter findet Olaf doof. 3 Ilka findet ihren Stiefvater nett. 4 Jetzt findet Peter Olaf super! 5 Ich finde „Meyerstraße" furchtbar!

Further practice of the language and vocabulary of this unit is given on the following pages:
Lesen/Schreiben: pp. 166–167

All the vocabulary and structures from this chapter are listed on the **Wörter** pages 46–47. These can be used for revision by covering up either the English or the German. Students can check here to see how much they remember from the chapter.

Assessment materials for Chapters 3 and 4 are available after Chapter 4.

Further speaking and grammar practice on the whole chapter is provided on pp. 22–23 of the **Workbook**.

Workbook

Logo! 4 3 Wir haben frei!

p. 16

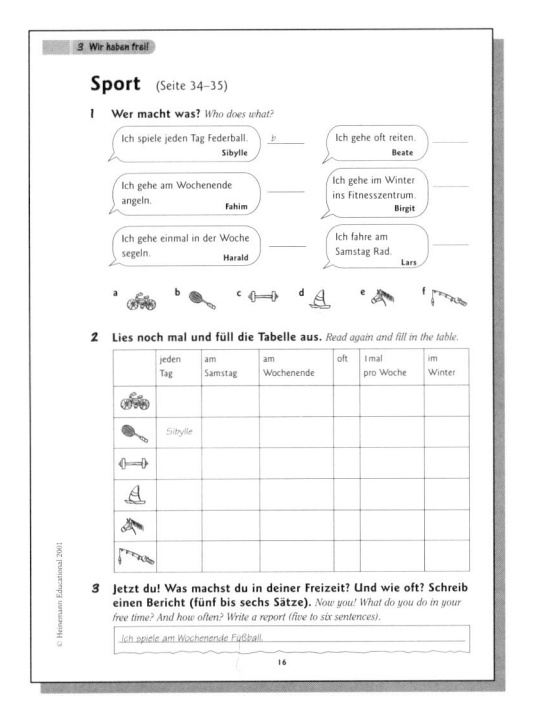

p. 17

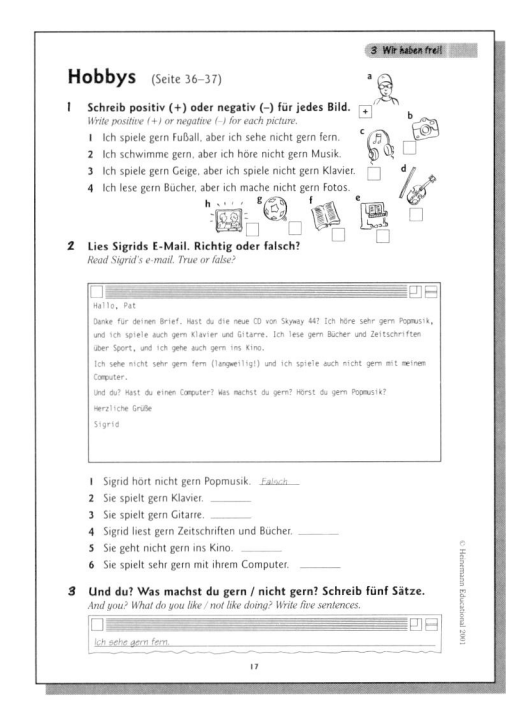

1 Sibylle b; Beate e; Fahim f; Birgit c; Harald d; Lars a
2 Sibylle: badminton, jeden Tag Lars: cycling, am Samstag Fahim: fishing, am Wochenende Beate: riding, oft; Harald: sailing, 1 x Woche; Birgit: fitness, im Winter
3 Open-ended. 1 mark per correct sentence. Ignore minor errors.

1 a+, b–, c–, d+, e–, f+, g+, h–
2 1 falsch, 2 richtig, 3 richtig, 4 richtig, 5 falsch, 6 falsch
3 Open-ended. 1 mark per correct sentence. Ignore minor errors.

p. 18

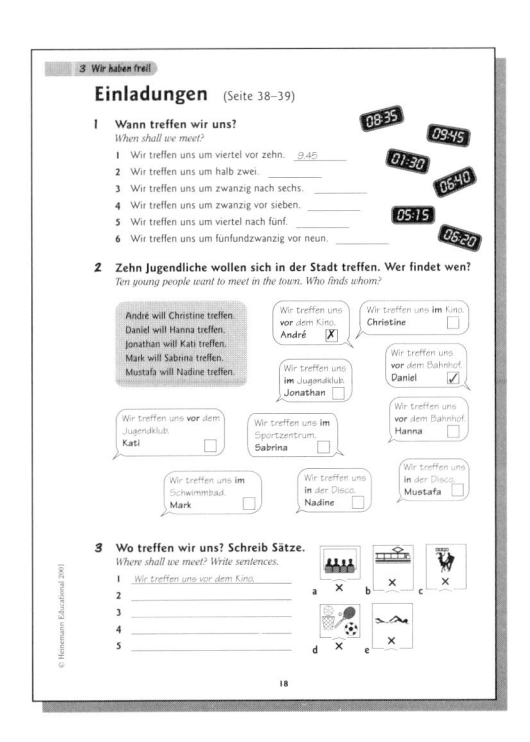

p. 19

1 1 9.45, 2 01.30, 3 06.20, 4 06.40, 5 05.15, 6 08.35
2 Daniel und Hanna; Mustafa und Nadine
3 1 Wir treffen uns vor dem Kino. 2 Wir treffen uns im Bahnhof. 3 Wir treffen uns in der Disco. 4 Wir treffen uns vor dem Sportzentrum. 5 Wir treffen uns im Schwimmbad.

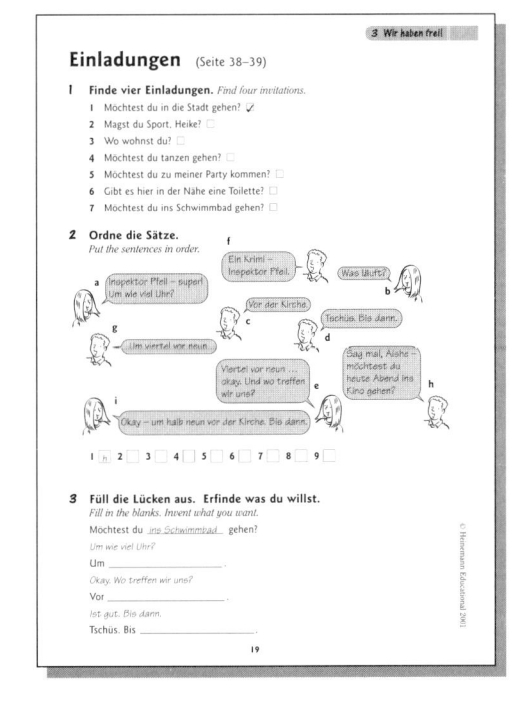

1 1, 4, 5, 7
2 1 h, 2 b, 3 f, 4 a, 5 g, 6 e, 7 c, 8 i, 9 d
3 Any substitutions are acceptable, provided that they make sense and are reasonably logical. Ignore minor errors.

p. 20

1 1 e, 2 d, 3 b, 4 c, 5 a
2 1 Ich kann nicht schwimmen gehen, weil ich müde bin. 2 Ich kann nicht ins Kino gehen, weil ich kein Geld habe. 3 Ich kann nicht zum Fußballspiel gehen, weil ich krank bin. 4 Ich kann nicht in die Stadt gehen, weil ich zu viele Hausaufgaben habe. 5 Ich kann nicht in die Disco gehen, weil ich meine Haare waschen muss.
3 Any excuse is acceptable provided that it is grammatically correct and makes sense. Allow funny excuses!

p. 21

1 1 d, 2 b, 3 e, 4 a, 5 c,
2 Carsten: ja Maja: nein Janina: ja Nassim: ja
3 Carsten: Geld, Geld, Geld; Unsere Straße. Janina: Bedrohte Tiere. Maja: nichts. Nassim: Fußballwoche.

p. 22

p. 23

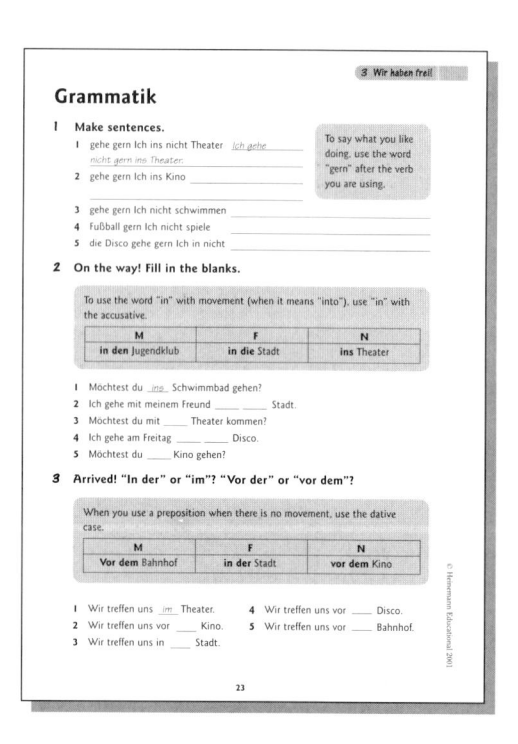

1 1 Ich gehe nicht gern ins Theater. 2 Ich gehe gern ins Kino. 3 Ich gehe nicht gern schwimmen. 4 Ich spiele nicht gern Fußball. 5 Ich gehe nicht gern in die Disco.
2 1 ins, 2 in die, 3 ins, 4 in die, 5 ins
3 1 im, 2 dem, 3 der, 4 der, 5 dem

50

4 Urlaub (pp. 48–61)

Topic area	Key language	Grammar	Language skills
4.1 Woher kommst du? (pp. 48–49) Talk about countries, towns and nationalities	*In welchem Land ist …?* [European towns] *ist in* [countries]. *Ich bin* [nationalities]. *Aus welchem Land kommst du? Ich komme aus Großbritannien / aus den USA / aus der Schweiz. Er/Sie ist … Er/Sie kommt aus …*	Masculine and feminine forms of nationalities	*German towns and seas*
4.2 Das Wetter (pp. 50–51) Talk about the weather	*Wie ist das Wetter in …? Es ist kalt/kühl/nass/neblig/ sonnig/stürmisch/trocken/warm/windig/wolkig. Es blitzt/donnert/regnet/friert/schneit. Es gibt Schnee/Frost/ Gewitter/Nebel/Regen/Schauer/Sonne/Sturm/Wind. Die Sonne scheint. Es sind 25 Grad.*	First, second and third person of *sein*.	Advice on listening for essential information rather than qualifying words.
4.3 Die letzten Ferien (pp. 52–53) Describe a holiday in the past	*Ich bin / Wir sind mit meiner Familie / meinen Freunden gefahren. Ich war / Wir waren in* [+ countries]. *Ich bin / Wir sind eine Woche geblieben. Ich bin / Wir sind* [types of transport] *gefahren/geflogen. Ich habe / Wir haben* [types of holiday places] *übernachtet/gewohnt. Das Wetter war …*	*Ich* and *wir* forms of the perfect tense (*sein* and *haben*)	Advice to use *wir* form when describing holidays.
4.4 Urlaubsspaß (pp. 54–55) Say what you did on holiday	*Ich bin / Du bist / Er/Sie ist / Wir sind ausgegangen/ gefahren/geschwommen/gewandert/spazieren/gegangen/. Ski gefahren. Ich habe / Du hast / Er/Sie hat / Wir haben gemacht/gegessen/angesehen/gespielt/geangelt/getanzt/ getroffen. Ich war am ersten/zweiten/nächsten Tag / am Abend gewandert. Ich war … Es war …*	*Ich, du, er/sie* and *wir* forms of perfect tense (*sein* and *haben*) Imperfect tense to say 'was' (*ich war, es war …*)	
4.5 Unterkunft (pp. 56–57) Find and book accommodation	*Haben Sie ein Zimmer frei? Wieviel kostet ein Einzel/ Doppelzimmer? Ich möchte ein Doppelzimmer reservieren. Ich möchte Halbpension/Vollpension / 2 Nächte bleiben. Ist das Zimmer mit Bad/Dusche/ Fernsehen/Telefon/Radio? Gibt es einen Lift / ein Restaurant / einen Parkplatz? Um wieviel Uhr ist das Frühstück/Abendessen? Kann ich bitte die Rechnung / meinen Schlüssel haben / zahlen?*		Advice on writing a letter to book a hotel room
4.6 Die Dusche ist kalt! (pp. 58–59) Deal with problems with accommodation	*Der Fernseher/Aufzug ist kaputt. Das Zimmer ist schmutzig / zu klein / zu laut / zu teuer. Die Dusche ist kalt. Das Essen war furchtbar. Ich möchte mit den Direktor sprechen / mein Geld zurück haben.*	Using *war* in a letter of complaint	Writing a formal letter
Lesen/Schreiben (pp. 168–169)			Reading and Writing skills

- The vocabulary and structures taught in Chapter 4 are summarised on the **Wörter** pages of the Student's Book, pp. 60–61.
- Further Speaking practice on the language of the chapter is provided on **Sprechen** p. 63.
- Coursework pages relating to this chapter can be found on pp. 154–155 of the Student's Book.
- For a selection of assessment tasks for Chapters 3 & 4, please refer to the separate Assessment Pack for your chosen examination board: AQA, OCR or Edexcel.

1 Woher kommst du? (pp. 48–49)

Students will learn how to:
- talk about countries, towns and nationalities

Key language	Grammar points
In welchem Land ist …?	• masculine and feminine forms of nationalities
Ich bin Amerikaner/ Amerikanerin (usw.)	
Aus welchem Land kommst du?	**Language skills**
Ich komme aus Großbritannien / aus den USA / aus der Schweiz (usw.)	• German towns and seas
Er/Sie ist Engländer/ Engländerin (usw.)	**Resources**
Er/Sie kommt aus …	• Cassette B Side A
	• Workbook p. 24
	• Sprechen p. 63, Gespräch 1

Before starting this spread, ask students to brainstorm all the German names for European countries that they can remember, as well as the names of German and other European cities. This is important because some students can be remarkably sketchy about European geography!

The teacher should take responsibility in this chapter for ensuring correct pronunciation and intonation, to avoid the temptation to pronounce everything in the English way (e.g. London, Paris).

1 Hör zu. Richtig oder falsch? (Listening)
Students listen to the tape and write down whether the sentences are true or false. The map is provided for reference, but students should be asked to do this exercise as pure listening, without referring to the map.

Answers

1 falsch, 2 falsch, 3 richtig, 4 falsch, 5 richtig, 6 richtig, 7 falsch, 8 richtig

– So, Leute, heute geht's um Städte und Länder. In welchem Land ist München?
– München ist in Deutschland, Herr Wolf.
– Ist Köln auch in Deutschland?
– Ja, natürlich!
– Gut! Und in welchem Land ist Marseille?
– Marseille ist in Frankreich, Herr Wolf.
– Ist Berlin in Frankreich?
– Nein! Berlin ist in Deutschland.
– Gut! Und in welchem Land ist Avila?
– Äh … Avila … Ist Avila in Italien?
– Nein!
– Avila ist in Spanien. Und Madrid ist auch in Spanien.
– Richtig! Und wo ist Arhus?
– Arhus ist in Dänemark.
– Und Kopenhagen ist die Hauptstadt von Dänemark.

2 Partnerarbeit. (Speaking)
Pairwork activity in which students ask and answer questions about cities and countries. The "spaghetti" puzzle is there to help out if there are any doubts about the facts!

Grammatik: Masculine and feminine forms of nationalities
Point out that this list will be especially useful in Listening and Reading Tests, where they might have to identify someone's gender or nationality.

3a Hör zu. Wer ist wer? (1–8) (Listening)
Students listen to the tape as often as necessary and look at the pictures in order to identify who is speaking.

Answers

1 f, 2 e, 3 d, 4 a, 5 g, 6 b, 7 h, 8 c

1 Ich bin Italiener. Ich komme aus Italien.
2 Ich bin Spanier. Ich komme aus Spanien.
3 Ich bin Engländerin. Ich komme aus Großbritannien.
4 Ich bin Amerikaner. Ich komme aus den USA.
5 Ich bin Österreicherin. Ich komme aus Österreich.
6 Ich bin Irin. Ich komme aus Irland.
7 Ich bin Schweizer. Ich komme aus der Schweiz.
8 Ich bin Holländer. Ich komme aus den Niederlanden.

Tip box
A list for students of German towns and seas which have English equivalents. They may not have realised that both exist.

3b Partnerarbeit. Mach für jede Person in Übung 3a einen Dialog. (Speaking)
Students create short dialogues based on the illustrations from Exercise 3a. Make sure they take it in turns to start the dialogue. They then adapt the same conversation to their own real life situation.

3c Schreib für jede Person in Übung 3a zwei Sätze. (Writing)
Students now write out the information about the illustrations from Exercise 3a, finally writing about themselves as well.

Answers

a Brian ist Amerikaner. Er kommt aus den USA. b Mary ist Irin. Sie kommt aus Irland. c Johan ist Holländer. Er kommt aus Holland. d Susie ist Engländerin. Sie kommt aus Großbritannien. e Paco ist Spanien. Er kommt aus Spanien. f Giovanni ist Italiener. Er kommt aus Italien. g Maria ist Österreicherin. Sie kommt aus Österreich. h Hannes ist Schweizer. Er kommt aus der Schweiz.

Further practice of the language and vocabulary of this unit is given on the following pages:
Sprechen: p. 63
Workbook: p. 24

2 Das Wetter (pp. 50–51)

Students will learn how to:
- talk about the weather

Key language	Grammar points
Wie ist das Wetter in ...?	• first, second and third person of *sein*
Es ist kalt/kühl/nass/neblig/sonnig/stürmisch/trocken/warm/windig/wolkig	**Language skills**
Es donnert und blitzt	• advice to listen for essential information only
Es regnet	
Es schneit/friert	**Resources**
Es gibt Schnee	• Cassette B Side A
Es sind 25 Grad	• Workbook p. 25
Die Sonne scheint	

Before starting this spread, elicit as many weather expressions as students can remember from earlier in the course. Mime and sound effects can be used, as well as any previously-used flashcards or OHP transparencies that are available.

1a Hör zu. Welches Bild ist das? (1–8)
(Listening)
Students listen to the tape and write down letters to identify the types of weather being described.

Answers
1 g, 2 b, 3 a, 4 e, 5 f, 6 h, 7 d, 8 c

1 – Hallo Mutti! Hier spricht Angela!
  – Hallo Angela! Wo bist du denn?
  – Ich bin in der Schweiz und es ist sehr kalt!
2 – Hallo Olli! Hier in Spanien ist es sehr warm.
3 – Na, Klaus, wie ist das Wetter in England?
  – Es regnet, natürlich.
4 – Hier in Österreich ist es sehr windig!
5 – Wie ist das Wetter in München?
  – Es ist neblig.
6 – Ist es schön in Norwegen?
  – Nein, es ist stürmisch!
7 – Ist es kalt in Italien?
  – Nein, es ist sonnig!
8 – Wo bist du, Silke?
  – In Holland. Hier ist es wolkig.

1b Hör nochmal zu und schreib das Land auf.
(Listening)
Students now listen to the tape again and note down in German which country each person is in.

Answers
1 Schweiz, 2 Spanien, 3 England, 4 Österreich, 5 Deutschland, 6 Norwegen, 7 Italien, 8 Holland

Tip box
Advice to students to listen out for key words and not to let qualifying words distract them.

2a Partnerarbeit. (Speaking)
Students use the weather map provided to ask and answer questions about the weather in the various countries. They can do them in any order but must remember to do the exercise both ways round (i.e. so it isn't just one doing all the work!).

2b Lies die Sätze. Welches Land ist das?
(Reading)
This exercise refers to the same weather map as in Exercise 2a. Students identify which country is being referred to and write it down in German.

Answers
1 Polen, 2 Deutschland, 3 Großbritannien, 4 Spanien, 5 Italien, 6 Frankreich, 7 Holland, 8 Belgien

2c Schreib die Antworten auf. (Writing)
Also using the same weather map, students now write down what the weather is like in each country.

Answers
1 Es ist stürmisch. / Es donnert und blitzt. 2 Es ist warm. / Es sind 25 Grad. 3 Es ist kalt. / Es sind 5 Grad. 4 Es ist sonnig. / Die Sonne scheint. 5 Es ist windig. / Der Wind ist stark. 6 Es regnet. / Es ist nass. 7 Es ist neblig. / Man kann nicht gut sehen! 8 Es schneit. / Es gibt Schnee.

2d Wer ist wo? Sieh dir die Karte noch einmal an. Schreib die Namen der Länder auf.
(Reading, Writing)
A final activity based on the same map. Students now read some extracts from postcards and work out where the correspondents are writing from.

Answers
1 Oskar ist in Spanien. 2 Maike ist in Großbritannien. 3 Kai ist in Deutschland. 4 Mani ist in Frankreich. 5 Stefanie ist in Polen.

Grammatik: Summary of the first, second and third person of *sein*
A reminder of the parts of *sein* which have been used in the first two spreads.

Further practice of the language and vocabulary of this unit is given on the following pages:
Workbook: p. 25

Logo! 4 4 Urlaub

3 Die letzen Ferien (pp. 52–53)

Students will learn how to:
- describe a holiday in the past

Key language	Ich war/Wir waren in …
Ich bin / Wir sind … mit meiner Familie/(meinen) Freunden gefahren eine Woche / zwei Wochen dort geblieben mit dem Auto/Bus/Rad/Zug gefahren mit dem Flugzeug geflogen Ich habe / Wir haben in einem Hotel/Wohnwagen / auf einem Campingplatz übernachtet/gewohnt	Das Wetter war … **Grammar points** • *ich* and *wir* forms in the perfect tense (verbs with *sein* and *haben*) **Language skills** • advice to use *wir* forms of verbs when describing holidays **Resources** • Cassette B Side A • Workbook pp. 26–27

Introduce the spread by telling students that they will be practising using the perfect tense to talk about the past. Emphasise that it is essential for them to use a few correct past tense expressions if they want to achieve a good grade and that this spread contains some ideal ones to learn.

1a Hör zu und lies. Welche vier Buchstaben passen zu Jasmin, zu Benjamin und zu Samira? (Listening, Reading)

Because this is more complicated than any previous task, students may look at the text as well as listening to the tape. Make sure that they understand that they are to write down FOUR letters for each speaker, indicating the **transport**, the **accommodation**, the **length of time** and the **weather**.

Answers
Jasmin c, e, h, j, **Benjamin** b, d, i, l, **Samira** a, f, g, k

> – Ich war mit meinen Freunden in Spanien. Wir sind mit dem Zug dorthin gefahren und sind zwei Wochen dort geblieben. Wir haben in einem Wohnwagen übernachtet. Das Wetter war super!
> – Ich war mit meiner Familie in Polen. Wir sind mit dem Auto dorthin gefahren und sind drei Wochen dort geblieben. Wir haben auf einem Campingplatz gewohnt. Es war okay, aber das Wetter war schlecht.
> – Ich war eine Woche mit meiner Freundin in Amerika, in Kalifornien. Wir sind mit dem Flugzeug geflogen und wir sind eine Woche dort geblieben. Wir haben in einem Hotel gewohnt. Das Wetter war schön warm.

1b Partnerarbeit. Du bist Benjamin oder Samira. Beantworte die Fragen. Hier sind Jasmins Antworten. (Speaking)

Again, a more complicated speaking task than has previously been attempted, which is why a full transcript has been provided. This one should be read aloud in pairs, as a preparation for constructing the other two dialogues, based on the information in the speech bubbles on page 52. Partners should both attempt both sides of each dialogue. Some may perform them to the class.

Grammatik: The formation of *ich* and *wir* forms of the perfect tense for verbs with *sein* and *haben*

Students are formally presented with information about the perfect tense, at the moment only in the *wir* and *ich* forms, the ones they are most likely to use at Foundation level.

Tip box: Advice to use *wir* as well as *ich*

Ask students to avoid endless lists of sentences beginning *Ich …*, especially in the Speaking Test, by using *Wir* occasionally. Take the opportunity to practise the correct pronunciation of *Ich*.

Ask students to contribute as many expressions as they can beginning *Ich* and then to change them into the *Wir* form.

2a Was sagt Uli? Lies die E-Mail und schreib *richtig* oder *falsch*. (Reading)

Students read the e-mail and decide whether the sentences are true or false.

Answers
1 falsch, 2 falsch, 3 richtig, 4 falsch, 5 falsch, 6 richtig

2b Du bist Lars. Schreib eine E-Mail zurück. Ersetze die braunen Wörter. (Writing)

A quite challenging writing task, in which students adapt the printed e-mail with the help of some suggested pieces of language. The more able can then make one up as well.

Further practice of the language and vocabulary of this unit is given on the following pages:
Workbook: pp. 26–27

4 Urlaubsspaß (pp. 54–55)

Students will learn how to:
- say what they did on holiday

Key language	Grammar points
Ich bin / Du bist / Er/Sie ist / Wir sind ... ausgegangen/ geschwommen/ gewandert/ spazierengegangen/ Ski gefahren Ich habe / Du hast / Er/Sie hat / Wir haben ... geangelt/getanzt/ Freunde getroffen ... gemacht/gegessen/ angesehen/gespielt am ersten/zweiten/ nächsten Tag Ich war in Spanien Es war warm	• *ich, du, er/sie* and *wir* forms of perfect tense (*sein* and *haben*) • *ich/es war* ... **Resources** • Cassette B Side A • Workbook p. 28 • Sprechen p. 63, Gespräch 2 • Lesen/Schreiben A + B pp. 168–169 • Kursarbeit pp. 154–155

Before starting this spread, remind students about the perfect with *sein* and see how many things they are able to say about what they did during a past holiday. The teacher can start them off by relating a few things he or she did.

1a Was passt zusammen? (Reading)
Students link perfect tense sentences to pictures by noting down letters.

Answers
1 b, 2 d, 3 i, 4 e, 5 a, 6 g, 7 f, 8 h

1b Hör zu. Wer hat was gemacht? (1–3) (Listening)
Using the same picture prompts, students listen to the tape as often as they need in order to identify THREE pieces of information about each interviewee.

Answers
1 g, d, e, 2 h, f, a, 3 i, c, b

> 1 – Jasmin, du warst in Spanien. Was hast du in Spanien gemacht?
> – Wir sind am ersten Tag ins Museum gegangen. Das war sehr langweilig! Aber am zweiten Tag sind wir ins Freibad gegangen. Das war toll!
> 2 – Und du, Benjamin? Was hast du in Polen gemacht?
> – Wir haben eine Rundfahrt gemacht. Das war nicht sehr interessant! Aber wir sind auch in eine Diskothek gegangen. Das war super!
> 3 – Und du, Samira? Wie war es in Kalifornien?
> – Es war herrlich! Ich bin ins Fitnesszentrum gegangen und ich habe natürlich viele Fotos gemacht.

2 Lies den Brief und beantworte die Fragen. Schreib nur ein Wort für jede Antwort. (Reading)
This is a denser piece of reading practice but the task is straightforward. Students write down one-word answers. It is suitable for individual work or homework. More able students can be encouraged to answer in full sentences.

Answers
1 Mallorca, 2 Palma, 3 Stadt, 4 Restaurant, 5 Fisch, 6 Meer, 7 Hotel, 8 Konzert, 9 Musik, 10 Strand

3a Partnerarbeit. (Speaking)
Now students put the new material to use in a guided dialogue with picture prompts. Make sure they conduct the activity both ways round.

Grammatik: The *ich, du, er/sie* and *wir* forms in the perfect tense (with *sein* and *haben*)
This expands the explanation of the use of the perfect tense so that students can also use it in the third person, enabling them to talk about friends and other family members.

Grammatik: Using the imperfect tense to say 'was' (*ich war, es war*)
A further reminder about the use of the imperfect tense of *sein*. Give students some practice in this by asking for sentences starting *Ich bin* and *Es ist* and asking for them to be changed into the past.

3b Schreib einen Bericht über den Dialog in Übung 3a. (Writing)
Students get their first opportunity to write a report in the perfect tense, using the information in the speaking activity. Afterwards, ask them to write a similar paragraph telling their own holiday experiences. It doesn't have to be true, but it will be essential both for Speaking and Writing Tests. This work will need to be marked and kept for reference.

Further practice of the language and vocabulary of this unit is given on the following pages:
Sprechen: p. 63
Lesen/Schreiben A + B: pp. 168–169
Workbook: p. 28

The activities of this unit form an ideal introduction to coursework preparation. For further information and guidelines about the preparation of coursework on this topic, please refer to the **Coursework** spread pp. 154–155.

Logo! 4 4 Urlaub

5 Unterkunft (pp. 56–57)

Students will learn how to:
- book accommodation

Key language
Haben Sie ein Zimmer frei?
Ich möchte ein Doppelzimmer reservieren
Halbpension/Vollpension
Wie viel kostet ein Einzel/Doppelzimmer?
Ich möchte zwei Nächte bleiben
Ist das Zimmer mit … Bad/Dusche/Fernsehen/Radio/Telefon?
Ist das Zimmer inklusive Frühstück?
Um wie viel Uhr ist Frühstück/Abendessen?
Gibt es ein Lift / ein Restaurant / einen Parkplatz?
Kann ich bitte … die Rechnung / meinen Schlüssel haben? zahlen?

Language skills
- advice on writing a letter to book a hotel room

Resources
- Cassette B Side A
- Workbook p. 29
- Sprechen p. 63, Rollenspiel

Some students may be encountering this transactional topic for the first time. The introduction can take the form of eliciting, in English, what sort of expressions and vocabulary would be useful for booking accommodation.

1a Hör zu und lies. Welches Zimmer nimmt Herr Franz? (Listening, Reading)

As the task is straightforward (selecting one room from a selection of four), students can cover up the script and treat this as a "pure" listening task. Afterwards, they can practise the dialogue in pairs.

Answer

Zimmer c

– Guten Abend! Haben Sie ein Zimmer frei?
– Für wie viele Personen?
– Für zwei Personen.
– Ja, wir haben im ersten Stock ein Doppelzimmer frei.
– Ist das Zimmer mit Bad?
– Nein, nicht mit Bad, mit Dusche. Natürlich hat das Zimmer Fernsehen, Radio und Telefon.
– Hat das Zimmer zwei Einzelbetten?
– Nein, ein Doppelbett.

1b Hör zu und wähle die richtige Antwort. (Listening)

The conversation continues and students answer some multiple-choice questions while listening to the tape as often as necessary.

Answers

1 a, 2 a, 3 b, 4 b

– Was kostet ein Doppelzimmer pro Nacht?
– Sechzig Euro.
– Hmm … Ist das mit Frühstück?
– Jawohl.
– Gut. Ich nehme das Zimmer. Kann ich jetzt zahlen?
– Gern. Haben Sie eine Kreditkarte?
– Ja. Bitte schön. Wo ist das Restaurant?
– Hier vorne.
– Um wie viel Uhr ist das Abendessen?
– Von sechs bis acht Uhr.

2 Partnerarbeit. (Speaking)

Students create a hotel dialogue in pairs with the help of the Key Language box and some picture prompts. Make sure both students get the chance to play both roles.

3a Lies den Brief und beantworte die Fragen auf Englisch. (Reading)

Students read a letter to a hotel and answer comprehension questions in English.

Answers

1 two, 2 one double, one twin, 3 8th July, 4 two nights 5 bath, TV, 6 breakfast and evening meal, 7 Is there a lift? How much does a room cost? What time is breakfast? 8 female

Tip box: Advice on writing a letter to book a hotel room

This offers some useful advice on how students can ask for the necessary information.

3b Schreib einen Brief an ein Hotel. Benutze den Brief in Übung 3a und ändere die braunen Wörter. (Writing)

Now students write a similar letter to a hotel, using the same template but changing the content as indicated. Afterwards, they should write another similar letter of their own invention.

Teachers should draw attention to aspects of writing formal letters in German.

Further practice of the language and vocabulary of this unit is given on the following pages:
Sprechen: p. 63
Workbook: p. 29

6 Die Dusche ist kalt! (pp. 58–59)

Students will learn how to:
- complain about service in a hotel

Key language	Grammar points
Der Fernseher / Der Aufzug ist kaputt. Das Zimmer ist schmutzig / zu klein / zu laut / zu teuer. Die Dusche ist kalt. Das Essen war furchtbar. Ich möchte mit dem Direktor sprechen / mein Geld zurück haben.	• using *war* in a letter of complaint **Language skills** Writing a formal letter **Resources** • Cassette B Side A

Introduce this spread by inviting suggestions for things that students might want to complain about in a hotel. Elicit as much useful German vocabulary as they can remember.

1 Hör zu. Was passt zusammen? (1–6)
(Listening)
Students listen to the tape and write letters to link each complaint to the appropriate illustration.

Answers
1 c, 2 a, 3 f, 4 b, 5 e, 6 d

> 1 Die Dusche ist kalt!
> 2 Der Fernseher ist kaputt!
> 3 Das Zimmer ist zu laut!
> 4 Das Zimmer ist schmutzig!
> 5 Der Aufzug ist kaputt!
> 6 Das Zimmer ist zu klein!

2 Partnerarbeit. (Speaking)
Students construct brief dialogues (this is also an information gap activity) based on the pictures from Exercise 1, tackled in any order they wish.

3 Lies den Brief und schreib *richtig* oder *falsch*.
(Reading)
Students read the letter and note down whether the statements are true or false.

Answers
1 falsch, 2 falsch, 3 falsch, 4 falsch, 5 falsch, 6 richtig

Grammatik: the use of *war* when writing in the past
Remind students that, more often or not, a letter of complaint will refer to something which happened in the past.

4 Schreib einen Brief an ein Hotel. (Writing)
A fairly challenging task in which students write a similar letter to the one in Exercise 3, based on new information. More able students can then invent a letter of their own.

All the vocabulary and structures from this chapter are listed on the **Wörter** pages 60–61. These can be used for revision by covering up either the English or the German. Students can check here to see how much they remember from the chapter.

Assessment materials for Chapters 3 and 4 are available after Chapter 4.

Further speaking and grammar practice on the whole chapter is provided on p. 30–31 of the **Workbook**.

Kursarbeit

Logo! 4 4 Urlaub

4 Die Ferien (pp. 154–155)

The coursework section in *Logo! 4 Grün* gives regular, guided practice in preparing for the coursework element of the GCSE examination. It is cross-referenced to relevant sections in the core units. Each double-page spread is linked to a GCSE theme, and always starts with a model text on that theme (at a higher level than that expected by the student). This text acts as a stimulus to give students ideas about what they might include in their own piece of work. Students are encouraged to look at the detail of the text through the structured reading activities. They are gradually guided to produce good German sentences in the various activities, through to the final task in which they are asked to produce an extended piece of writing.

The *Hilfe* column is a feature on all the spreads. It shows students language they might include and particular structures that will raise the level of their writing. It is important to remind students who are capable of achieving a grade at the upper end of the Foundation level that they should always include examples of two or three tenses in their writing.

This spread guides students to produce an extended piece of writing on the topic of holidays.

1 Schreib die unterstrichenen Wörter auf Deutsch und Englisch hin.

Students write out the underlined words in German and English using a glossary or dictionary if necessary.

Answers

Urlaub = holiday; Sommerferien = summer holidays; sportlich = sporty; Manchmal = Sometimes; Spanien = Spain; Griechenland = Greece; Dänemark = Denmark; Schweden = Sweden; Wochen = weeks; hübsche = pretty; Österreich = Austria; später = later; Flughafen = airport; Flug = flight; Reisebus = tourist bus; Stadtrand = outskirts/edge of town; Gäste = guests; Freibad = open-air swimming pool; Radtouren = cycle rides; meistens = mostly; nie = never; immer = always; traurig = sad; Hoffentlich = Hopefully; nächstes Jahr = next year

2 Schreib diese Ausdrücke auf Deutsch. Sie sind im Text grün.

Students find and write the German equivalents of the English expressions listed. They are all in green in the text.

Answers

1 Ich mag die Sommerferien. 2 Ich bin sehr sportlich. 3 Manchmal fahren wir nach England. 4 Meine Familie und ich sind dieses Jahr für zwei Wochen nach Kitzbühel gefahren. 5 Der Flug war sehr gut. 6 Das Hotel war am Stadtrand. 7 Das Essen war spitze. 8 Ich bin im Freibad oft geschwommen. 9 Das Wetter war meistens gut. 10 Dieser Urlaub war prima.

3 Du bist Udo. Beantworte diese Fragen.

Students answer the questions as if they were Udo.

Answers

1 Ja, ich **bin** sehr **sportlich**. 2 Ich **spiele** Tennis, **gehe** oft schwimmen, und **fahre** in den Ferien Rad. 3 Kitzbühel ist eine **kleine**, **hübsche** Stadt in **Österreich**. 4 Der **Flug** war sehr gut und nicht zu **lang**. 5 Wir **sind** vom Flughafen mit **einem** Reisebus zum Hotel gekommen. 6 Das Hotel **war** am Stadtrand. 7 Das **Wetter** war meistens **gut**. 8 Dieser Urlaub **war prima**.

4 Schreib einen Bericht über deinen Urlaub.

Students should now be ready to write about their holidays using the support in the *Hilfe* column.

Hilfe
Help for students when writing about their holidays:
- write in a logical order
- use some time phrases, with the verb in second position
- include opinions

Workbook

p. 24

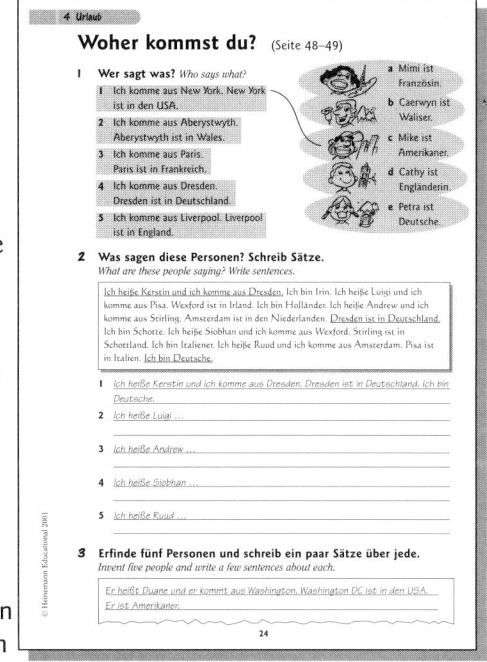

1 **1** c, **2** b, **3** a, **4** e, **5** d,
2 **1** Ich heiße Kerstin und ich komme aus Dresden. Dresden ist in Deutschland. Ich bin Deutsche.
2 Ich heiße Luigi und ich komme aus Pisa. Pisa ist in Italien. Ich bin Italiener.
3 Ich heiße Andrew und ich komme aus Stirling. Stirling ist in Schottland. Ich bin Schotte.
4 Ich heiße Siobhan und ich komme aus Wexford. Wexford ist in Irland. Ich bin Irin.
5 Ich heiße Ruud und ich komme aus Amsterdam. Amsterdam ist in den Niederlanden. Ich bin Holländer.
3 Open-ended, 1 mark per correct sentence. Overlook minor errors.

p. 25

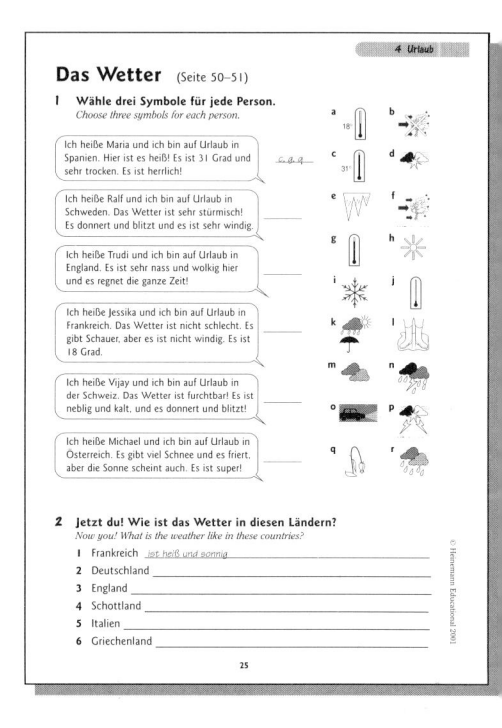

1 Maria – c, g, q; Ralf – f, n, p; Trudi – l, m, r; Jessika – a, b, k; Vijay – j, o, p; Michael – e, i, h
2 Open-ended. 1 mark per correct sentence. Overlook minor errors.

p. 26

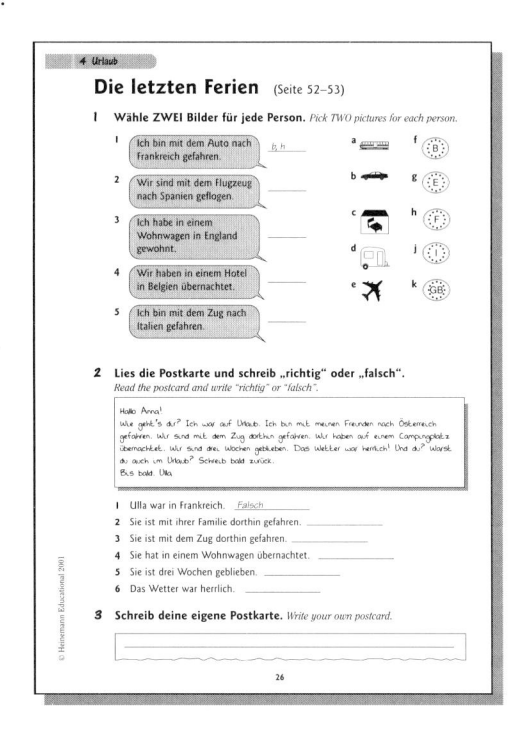

1 **1** b, h, **2** e, g, **3** d, k, **4** c, f, **5** a, j
2 **1** falsch, **2** falsch, **3** richtig, **4** falsch, **5** richtig, **6** richtig
3 Open-ended. 1 mark per correct sentence. Overlook minor errors.

p. 27

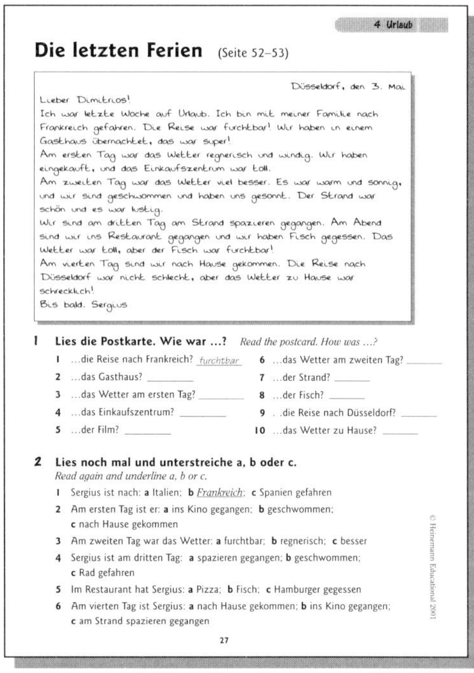

1 **1** furchtbar, **2** super, **3** regnerisch und windig, **4** toll, **5** langweilig, **6** viel besser, **7** schön, **8** furchtbar, **9** nicht schlecht, **10** schrecklich
2 **1** b, **2** a, **3** c, **4** a, **5** b, **6** a

Logo! 4 4 Urlaub

p. 28

1 1 b, 2 c, 3 d, 4 e, 5 a
2 Lieber Paul! Ich bin hier in **Paris** mit **meiner Familie**. Wir finden es **sehr gut**. Wir sind am ersten Tag **Rad gefahren**. Wir haben **eine Rundfahrt gemacht** und **Fotos gemacht**. Es war wunderbar. Am Abend sind wir **in die Disco gegangen**. Am zweiten Tag haben wir **geangelt**, und danach haben wir **die Stadt angesehen**. Am Abend haben wir **Freunde getroffen** und wir sind **ins Restaurant** gegangen. Morgen kommen wir nach Hause. Langweilig! Bis bald. Erich
3 Open-ended. 1 mark per correct sentence. Overlook minor errors.

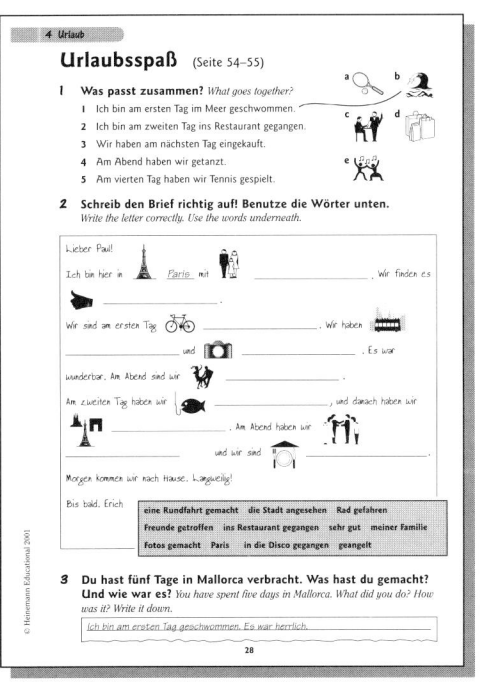

p. 29

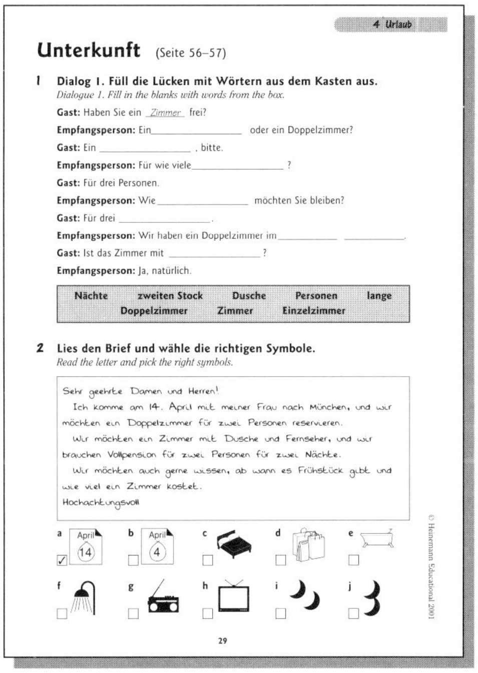

1 Zimmer, Einzelzimmer, Doppelzimmer, Personen, lange, Nächte, zweiten Stock, Dusche
2 a, c, f, h, i

p. 30

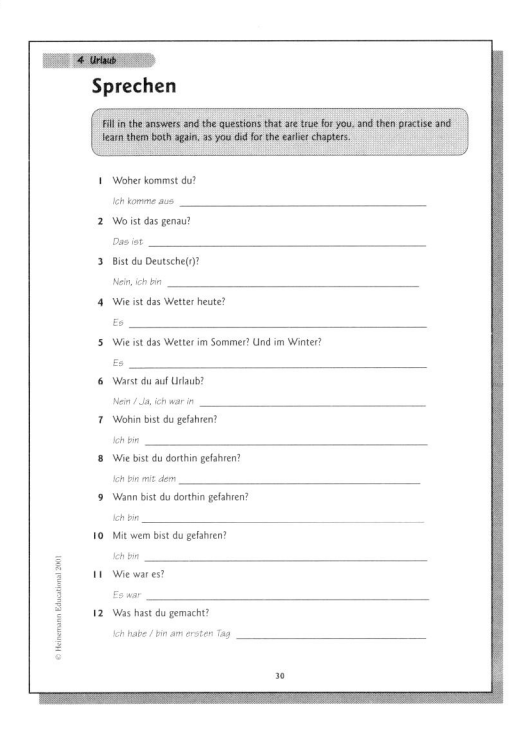

p. 31

1 1 Italienerin, 2 Österreicher, 3 Ire, 4 Schweizerin, 5 Französin
2 1 Ich bin mit dem Bus gefahren. 2 Wir sind mit dem Flugzeug geflogen. 3 Ich habe in einem Hotel übernachtet. 4 Wir sind drei Wochen geblieben. 5 Er hat auf einem Campingplatz gewohnt.
3 1 waren, 2 war, 3 war, 4 waren, 5 war

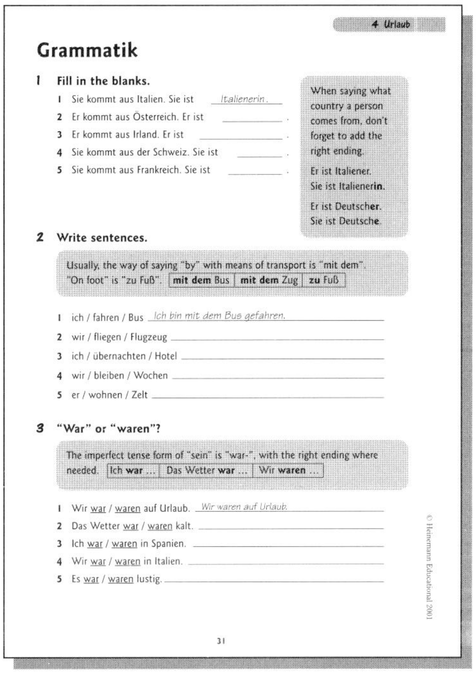

5 Meine Stadt (pp. 64–77)

Topic area	Key language	Grammar	Language skills
5.1 Wo ich wohne (pp. 64–65) Talk about home town and transport	*Ich wohne in … Das ist eine Kleinstadt/Großstadt / ein Dorf. … liegt in Norddeutschland. Es gibt einen Bahnhof / eine Kirche / ein Krankenhaus* [other places]. *… hat … Einwohner. In Logostadt gibt es / haben wir … / viele … / einige …* .	Use of *kein* in the accusative (*einen, eine, ein*) *Es gibt … + accusative*	
5.2 Logostadt (pp. 66–67) Say what there is to do	*Man kann (nicht) gut einkaufen / essen gehen / sport treiben. Es gibt (nicht) viele Geschäfte / (kein) Kino / (k)eine Disko usw. Ich fahre mit dem Bus/Zug/ Auto/Rad. Ich gehe zu Fuß. Ich fliege mit dem Flugzeug.*	Reminder of the useful phrases: *man kann … , es gibt …* . Revision of *mit dem/der* used with forms of transport	
5.3 Wie komme ich? (pp. 68–69) Ask and give directions	*Gehen Sie geradeaus/links/rechts / über die Ampel/Brücke. Nehmen Sie die erste (usw.) Straße links/rechts. Es ist auf der linken/rechten Seite / am Ende der Straße. Wie komme ich am besten zum/zur* [places in a town]?	*zum/zur* used with places to mean 'to the' Imperative: *Sie*	
5.4 Transportmöglichkeiten (pp. 70–71) Get around by public transport	*Wie fahre ich am besten zum (Flughafen / zur Stadtmitte / nach Berlin? Fahren Sie mit dem Bus/Zug / mit der U-S-/Straßenbahn? Haben Sie eine Broschüre/ Hotelliste? Haben Sie einen Fahrplan für die Bahn/ Busse? Haben Sie einen Stadtplan von …?*	Using *nach* with named towns and *zum/zu der* with other places in a town	*kostenlos* used to say something is free
5.5 Die Bundesbahn (pp. 72–73) Ask for information at a train station	*Wann fährt der Zug nach …? Von welchem Gleis? Einmal/Zweimal, bitte. Einfach oder hin und zurück? Erste oder zweite Klasse? Was kostet die Karte? Wann kommt der Zug in .. an? Muss ich umsteigen?* Signs in a station		Advice on phrases to use for dialogues when buying train/plane and bus tickets
5.6 Willkommen in unserer Stadt (pp. 74–75) Describe and compare towns	*… ist eine große Stadt / eine Kleinstadt. … hat … Einwohner. … ist alt/historisch/ruhig/modern/ruhig. größer, kleiner, älter, moderner, ruhiger, lebendiger, besser, teurer, billiger*	Comparatives (used to describe towns)	
Lesen/Schreiben (pp. 170–171)			Reading and Writing skills

- The vocabulary and structures taught in Chapter 5 are summarised on the **Wörter** pages of the Student's Book.
- Further Speaking practice on the language of the chapter is provided on **Sprechen** pp. 92–93.
- Coursework pages relating to this chapter can be found on pp. 156–157 of the Student's Book.
- For a selection of assessment tasks for Modules 5 and 6, please refer to the separate Assessment Pack for your chosen examination board: AQA, OCR or Edexcel.

Logo! 4 5 Meine Stadt

1 Wo ich wohne (pp. 64–65)

Students will learn how to:
- talk about their home town and transport

Key language
Ich wohne in …
Das ist …
  eine Kleinstadt
  eine Großstadt
  ein Dorf
… liegt in (Nord)england
Es gibt …
  einen Bahnhof
  eine Kirche
  ein Krankenhaus
(Logostadt) hat ungefähr (6 000) Einwohner
In (Logostadt) gibt es/haben wir … einen Dom/Fluss/Marktplatz/Park/Supermarkt/Zoo
eine Tankstelle/Universität
ein Rathaus/Einkaufszentrum/Museum/Schloss
viele Geschäfte/einige Schulen

Grammar points
- *kein* in the accusative (keinen, keine, kein)
- *Es gibt* + accusative

Resources
- Cassette B Side A
- Workbook p. 32

Before starting this spread, explain that it is about places in a town and ask students to mention as many of these as they can remember. Use any appropriate flashcards and OHP transparencies that are available.

1 Hör zu. Wer wohnt in Logostadt? Wer wohnt nicht in Logostadt? Schreib ja oder nein. (Listening)

Before starting on this listening, make sure students understand precisely how the task works: They will hear six people, some of whom live in Logostadt and some of whom don't. They must work out who does and who doesn't and write *Ja* or *Nein*.

Answers
1 nein, 2 ja, 3 nein, 4 ja, 5 nein, 6 nein

1 In meiner Stadt gibt es einen Fluss. Was? Einen Zoo? Nein, wir haben keinen Zoo!
2 Wir haben ein Rathaus, einen Marktplatz und auch ein Schloss.
3 Das Museum ist interessant. Kann man mit dem Zug dorthin fahren? Nein, es gibt keinen Bahnhof.
4 Der Park ist schön, und der Fluss auch.
5 Wir haben einen Dom und ein Sportzentrum.
6 Meine Stadt ist toll! Wir haben viele Geschäfte und einen Park. Was? Ein Schloss? Nein, es gibt kein Schloss.

Grammatik: The use of *kein* in the accusative (keinen, keine, kein)

Point out to students that this sometimes rather baffling construction can be vital for understanding, so they must listen out very carefully for it.

2 Lies die Broschüre. Sind die Sätze falsch oder richtig? (Reading)

Students read this extract from a brochure about this fictitious town and say whether the accompanying sentences are true or false.

Answers
1 falsch, 2 falsch, 3 falsch, 4 falsch, 5 falsch, 6 richtig

3 Partnerarbeit. (Speaking)

Students construct three dialogues about towns. First, they should read aloud the one about Malton and then do the others on the same basis.

4 Beschreib deine Stadt. (Writing)

Students now describe their own town or village, using information from the Key Language box. It must be written down, corrected and learnt for future reference. The more able should be encouraged to add in as much extra information as they are confident about.

Further practice of the language and vocabulary of this unit is given on the following pages:
Workbook: p. 32

2 Logostadt (pp. 66–67)

Students will learn how to:
- say what there is to do

Key language	Grammar points
Man kann (nicht) gut ...	• reminder of *man kann*
einkaufen	... and *es gibt* ...
essen gehen	• *mit dem/der* used with
Sport treiben	modes of transport
Es gibt ...	
(nicht) viele Geschäfte	**Resources**
(k)ein Kino/(k)eine	• Cassette B Side A
Disco usw.	• Workbook pp. 33–35
Ich fahre ...	• Sprechen p. 92,
mit dem Bus/Zug/	Gespräch +
Auto/Rad	Rollenspiel 1
Ich gehe zu Fuß	• Kursarbeit pp.
Ich fliege mit dem	156–157
Flugzeug	

Start the spread by brainstorming in German what there is to do in the nearest town to where the students live.

1a Was passt zusammen? (Reading)
Students read the sentences about Logostadt and match them to the illustrations by writing down letters.

Answers
1 b, 2 e, 3 d, 4 a, 5 c, 6 f

1b Hör zu. Was gibt es zu tun? (1–6) (Listening)
Students listen to six sentences and again match them to the illustrations in Exercise 1a by writing down letters.

Answers
1 f, 2 d, 3 a, 4 e, 5 c, 6 b

1 Man kann gut essen gehen. Wir haben eine Pizzeria und viele Restaurants.
2 Man kann gut Sport treiben. Wir haben einen Tennisplatz und ein Sportzentrum.
3 Die Stadt ist sehr gut für junge Leute. Es gibt viele Discos und Clubs.
4 Man kann gut einkaufen. Wir haben einen großen Supermarkt und ein Einkaufszentrum.
5 Meine Stadt ist nicht gut für junge Leute. Wir haben keine Disco und kein Kino.
6 Hier ist es toll für Touristen. Es gibt einen Dom und auch ein Schloss.

2a Partnerarbeit. (Speaking)
Students construct three dialogues about towns and what there is to do in them, based on the illustrations. The first one is done for them, so they should start by reading it in pairs, before substituting other pieces of information for the other two dialogues. These can be written down if wished.

Wiederholung: A reminder of the useful expressions *Man kann ...* and *Es gibt ...*
Point out how vital these expressions are for saying what there is to do.

2b Beantworte die Fragen in Übung 2a für DEINE Stadt. (Writing)
A template is provide for students to write a brief description of what there is to do in their own nearest town.

3a Wie kommt man nach Logostadt? Was passt zusammen? (Reading)
Before tackling this exercise, elicit as many forms of transport as possible from the students without looking at the page. In the exercise, they match transport phrases to pictures by writing letters.

Answers
1 a, 2 c, 3 d, 4 b, 5 f, 6 e

3b Hör zu. Wer kommt wie nach Logostadt? (1–6) (Listening)
Students listen to the tape and write down letters to match the forms of transport to the same pictures from Exercise 3a.

Answers
1 f, 2 b, 3 d, 4 e, 5 a, 6 c

1 – Richard, wie kommst du in die Stadt?
  – Zu Fuß.
2 – Und du, Bettina?
  – Ich fahre mit dem Auto.
3 – Wie kommst du nach Logostadt, Uli?
  – Ich? Ich fahre mit dem Zug.
4 – Und du, Margret?
  – Ich fahre mit dem Rad.
5 – Du, Mike?
  – Ich fliege mit dem Flugzeug.
  – Was?!
  – Ja, wirklich!
6 – Und wie fährst du, Gitti?
  – Ich fahre mit dem Bus.

4a Partnerarbeit. Und du? Wie kommst du in die Stadt? (Speaking)
Students construct simple questions and answers about forms of transport. This exercise needs to be done twice, with students swopping roles.

4b Schreib die Sätze aus. (Writing)
Finally, the answers to Exercise 4a must be written down.

Answers
1 Ich fahre mit dem Bus. 2 Ich fahre mit dem Auto.
3 Ich gehe zu Fuß. 4 Ich fahre mit dem Zug. 5 Ich fahre mit dem Rad.

Grammatik/Wiederholung: A reminder to use *mit dem/der* when describing modes of transport
Make sure students realise that they mustn't use other prepositions such as *auf* or *in*.

> Further practice of the language and vocabulary of this unit is given on the following pages:
> Sprechen: p. 92
> Workbook: pp. 33–35
>
> The activities of this unit form an ideal introduction to coursework preparation. For further information and guidelines about the preparation of coursework on this topic, please refer to the **Coursework** spread pp. 156–157.

3 Wie komme ich ...? (pp. 68–69)

Students will learn how to:
- find the way

Key language	Grammar points
Gehen Sie ...	• *zum/zur* used to mean 'to the'
geradeaus	• imperative with *Sie*
links/rechts	
über die Ampel/Brücke	**Resources**
Nehmen Sie ...	• Cassette B Side A
die erste (usw.) Straße	• Workbook p. 36
links/rechts	• Sprechen p. 92,
Es ist ...	Rollenspiel 2
auf der rechten/linken Seite	
am Ende der Straße	
Wie komme ich am besten zum Bahnhof / zur Tankstelle (usw.)?	

Before starting this spread, point out that it is a topic particularly beloved of GCSE examiners. It is also very useful if students need to find the way anywhere while staying in a German-speaking country.

Students will no doubt remember *rechts* and *links*. Find out how many other directions they remember by using mime or a simple line plan on the blackboard or OHP.

1a Lies die Sätze und finde die Gebäude. (Reading)

Students read five directions from speech bubbles and identify where the people are going to by writing down a letter from the map on the previous page. Teachers can use this map for more practice in giving and understanding directions.

Answers
1 d, 2 i, 3 f, 4 e, 5 c

Grammatik: *zum/zur* ...

This reminds students to use *zum* with masculine and neuter words and *zur* with feminine words. Call out names of places and get students to say whether they would say *zum* or *zur*:
Teacher: die Kirche.
Student: zur Kirche.
Teacher: Richtig. das Rathaus.
Student: zum Rathaus, usw.

1b Hör zu. Finde die Gebäude. (1–5) (Listening)

Now students find five more places on the map, this time on the basis of listening to the tape as often as necessary.

Answers
1 b, 2 j, 3 g, 4 h, 5 a

1 – Gibt es hier in der Nähe ein Krankenhaus?
  – Ja, gehen Sie immer geradeaus.
2 – Gibt es ein Informationsbüro in der Stadt?
  – Jawohl. Gehen Sie geradeaus über die Brücke. Nehmen Sie dann die erste Straße links.
3 – Ist das Museum weit von hier?
  – Nein, nehmen Sie die erste Straße links. Das Museum ist am Ende der Straße.
4 – Gibt es hier in der Nähe eine Tankstelle?
  – Ja. Fahren Sie geradeaus, über die Ampel. Nehmen Sie dann die erste Straße links.
5 – Entschuldigen Sie, wo ist die nächste Post?
  – Am Ende der zweiten Straße rechts.

2a Partnerarbeit. (Speaking)

This speaking practice is based on the illustrations provided in the dialogue, not the original map. The exercise must be done both ways round and more able students encouraged to invent similar dialogues of their own.

2b Schreib die Antworten aus Übung 2a auf Deutsch auf. (Writing)

Students write down the answers to Exercise 2a.

Answers
1 Nehmen Sie die dritte Straße links. 2 Gehen Sie geradeaus. 3 Nehmen Sie die zweite Straße links. 4 Nehmen Sie die vierte Straße rechts. 5 Nehmen Sie die erste Straße rechts. 6 Nehmen Sie die zweite Straße links.

Further practice of the language and vocabulary of this unit is given on the following pages:
Sprechen: p. 92
Workbook: p. 36

4 Transportmöglichkeiten
(pp. 70–71)

Students will learn how to:
- get around by public transport

Key language	Grammar points
Wie fahre ich am besten … zum (Flug)hafen / zur Stadtmitte / nach Berlin? Fahren Sie … mit dem Bus/Zug mit der U-/S-/Straßenbahn Haben Sie … eine Broschüre/ Hotelliste? einen Fahrplan für die Bahn? einen Stadtplan von …?	• using *nach* with a named town, otherwise *zum/zur* for places **Resources** • Cassette B Side A • Workbook p. 37 • Sprechen p. 92, Rollenspiel 3 + 4

Before starting this spread, explain that students will be learning various useful expressions for moving around in a German city. Elicit in English what sorts of questions would be useful.

1 Im Informationsbüro. Wer möchte was? (Reading)
Students link the questions in the speech bubbles to the illustrations by writing down letters. Tell students about the two other words for Tourist Office, *Verkehrsamt* or *Verkehrsverein*, either of which they may need to recognise.

Answers
1 d, 2 c, 3 a, 4 f, 5 b, 6 e

2 Hör zu. Welches Bild passt zu welchem Dialog? (1–5) (Listening)
Students listen to these taped dialogues as often as necessary in order to link them to the pictures by writing down letters.

Answers
1 e, 2 d, 3 c, 4 b, 5 a

1 – Wie fahre ich am besten zum Krankenhaus?
   – Fahren Sie mit der Straßenbahn Linie 5.
2 – Wie fahre ich am besten zum Flughafen?
   – Fahren Sie mit der U-Bahn Linie 2.
3 – Wie fahre ich am besten zur Stadtmitte?
   – Fahren Sie mit dem Bus Linie 25.
4 – Wie fahre ich am besten nach Hamburg?
   – Fahren Sie mit dem Zug.
5 – Wie fahre ich am besten zum Schloss?
   – Fahren Sie mit der S-Bahn Linie 12.

Grammatik: *Nach* + named town, *zum/zur* for other places
Point out that misuse of *zu* and *nach* is a particularly common error which can easily be avoided.

3 Partnerarbeit. (Speaking)
Students construct questions and answers about the best way to get to places, based on illustrations. They should take it in turn to ask the questions.

4 Was kostet das? (Reading)
Students identify the items from the pictures and note down the prices.

Answers
1 €1.00, 2 €1.50, 3 €0.50, 4 €2.50, 5 kostenlos, 6 kostenlos

Tip box: *kostenlos*
This word often crops up in exams. Students are sometimes tempted to use an incorrect word such as *frei*.

5 Partnerarbeit. (Speaking)
Students construct a series of short dialogues asking for items in a Tourist Office. These dialogues need to be done both ways round. More able students can write the questions out.

Further practice of the language and vocabulary of this unit is given on the following pages:
Sprechen: p. 92
Workbook: p. 37

5 Die Bundesbahn (pp. 72–73)

Students will learn how to:
- ask for information at a train station

Key language	Language skills
Wann fährt der Zug nach …?	• help for dialogues involving buying train/bus and plane tickets
Um … Uhr	
Von welchem Gleis?	
Einmal/Zweimal, bitte	
Einfach oder hin und zurück?	**Resources**
Erste oder zweite Klasse?	• Cassette B Side A
Was kostet die Karte?	• Workbook p. 38
Wann kommt der Zug in … an?	• Sprechen p. 93, Rollenspiel 5
Muss ich umsteigen?	
[+ signs at a station]	

As this is a topic which they will have encountered before, ask students, before starting this spread, to try and remember as many expressions as they can for asking for information about trains, buying tickets, etc.

1a Hör zu und lies. Wähle die richtige Antwort. (Listening, Reading)

This can either be done initially as a "pure" listening activity, with the script covered up, or with students following the text as they listen. They listen as often as necessary in order to choose the correct multiple-choice answers.

Answers

1 Bornholm, 2 14 Uhr 30, 3 4, 4 hin und zurück, 5 €10,50, 6 16 Uhr 45, 7 in Strande

– Guten Tag! Wann fährt der nächste Zug nach Bornholm?
– Um 14.30 Uhr.
– Von welchem Gleis?
– Gleis 4.
– Einmal bitte.
– Einfach oder hin und zurück?
– Hin und zurück. Was kostet die Karte?
– € 10,50
– Wann kommt der Zug in Bornholm an?
– Um 16. 45 Uhr.
– Muss ich umsteigen?
– Ja, in Strande.

1b Hör zu und wähle die richtige Antwort. (1–7) (Listening)

Students listen to the tape, which contains different information. However, they still select from the multiple choice answers in Exercise 1a.

Answers

1 Bromberg, 2 14 Uhr 40, 3 14, 4 einfach, 5 €15, 6 14 Uhr 54, 7 nicht

– Guten Tag! Wann fährt der nächste Zug nach Bromberg?
– Um 14.40 Uhr.
– Von welchem Gleis?
– Gleis 14.
– Einmal bitte.
– Einfach oder hin und zurück?
– Einfach. Was kostet die Karte?
– 15 Euro.
– Wann kommt der Zug in Bromberg an?
– Um 14. 54 Uhr.
– Muss ich umsteigen?
– Nein.

2 Partnerarbeit. (Speaking)

Working in pairs, students construct six dialogues at a rail station booking office, based on the timetable provided.

3a Schreib die Gespräche auf. (Writing)

Students write down three dialogues based on the prompts provided. Whenever names of towns, etc, which may be unfamiliar to students, crop up, as they do here, make sure they are aware of the correct pronunciation.

Answers

1
Einmal nach Stuttgart, bitte.
Einfach oder hin und zurück?
Einfach.
Erste oder zweite Klasse?
Zweite Klasse, bitte.
Bitte schön.
Was kostet die Karte?
12 Euro.
Muss ich umsteigen?
Ja, in Koblenz.

2
Zweimal nach Wismar, bitte.
Einfach oder hin und zurück?
Hin und zurück.
Erste oder zweite Klasse?
Zweite Klasse, bitte.
Was kostet die Karte?
95 Euro.
Muss ich umsteigen?
Nein.

3
Einmal nach Kiel, bitte.
Einfach oder hin und zurück?
Einfach.
Erste oder zweite Klasse?
Erste Klasse, bitte.
Was kostet die Karte?
35 Euro.
Muss ich umsteigen?
Ja, in Hamburg.

3b Übe die Gespräche aus Übung 3a mit einem Partner / einer Partnerin. (Speaking)
Students now use the dialogues from Exercise 3a for further speaking practice.

Tip box: Useful language for buying tickets
This lists the expressions which students must learn in preparation for their Speaking Test.

4 Welche Schilder haben welche Bedeutung? (Reading)
Students should use the glossary or dictionaries to help them work out the English meanings of these station signs. Point out how useful these will be in real life as well as in the Reading Test in their exam.

Answers
1 c, 2 d, 3 i, 4 b, 5 j, 6 e, 7 f, 8 g, 9 h, 10 a

Further practice of the language and vocabulary of this unit is given on the following pages:
Sprechen: p. 93
Workbook: p. 38

6 Willkommen in unserer Stadt (pp. 74–75)

Students will learn how to:
- describe and compare towns

Key language	Grammar points
... ist ...	• introduction to comparatives
eine große Stadt/ Kleinstadt	
... hat ... Einwohner	**Resources**
... ist alt/historisch/ ruhig/modern/lebendig	• Cassette B Side A
größer/kleiner als ...	• Lesen/Schreiben A + B pp. 170–171
älter/moderner als ...	
ruhiger/lebendiger als ...	
besser	

Introduce this spread by asking a few simple oral questions like *Ist Berlin in Frankreich?*, *Ist New York größer oder kleiner als Bristol?*, etc.

1 Welche Stadt ist das? Schreib *Bridport*, *Engelberg* oder *Delmenhorst*. (Reading)
Students read the extracts from brochures about three towns and note down which town each sentence refers to.

Answers
1 Bridport, 2 Delmenhorst, 3 Delmenhorst, 4 Bridport, 5 Bridport/Engelberg, 6 Delmenhorst, 7 Bridport, 8 Engelberg

Grammatik: An introduction to comparatives
For Foundation level, this selection of comparative forms should be sufficient without further explanation. Teachers who want to go into further detail can refer to the grammar section (page 185).

2 Partnerarbeit. (Speaking)
Students ask and answer questions using the comparative forms.

3 Vergleiche Bridport und Delmenhorst. (Writing)
Students compare aspects of two towns and write down the answers in full sentences.

Answers
1 Delmenhorst ist größer als Bridport. 2 Bridport ist kleiner als Delmenhorst. 3 Bridport ist älter als Engelberg. 4 Delmenhorst ist moderner als Bridport. 5 Bridport ist ruhiger als Delmenhorst. 6 Delmenhorst ist lebendiger als Bridport.

4 Hör zu und lies. Schreib *England* oder *Deutschland*. (Listening, Reading)
This can either be treated as a pure listening item (with the script covered up) or as a pure reading item, or both. Students are now being asked to tackle more flexible language at the upper end of Foundation level, but the answers are still one-word responses. More able students should be asked to write full sentences.

Answers
1 England, 2 England, 3 England, 4 Deutschland, 5 England, 6 England

– Der Schauspieler Freddi Frapp dreht einen Film in London. Na, Freddi, wie findest du England?
– England ist toll, aber London ist unheimlich teuer! Mein Hotel kostet £150 pro Nacht. Die Hotels in Deutschland sind billiger. Aber das englische Frühstück ist toll, mit Schinken, Spiegelei und Toast. Das ist viel besser als das deutsche Frühstück, mit nur Brötchen, Marmelade und Käse. Es regnet viel in England. Das englische Wetter ist schrecklich. In Deutschland gibt es nicht so viel Regen. Aber in Deutschland ist es kalt. Die Städte in England sind oft schmutzig. Das finde ich nicht gut. Deutschland ist ein sauberes Land. Aber die Leute in England sind immer nett und freundlich.

5 Beschreib diese Städte. (Writing)
Students write descriptions of two towns, based on information provided. They could also write a similar description of their own nearest town in a similar format. Encourage students to include as much information as they can. This work should be marked and retained for reference.

Answers

Kronberg ist eine Kleinstadt in Süddeutschland. Kronberg hat 30 000 Einwohner und ist historisch und ruhig. Kronberg ist kleiner als Frankfurt.

Frankfurt ist eine Großstadt in Süddeutschland. Frankfurt hat 650 000 Einwohner und ist modern und lebendig. Frankfurt ist größer als Kronberg.

Further practice of the language and vocabulary of this unit is given on the following pages:
Lesen/Schreiben A + B: pp. 170–171

All the vocabulary and structures from this chapter are listed on the **Wörter** pages 76–77. These can be used for revision by covering up either the English or the German. Students can check here to see how much they remember from the chapter.

Assessment materials for Chapters 5 and 6 are available after Chapter 6.

Further speaking and grammar practice on the whole chapter is provided on pp. 39–40 of the **Workbook**.

Kursarbeit

5 Stadt/Umgebung (pp. 156–157)

The coursework section in *Logo! 4 Grün* gives regular, guided practice in preparing for the coursework element of the GCSE examination. It is cross-referenced to relevant sections in the core units. Each double-page spread is linked to a GCSE theme, and always starts with a model text on that theme (at a higher level than that expected by the student). This text acts as a stimulus to give students ideas about what they might include in their own piece of work. Students are encouraged to look at the detail of the text through the structured reading activities. They are gradually guided to produce good German sentences in the various activities, through to the final task in which they are asked to produce an extended piece of writing.

The *Hilfe* column is a feature on all the spreads. It shows students language they might include and particular structures that will raise the level of their writing. It is important to remind students who are capable of achieving a grade at the upper end of the Foundation level that they should always include examples of two or three tenses in their writing.

This spread guides students to produce an extended piece of writing on the topic of a town.

1 Finde diese Ausdrücke im Text. Sie sind grün.
Students find and write out the German equivalents of the English expressions listed.

Answers

1 Andenken, 2 die Einkaufsstraßen, 3 Vergessen Sie nicht den Fotoapparat! 4 mit der Bahn, 5 eine herrliche Stadt, 6 freundliche Leute, 7 hier ist immer was los! 8 dreißig Kilometer von Gießen entfernt, 9 im Verkehrsamt, 10 Herzlich willkommen in Marburg!

2 Beantworte die Fragen auf Deutsch. Wähle *a*, *b* oder *c*.
Students choose the right answer for each question from the three alternatives given.

Answers

1 b, 2 a, 3 c, 4 b, 5 a, 6 c, 7 a, 8 b

3 Schreib eine Broschüre über eine andere Stadt.
Students should now be ready to write a brochure about a town, using the support in the *Hilfe* column.

Hilfe
Tips to help students to write a brochure:
- adapt language from the text provided
- use questions and short quotes
- add a labelled illustration of a town

Logo! 4 5 Meine Stadt

Workbook

p. 32

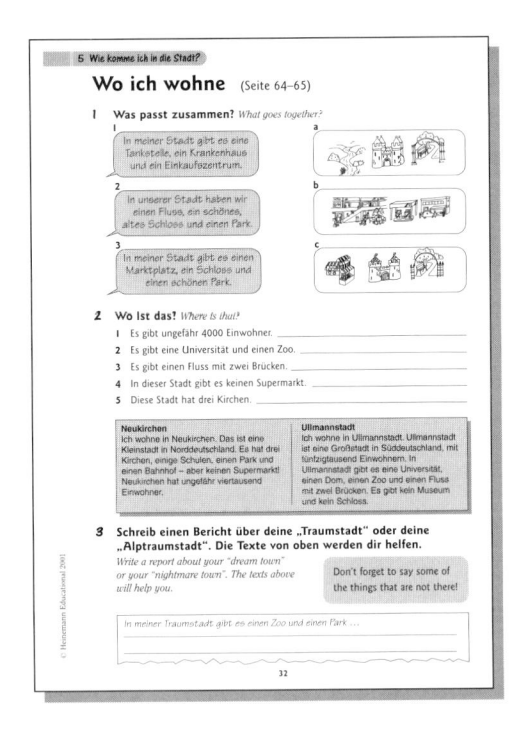

1 1 b, 2 a, 3 c
2 1 Neukirchen, 2 Ullmannstadt, 3 Ullmannstadt, 4 Neukirchen, 5 Neukirchen
3 Open-ended. 1 mark per correct sentence. Overlook minor errors.

p. 33

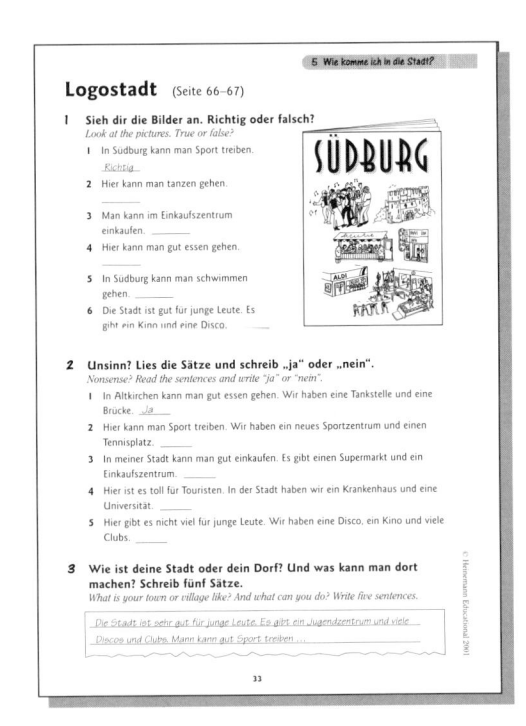

1 1 Richtig, 2 Richtig, 3 Falsch, 4 Richtig, 5 Falsch, 6 Richtig
2 1 Ja, 2 Nein, 3 Nein, 4 Ja, 5 Ja
3 Open-ended. 1 mark per correct sentence. Overlook minor errors.

p. 34

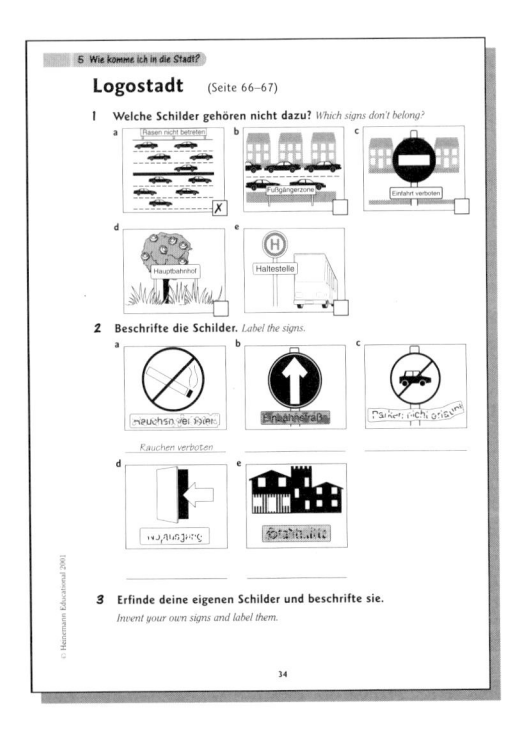

1 a, b, d
2 a Rauchen verboten, b Einbahnstraße, c Parken nicht erlaubt, d Notausgang, e Stadtmitte
3 Open-ended

p. 35

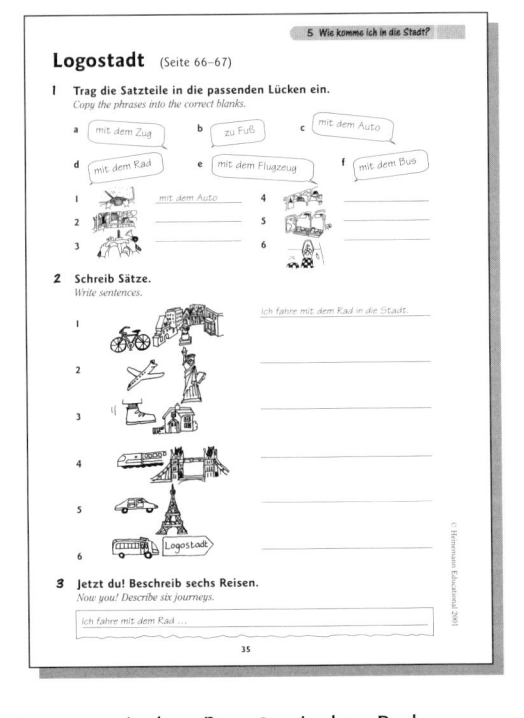

1 1 mit dem Auto, 2 mit dem Bus, 3 mit dem Rad, 4 mit dem Zug, 5 mit dem Flugzeug, 6 zu Fuß
2 1 Ich fahre mit dem Rad in die Stadt. 2 Ich fahre mit dem Flugzeug nach New York. 3 Ich gehe zu Fuß nach Hause. 4 Ich fahre mit dem Zug nach London. 5 Ich fahre mit dem Auto nach Paris. 6 Ich fahre mit dem Bus nach Logostadt.
3 Open-ended. Overlook minor errors.

p. 36

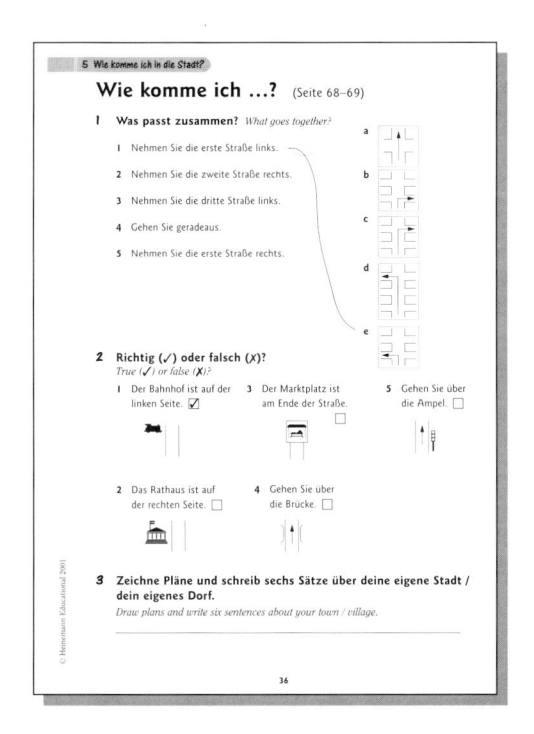

1 1 e, 2 c, 3 d, 4 a, 5 b
2 1 Richtig, 2 Falsch, 3 Richtig, 4 Richtig, 5 Richtig
3 Open-ended

p. 37

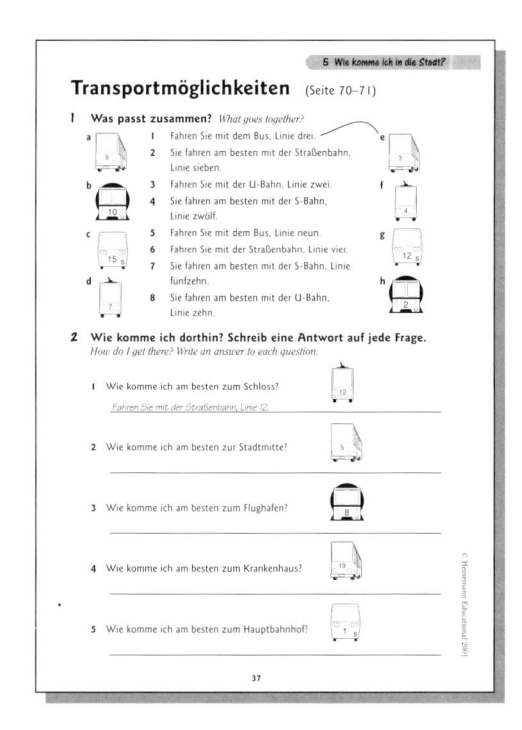

1 1 e, 2 d, 3 h, 4 g, 5 a, 6 f, 7 c, 8 b
2 1 Fahren Sie mit der Straßenbahn, Linie 12.
   2 Fahren Sie mit dem Bus, Linie 5.
   3 Fahren Sie mit der U-Bahn, Linie 8.
   4 Fahren Sie mit dem Bus, Linie 19.
   5 Fahren Sie mit der S-Bahn, Linie 1.

p. 38

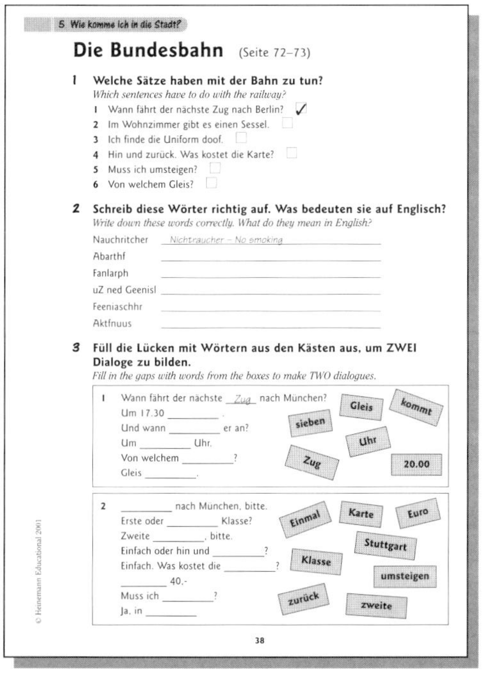

1 1, 4, 5, 6
2 Nichtraucher – No smoking
Abfahrt – Departures
Fahrplan – Timetable
Zu den Gleisen – To the platforms
Fahrscheine – Tickets
Auskunft – Information
3 Dialog 1
Wann fährt der nächste **Zug** nach München?
Um 17.30 **Uhr**.
Und wann **kommt** er an?
Um **20.00** Uhr.
Von welchem **Gleis**?
Gleis **sieben**.
Dialog 2
Einmal nach München, bitte.
Erste oder **zweite** Klasse?
Zweite **Klasse**, bitte.
Einfach oder hin und **zurück**?
Einfach. Was kostet die **Karte**?
Euro 40,–.
Muss ich **umsteigen**?
Ja, in **Stuttgart**.

p. 39

p. 40

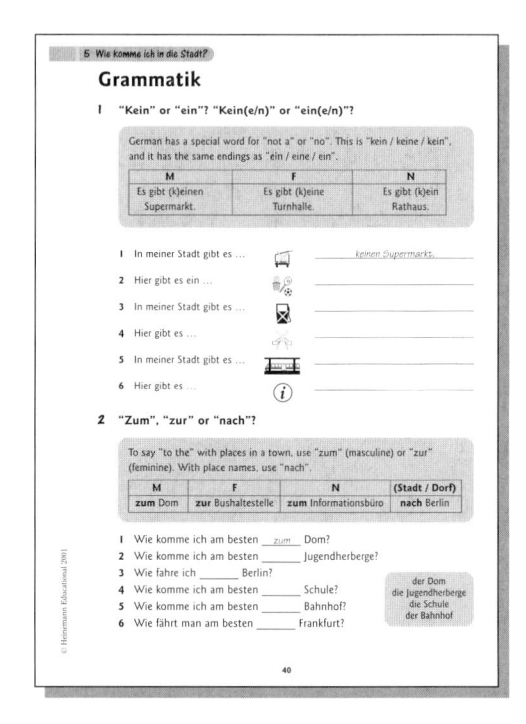

1 1 In meiner Stadt gibt es keinen Supermarkt. 2 Hier gibt es ein Sportzentrum. 3 In meiner Stadt gibt es keine Tankstelle. 4 Hier gibt es keine Brücke. 5 In meiner Stadt gibt es einen Bahnhof. 6 Hier gibt es ein Informationsbüro.

2 1 zum, 2 zur, 3 nach, 4 zur, 5 zum, 6 nach

6 Einkaufen (pp. 78–91)

Topic area	Key language	Grammar	Language skills
6.1 Geschäfte und Öffnungszeiten (pp. 78–79) Talk about shops and opening times	Types of shop *Wo ist der nächste Supermarkt? In der ... straße. Wann macht die Konditorei auf? Wann macht das Kaufhaus zu? Viertel vor/nach ... Halb ..., 18 Uhr dreißig, fünf vor halb fünf, fünf nach halb sieben.* Signs in shops		Times: *halb, Viertel vor/nach, fünf vor halb/fünf nach halb*
6.2 Preise, usw (pp. 80–81) Talk about food with numbers and prices	*Bitte schön? Ich möchte 500 Gramm Äpfel / 1 Kilo Erdbeeren / 6 Scheiben Käse / eine Packung Chips / eine Dose Cola / eine Flasche Weißwein / eine Tüte Milch.* [+ other food items]. *Sonst noch etwas? Ist das alles? Was macht das?*	Amounts and weights of foodstuffs Food packaging	
6.3 Im Kleidungsgeschäft (pp. 82–83) Shop for clothes	*Ich möchte einen roten Schal / eine graue Hose / ein gelbes Hemd / weiße Socken.* [+ other clothes and colours]. *Bitte schön. Welche Farbe/Größe? Was kostet das? Kann ich ... anprobieren? Der Rock ist zu klein/groß/teuer.*	Adjectival endings after *ein* in the accusative (*einen roten, eine rote, ein rotes*)	
6.4 Taschengeld (pp. 84–85) Talk about pocket money Find your way round a store	*Wie viel Taschengeld bekommst du? Ich bekomme € ... pro Monat/Woche. Was kaufst du damit? Ich kaufe Kassetten* (usw.). *Ich spare für die Ferien. Wo ist die ...abteilung? Im Erdgeschoss. In der ersten* (usw.) *Etage.*	Plurals *im / in der*	Advice to students to learn pocket money details for Speaking Test
6.5 Auf der Post (pp. 86–87) Cope at the post office	*Was kostet ein Brief / eine Postkarte / dieses Päckchen nach ...? Ich möchte eine Briefmarke zu ein Euro. Ich möchte ein Fax schicken. Kann man hier / Wo kann man telefonieren / einen Brief einwerfen / eine E-Mail schicken?*	*Ich möchte ...*	Meaning of *Ansichtskarte* Advice when posting a parcel Useful expressions with *kann*
6.6 Es ist nicht in Ordnung (pp. 88–89) How to complain in shops	*Ich habe diesen/diese/dieses ... gekauft. Er/Sie/Es ist kaputt/alt/schmutzig/zu groß / zu klein. Kann ich einen neuen/eine neue/ein neues ... haben? Ich möchte mein Geld zurück / mit dem Direktor sprechen.*	*Diese* Adjectives in the accusative	Asking for money back or to see the manager
Lesen/Schreiben (pp. 172–173)			Reading and Writing skills

- The vocabulary and structures taught in Chapter 6 are summarised on the **Wörter** pages of the Student's Book, 90–91.
- Further Speaking practice on the language of the chapter is provided on **Sprechen** pp. 93.
- For a selection of assessment tasks for Chapters 5 and 6, please refer to the separate Assessment Pack for your chosen examination board: AQA, OCR or Edexcel.

1 Geschäfte und Öffnungszeiten (pp. 78–79)

Students will learn how to:
- talk about shops and opening times

> **Key language**
> der Supermarkt
> die Apotheke
> die Bäckerei
> die Buchhandlung
> die Drogerie
> die Konditorei
> die Metzgerei
> das Kaufhaus
> das Schreibwarengeschäft
> Viertel vor/nach …
> halb neun
> achtzehn Uhr dreißig
> fünf vor halb fünf
> fünf nach halb sieben
> Wo ist die nächste Apotheke?
> In der …straße
> Wann macht die Apotheke auf?
> Wann macht die Apotheke zu?
> [+ signs in shops]
>
> **Language skills**
> Advice on giving times in German
>
> **Resources**
> - Cassette B Side B
> - Workbook p. 41
> - Sprechen p. 93, Rollenspiel 1

Before starting this spread, have a brief brainstorming session in German to elicit as many names of shops as students can remember.

1a Welches Geschäft ist das? (Reading)
Students identify shops from pictures and write down their names.

Answers
1 die Apotheke, **2** die Buchhandlung, **3** das Schreibwarengeschäft, **4** die Bäckerei, **5** die Metzgerei, **6** die Konditorei, **7** die Drogerie, **8** der Supermarkt

1b Hör zu. Welches Geschäft ist das? (1–5) (Listening)
Now students identify more shops, this time on the basis of listening to the tape. Again, they write down the names of the shops.

Answers
1 die Metzgerei, **2** die Konditorei, **3** die Drogerie, **4** das Kaufhaus, **5** der Supermarkt

> 1 Dieses Geschäft macht um Viertel vor acht auf und um achtzehn Uhr zu.
> 2 Dieses Geschäft macht um Viertel nach acht auf und um siebzehn Uhr dreißig zu.
> 3 Dieses Geschäft macht um neun Uhr auf und um achtzehn Uhr dreißig zu.
> 4 Dieses Geschäft macht um halb neun auf und um neunzehn Uhr zu.
> 5 Dieses Geschäft macht um acht Uhr auf und um achtzehn Uhr dreißig zu.

Tip box
An explanation of the use of *halb, Viertel nach/vor* and *(fünf) vor/nach halb (sieben)*.

Make sure students have plenty of practice in understanding and saying these forms, because they cause much confusion and could easily lead to awkward misunderstandings. Some practice is included in this tip box.

2 Partnerarbeit. (Speaking)
Working in pairs, students create dialogues about shops and their opening hours, based on some printed signs.

3 Was passt zusammen? (Reading)
Students must use the glossary or dictionaries to identify the English meanings of various signs. Emphasise the fact that this is just the sort of thing which crops up in the Foundation level Reading Test.

Answers
1 g, **2** c, **3** f, **4** d, **5** b, **6** i, **7** e, **8** a, **9** j, **10** h

> Further practice of the language and vocabulary of this unit is given on the following pages:
> Sprechen: p. 93
> Workbook: p. 41

Logo! 4 6 Einkaufen

2 Preise usw (pp. 80–81)

Students will learn how to:
- talk about numbers, prices and food

Key language	Salami
Bitte schön?	Schinken
Ich möchte …	Sprudel
250 Gramm Butter	Mineralwasser
500 Gramm Äpfel	Rotwein
1 Kilo Erdbeeren	Orangensaft
2 Kilo Kartoffeln	Sonst noch etwas?
6 Scheiben Käse	Ist das alles?
eine Packung Chips	Was macht das?
zwei Packungen Kekse	
eine Dose Cola	**Grammar points**
zwei Dosen Limonade	• amounts and weights
eine Flasche Weißwein	of foodstuffs
zwei Flaschen Bier	• food packaging
eine Tüte Milch	
zwei Tuten Apfelsaft	**Resources**
Bananen	• Cassette B Side B
Apfelsinen	• Workbook p. 42
Orangen	• Sprechen p. 93,
Kirschen	Rollenspiel 2
Tomaten	• Lesen/Schreiben A
Zucker	p. 172

Introduce this spread by making sure that students understand the situation with the euro. From February 2002, Germany, along with several other European countries, abandons its own currency to use the euro exclusively. Then ask students to see how many German words for food items they can remember. Any available flashcards and OHP transparencies can also be used.

1a Was kann man hier kaufen? (Writing)
With the help of the Key Language box, students identify items from a market stall and write down their German names.

Answers

1 Tomaten, 2 Kartoffeln, 3 Butter, 4 Kirschen, 5 Käse, 6 Orangen, 7 Äpfel, 8 Erdbeeren, 9 Zucker, 10 Bananen

Grammatik: Quantities
Help for students to ask for amounts or weights of foodstuffs and the various containers that food is packaged in. The teacher can call out items and invite students to suggest suitable amounts, e.g:
Teacher: Käse.
Student: 250 Gramm.
Teacher: Chips.
Student: Eine Packung, usw.

1b Partnerarbeit (Speaking)
In pairs, students conduct brief shopping conversations, based on the illustrations provided and using the appropriate amounts and containers. These must be done both ways round.

2 Hör zu. Was kosten die Picknicksachen? Schreib die Preise auf. (Listening)
Students listen to six announcements in a supermarket and write down the prices of the items.

Answers

1 €0,99, 2 €3,30, 3 €1,75, 4 €1,48, 5 €1,60, 6 €0,75

1 Wollen Sie ein Picknick machen? Dann haben wir ein Top-Angebot für Sie: Zwei Packungen Knüsti-Chips für nur 99 Cent.
2 Super-Käse aus der Schweiz. 500 Gramm für nur 3,30 Euro. Perfekt für Ihr Picknick!
3 In unserer Bäckerei bekommen Sie zehn Brötchen für nur 1,75 Euro.
4 Sechs Scheiben Salami für nur 1,48 Euro.
5 Obst ist gut! Sechs Bananen für 1,60 Euro!
6 Und zu trinken: 4 Dosen Limonade für nur 75 Cent.

3 Partnerarbeit. (Speaking)
Using a provided template, students conduct six shopping conversations based on illustrations.

4 Schreib eine Einkaufsliste. (Writing)
Remind students that this is a very typical Foundation Writing Test task. They must write a shopping list consisting of the items illustrated. Afterwards, they can make a shopping list of their own (perhaps for homework).

Answers

2 Packungen Chips, 4 Brötchen, 500 Gramm Erdbeeren, 1 Flasche Weißwein, 6 Scheiben Käse, 1 Dose Cola, 10 Eier

---

Further practice of the language and vocabulary of this unit is given on the following pages:
Sprechen: p. 93
Lesen/Schreiben A: p. 172
Workbook: p. 42

3 Im Kleidungsgeschäft
(pp. 82–83)

Students will learn how to:
- shop for clothes

Key language
Ich möchte ...
   einen roten Schal/ Pullover/Rock
   einen grünen Mantel
   eine graue Hose/Jacke/ Bluse
   eine schwarze Jeans
   ein gelbes Hemd
   ein blaues Kleid
   weiße Socken
   braune Schuhe/ Handschuhe
Bitte schön
Welche Farbe/Größe?
Was kostet das?

Kann ich ... anprobieren?
Der Rock ist ...
zu klein/groß/teuer

Grammar points
- Adjective endings after *ein* in the accusative (*einen roten, eine rote, ein rotes*)

Resources
- Cassette B Side B
- Workbook p. 43
- Sprechen p. 93, Rollenspiel 3

As this spread revises both colours and items of clothing, elicit as many of both as students can remember before starting the spread. Use whatever realia, classroom items, flashcards or OHP transparencies are available.

1 Welche Farbe haben die Sachen? Schreib Sätze. (Writing)
Students write about items of clothing and their colours. This is the first time that students are asked to provide their answers in sentences rather than letters or single words. The task is not difficult, however, as all the words are provided on the page.

Answers
1 Das Hemd ist gelb. 2 Die Hose ist grau. 3 Der Rock ist grün. 4 Die Bluse ist weiß. 5 Die Jeans ist blau. 6 Die Krawatte ist rot.

2 Hör zu. Was kaufen diese Personen? Schreib die Tabelle ab und füll sie aus.
(Listening, Reading)
Students copy out the table and insert the details of size, colour and price while listening to the four conversations as often as they need to. The first one is done for them and they can use the printed dialogue for reading practice.

A photocopiable grid is available for this exercise. (p.139)

Answers
1 Hemd, 41, weiß, €20,–, 2 Hose, 35, grau, €35,50, 3 Rock, 40, rot, €50,–, 4 Bluse, 36, grün, €37,50

---

1 – Guten Tag! Ich möchte ein Hemd, bitte.
  – Welche Größe bitte?
  – Größe 41.
  – Und welche Farbe?
  – Weiß, bitte.
  – Dieses Hemd hier kostet €20.
2 – Guten Tag! Ich möchte eine Hose, bitte.
  – Ja. Welche Farbe bitte?
  – Grau.
  – Grau ... Und welche Größe?
  – 35.
  – 35 ... Hmm ... Diese Hose kostet €35,50.
3 – Guten Tag.
  – Guten Tag. Ich möchte einen Rock für eine Party.
  – Ein Rock? Kein Problem. Welche Farbe?
  – Rot.
  – Hmm, einen roten Rock. Welche Größe haben Sie?
  – 40.
  – Vierzig ... Moment ... Dieser Rock kostet €50.
4 – Guten Tag.
  – Guten Tag! Ich möchte eine Bluse, bitte.
  – Eine Bluse? Natürlich. Welche Farbe?
  – Grün.
  – So, eine grüne Bluse ... Welche Größe haben Sie?
  – 36.
  – Diese Bluse in Größe 36 kostet €37,50.

Grammatik: Adjectival endings after *ein* in the accusative
Teachers wishing to go into further detail on adjective endings can refer to the grammar section (page 184).

3 Wünsche dir diese Sachen zu Weihnachten. (Writing)
Based on the information in the Key Language box, students write a Christmas list. Again, this is a typical Foundation level Writing task.

Answers
1 Ich möchte eine weiße Bluse. 2 Ich möchte ein rotes Hemd. 3 Ich möchte eine blaue Jeans. 4 Ich möchte braune Schuhe. 5 Ich möchte eine blaue Krawatte.

4 Partnerarbeit. (Speaking)
In pairs, students conduct eight clothes shopping conversations based on the information provided in the illustrations.

5a Was sagen diese Personen? (Writing)
Students write down customers' complaints similar to those in the main picture.

Answers
1 Das Hemd ist zu klein. 2 Das Kleid ist zu groß. 3 Die Krawatte ist zu teuer.

Logo! 4 6 Einkaufen

5b Hör zu und wähle die richtige Antwort.
(Listening)
Students listen to some shopping dialogues and identify what the problems are.

Answers

1 zu klein, 2 zu groß, 3 zu teuer

1 – Kann ich eine Hose anprobieren?
 – Natürlich.
 – Nein, sie ist zu klein.
2 – Kann ich einen Pullover anprobieren?
 – Gern.
 – Nein, er ist zu groß.
3 – Kann ich einen Rock anprobieren?
 – Natürlich.
 – Ja, der Rock sitzt perfekt. Was kostet er?
 – € 250,–.
 – Was? Das ist zu teuer!

5c Partnerarbeit. (Speaking)
Students create three dialogues about trying on clothes.

Further practice of the language and vocabulary of this unit is given on the following pages:
Sprechen: p. 93
Workbook: p. 43

4 Taschengeld (pp. 84–85)

Students will learn how to:
- spend pocket money and find their way around a store

Key language
Wie viel Taschengeld bekommst du?
Ich bekomme € .. pro Monat/Woche
Was kaufst du damit?
Ich kaufe …
Kassetten/CDs/Bonbons/ Kleider
Ich spare für die Ferien
Wo ist die …
 Herrenabteilung
 Sportabteilung
 Schreibwarenabteilung
 Damenabteilung
 Schuhabteilung
 Süßwarenabteilung
Im Erdgeschoss
In der ersten/zweiten/ dritten Etage

Grammar points
- Plurals
- *im / in der*

Language skills
- advice to learn pocket money details for Speaking Test

Resources
- Cassette B Side B
- Workbook pp. 44–45
- Sprechen p. 93, Gespräch
- Lesen/Schreiben B p. 173

Before starting this spread, ask students for suggestions, in German if possible, for what they might spend their pocket money on.

1a Was passt zusammen? (Reading)
Introduce the vocabulary by asking students to link the words to the pictures by writing down letters.

Answers
1 g, 2 e, 3 a, 4 f, 5 c, 6 b, 7 d, 8 h

1b Hör zu. Wer bekommt was? Schreib die Tabelle ab und füll die Lücken aus. (Listening)
Students copy out the table and fill in the information about the amount of pocket money the speakers get and what they buy with it. The answers are letters referring to items in Exercise 1a, but more able students can write the answers in German.

A photocopiable grid is available for this exercise. (p.139)

Answers
1 Ines, € 10,–, f, 2 Roland, € 50,–, a + b, 3 Anni, € 40,–, d, 4 Sven, € 12,50, spare es, 5 Paul, € 100,–, e

– Unsere Diskussion am Telefon heute: Taschengeld!
1 – Hi, Uli. Hier spricht Ines.
 – Hallo Ines. Wie viel Taschengeld bekommst du?
 – Ich bekomme € 10,– pro Woche.
 – So, und was kaufst du damit?
 – Ich kaufe Bonbons.

2 – Danke, Ines. Und du, Roland? Wie viel bekommst du?
 – Ich bekomme € 50,– pro Monat.
 – Und was kaufst du?
 – Ich bin Musikfan. Ich kaufe CDs und Kassetten.
3 – Gut, und wer kommt jetzt?
 – Anni aus Oldenburg. Ich bekomme nur € 40,– pro Monat und ich kaufe Kleider damit!
4 – Und du, Sven, was kaufst du mit deinem Taschengeld?
 – Nichts. Ich bekomme € 12,50 pro Woche und ich spare es.
5 – Zum Schluss noch Paul. Wie viel bekommst du und was kaufst du?
 – Ich habe Glück. Ich bekomme von meinen Eltern € 100,– Taschengeld pro Monat. Ich kaufe Spiele für meinen Computer.

2 Partnerarbeit. (Speaking)
Students use the prompts to create dialogues about pocket money. They can also put together a true version for their own situations.

3a Lies die E-Mail. Schreib die Sprechblase ab und füll die Lücken aus. (Reading)
Students copy out the speech bubble complete with the information from the e-mail.

Answers
Ich bekomme € **60** pro **Monat**. Ich spare € **25** für **einen Computer**. Ich kaufe **Zeitschriften, Bonbons** und **Kleider**.

3b Jetzt bist du dran! Schreib eine E-Mail zurück. (Writing)
Students write down and learn their personal version with the information as it applies to them.

Tip box
Advice to students to learn their answer to use for the Speaking Test.

4 Wo findet man diese Sachen? (Reading)
Students note down in German the departments in which the illustrated items can be found. More able students can write full sentences: *Eine Jacke findet man in der Herrenabteilung.*

Answers
1 in der Herrenabteilung, 2 in der Sportabteilung, 3 in der Schreibwarenabteilung, 4 in der Damenabteilung, 5 in der Schuhabteilung, 6 in der Süßwarenabteilung

5 Hör zu. Wo ist die Abteilung? (1–6)
(Listening)
Students listen to the tape in order to find out which department is on which floor.

Logo! 4 6 Einkaufen

Answers
1 in der vierten Etage, **2** in der zweiten Etage, **3** im Erdgeschoss, **4** in der dritten Etage, **5** in der fünften Etage, **6** in der ersten Etage

1 – Entschuldigen Sie, wo ist die Sportabteilung?
 – In der vierten Etage.
2 – Wo ist die Herrenabteilung?
 – In der zweiten Etage.
3 – Entschuldigen Sie, wo ist die Schreibwarenabteilung?
 – Die Schreibwarenabteilung ist hier im Erdgeschoss.
4 – Wo ist die Damenabteilung?
 – Die Damenabteilung ist in der dritten Etage.
5 – Wo ist die Schuhabteilung?
 – In der fünften Etage.
6 – Wo ist die Süßwarenabteilung?
 – In der ersten Etage.

Further practice of the language and vocabulary of this unit is given on the following pages:
Sprechen: p. 93
Lesen/Schreiben B: p. 173
Workbook: pp. 44–45

5 Auf der Post (pp. 86–87)

Students will learn how to:
- ask for what they want at a post office

> **Key language**
> Was kostet ...
>   ein Brief / eine Postkarte /
>   dieses Paket / dieses
>   Päckchen nach
>   England?
> Ich möchte ...
>   eine Briefmarke zu
>   einem Euro
>   ein Fax schicken
> Kann man hier ...
> Wo kann man ...
>   telefonieren?
>   einen Brief einwerfen?
>   eine E-Mail schicken?
>
> **Grammar points**
> - *Ich möchte ...*
>
> **Language skills**
> - meaning of *Ansichtskarte*
> - what to say when posting a parcel
> - useful expressions: *Kann ich bitte ..., Kann man ..., Wo kann man...?*
>
> **Resources**
> - Cassette B Side B
> - Workbook p. 46
> - Sprechen p. 93, Rollenspiel 4

Before starting this spread, explain that this is a topic which is popular with examiners and also useful when staying in a German-speaking country. Brainstorm in English the types of thing one might want to say in a post office.

1 Was sagt man? (Reading)
Students must match the sentences in the speech bubbles to the pictures and copy out the sentences.

Answers
1 Wie viel kostet dieses Paket nach Frankreich? 2 Was kostet ein Brief nach Großbritannien? 3 Ich möchte fünf Briefmarken zu fünfzig Cent. 4 Was kostet eine Postkarte nach Amerika?

2 Hör zu und wähle die richtige Antwort.
(Listening)
Students listen to the tape as often as necessary in order to choose the correct multiple-choice answers.

Answers
1 a, 2 c, 3 a, 4 b, 5 c, 6 b, 7 b

- Guten Tag. Was kostet ein Brief nach England?
- Nach England? 75 Cent.
- Und eine Postkarte?
- 65 Cent.
- Ich möchte eine Briefmarke zu 75 Cent und fünf Briefmarken zu 65 Cent.
- Bitte schön.
- Und wie viel kostet dieses Päckchen, auch nach England?
- Moment ... 600 Gramm ... nach England ... Das macht € 3,25.
- So, was macht das?
- Also, ein Brief, fünf Postkarten, ein Päckchen, das macht € 7,25.

Tip boxes
The two tip boxes show the meaning of *Ansichtskarte* and give advice to students on what to say when posting a parcel.

3 Partnerarbeit. (Speaking)
In pairs, students practise post office dialogues based on the pictures.

4a Hör zu. Was passt zusammen? (1–4)
(Listening)
Students link typical post office questions to illustrations by writing down letters.

Answers
1 d, 2 b, 3 c, 4 a

1 Kann man hier telefonieren?
2 Ich möchte ein Fax schicken. Geht das?
3 Wo kann ich hier einen Brief einwerfen?
4 Kann ich hier eine E-Mail schicken?

4b Partnerarbeit. (Speaking)
Now the new sentences from Exercise 4a are practised in pairs.

Tip box
Useful expressions with *kann*, with a reminder that the infinitive goes to the end of the sentence.

4c Schreib die Fragen aus Übung 4b auf.
(Writing)
Students write down the new expressions.

Answers
1 Kann man hier eine E-Mail schicken? 2 Ich möchte ein Fax schicken. 3 Wo kann man einen Brief einwerfen? 4 Kann man hier telefonieren?

5 Was passt zusammen? (Reading)
Students link some post office expressions to pictures.

Answers
1 c, 2 d, 3 b, 4 e, 5 a

> Further practice of the language and vocabulary of this unit is given on the following pages:
> Sprechen: p. 93
> Workbook: p. 46

Logo! 4 6 Einkaufen

6 Es ist nicht in Ordung
(pp. 88–89)

Students will learn how to:
- complain in a shop

Key language	Ich möchte mit dem Direktor sprechen
Ich habe diesen Pullover/diese Hose/dieses Portemonnaie gekauft	**Grammar points** • *diese* • Adjectives in the accusative
Er/Sie/Es ist … Sie sind … kaputt/alt/schmutzig/ zu groß/zu klein	**Language skills** • asking for money back or to see the manager
Kann ich … einen neuen/eine neue/ein neues … haben? Ich möchte mein Geld zurück	**Resources** • Cassette B Side B

Start this spread by inviting students, in English, to suggest things they might complain about in a shop.

1 Hör zu. Wer hat welches Problem? (1–5) (Listening)
Students match complaints to pictures by writing down letters.

Answers
1 d, 2 b, 3 a, 4 e, 5 c

> 1 Ich habe heute Morgen dieses Brot gekauft, aber es ist alt. Kann ich bitte ein neues Brot haben?
> 2 Ich habe letzte Woche diese Bluse gekauft, aber sie ist zu groß. Kann ich bitte eine neue Bluse haben?
> 3 Guten Tag. Ich habe gestern dieses Hemd gekauft und es ist schmutzig. Kann ich bitte ein neues Hemd haben?
> 4 Ich habe gestern diese Handschuhe gekauft, aber sie sind kaputt. Kann ich bitte neue Handschuhe haben?
> 5 Ich habe neulich diesen Pullover gekauft, aber er ist zu klein. Kann ich bitte einen neuen Pullover haben?

2 Partnerarbeit. (Speaking)
Working in pairs, and based on the illustrations, students make short dialogues complaining about items and asking for replacements. The dialogues must be done both ways round.

Tip box: How to ask for money back or to see the manager
These two language items are only mentioned here. Draw students' attention to them because they may well come in useful.

3 Lies den Brief und wähle die richtige Antwort. (Reading)
Students read the letter from a consumer magazine and choose the correct answers. More able students should write out the full sentences.

Answers
1 teuer, 2 schön, 3 klein, 4 kaputt, 5 schmutzig, 6 muss das Geld

4 Schreib die Sätze aus Übung 2 auf. (Writing)
Students return to Exercise 2 and write out the complaints from the dialogues.

Answers
1 Ich habe diese Uhr gekauft, aber sie ist kaputt. Kann ich bitte eine neue Uhr haben? 2 Ich habe diesen Pullover gekauft, aber er ist zu groß. Kann ich bitte einen neuen Pullover haben? 3 Ich habe diese Bananen gekauft, aber sie sind alt. Kann ich bitte neue Bananen haben? 4 Ich habe diese Hose gekauft, aber sie ist schmutzig. Kann ich bitte eine neue Hose haben? 5 Ich habe diese Schuhe gekauft, aber sie sind zu klein. Kann ich bitte neue Schuhe haben? 6 Ich habe dieses Portemonnaie gekauft, aber es ist zu klein. Kann ich bitte ein neues Portemonnaie haben?

All the vocabulary and structures from this chapter are listed on the **Wörter** pages 90–91. These can be used for revision by covering up either the English or the German. Students can check here to see how much they remember from the chapter.

Assessment materials for Chapters 5 and 6 are available after Chapter 6.

Further speaking and grammar practice on the whole chapter is provided on pp. 47–48 of the **Workbook**.

Workbook

p. 41

1 der Supermarkt,
die Apotheke
die Buchhandlung,
die Konditorei,
das Kaufhaus,
das Schreibwarengeschäft
2 1 Nein, **2** Ja, **3** Ja, **4** Nein, **5** Nein, **6** Ja
3 1 Nein: 07.45 – 17.00, **2** Nein: 08.30 – 16.30,
3 Nein: 08.00 – 18.00, **4** Ja: 14.00 – 10.30

p. 42

1 €0,75, **2** €3,50, **3** €0,50, **4** €3,00, **5** €3,75,
6 €1,00,
2 **a** 7, **b** 3, **c** 6, **d** 2, **e** 5, **f** 4, **g** 1
3 Open-ended

p. 43

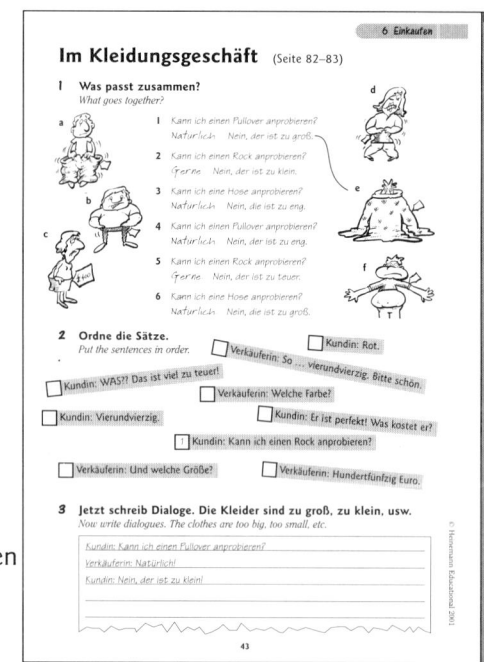

1 1 e, **2** d, **3** b, **4** f, **5** c, **6** a
2 *Kundin:* Kann ich einen Rock anprobieren?
Verkäuferin: Welche Farbe?
Kundin: Rot.
Verkäuferin: Und welche Größe?
Kundin: Vierundvierzig.
Verkäuferin: So … vierundvierzig. Bitte schön.
Kundin: Er ist perfekt! Was kostet er?
Verkäuferin: Hundertfünfzig Euro.
Kundin: WAS?? Das ist viel zu teuer!
3 Open-ended. Overlook minor errors.

p. 44

1 1 Karsten €55,
2 Claudia €50,
3 Turgut €25,
4 Rolf €15,
5 Anita €10
2 **Florian**: Ich bekomme €17,50 pro Woche von meiner Mutter. Ich kaufe Kleider und CDs. Ich spare €2,50.
Elena: Ich bekomme €10,00 pro Woche von meinem Vater. Ich kaufe Bonbons und Zeitschriften. Ich spare €1,00 pro Woche.
Yasemine: Ich bekomme €12,50 pro Woche, €5,00 von meiner Mutter, €7,50 von meinem Vater. Ich kaufe Zeitschriften, CDs, Kleider und Bonbons. Ich spare nichts.

p. 45

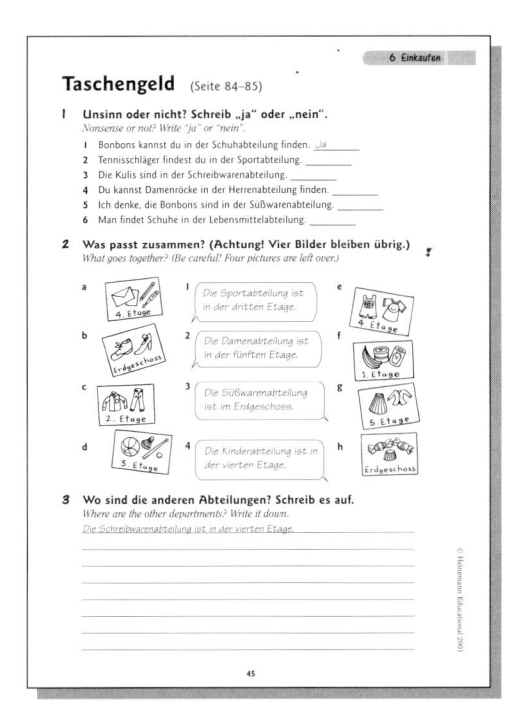

1 1 Ja, **2** Nein, **3** Nein, **4** Ja, **5** Nein, **6** Ja
2 1 d, **2** g, **3** h, **4** e
3 Die Schreibwarenabteilung ist in der vierten Etage.
Die Schuhabteilung ist im Erdgeschoss.
Die Herrenabteilung ist in der zweiten Etage.
Die Lebensmittelabteilung ist in der ersten Etage.

p. 46

1 1 ein Euro fünfzig Cent, **2** fünfundzwanzig Eurocent, **3** fünfzig Eurocent, **4** sechs Euro, **5** sieben Euro fünfzig Eurocent
2 1 e, **2** c, **3** a, **4** b, **5** d
3 1 Kann man hier ein Fax schicken? **2** Wo kann ich bitte eine E-Mail schicken? **3** Kann man hier telefonieren? **4** Wo kann ich einen Brief einwerfen? **5** Kann ich bitte drei Briefmarken haben?

p. 47

p. 48

1 1 Ich möchte zweihundertfünfzig Gramm Butter, bitte. **2** Ich möchte ein Kilo Bananen, bitte. **3** Ich möchte zwei Scheiben Käse, bitte. **4** Ich möchte fünfhundert Gramm Äpfel, bitte. **5** Ich möchte drei Scheiben Salami, bitte. **6** Ich möchte zwei Kilo Kartoffeln, bitte.
2 1 a, **2** b, **3** a, **4** a, **5** a, **6** c
3 1 grün, **2** grünes, **3** rot, **4** rote, **5** schwarzen, **6** schwarz

7 Freizeit und Urlaub (pp. 94–107)

Topic area	Key language	Grammar	Language skills
7.1 Imbiss und Café (pp. 94–95) Order a drink and a snack	*Ich habe Hunger/Durst. Er/Sie isst … und trinkt …. Ich möchte eine Portion Kartoffelsalat/Pommes frites mit Ketchup/Mayonnaise Senf / ein Wiener Schnitzel / eine Bratwurst / ein halbes Hähnchen / einen Apfelsaft/ Orangensaft / ein Stück Apfelkuchen mit/ohne Sahne / eine Tasse Kaffee/Schokolade / ein Kännchen/Glas Tee eine Cola/Limonade.*	*Ich habe Durst/Hunger*	
7.2 Im Restaurant (pp. 96–97) Go out for a meal	*Was für Getränke haben Sie? Ich möchte [food items]. Kann ich bitte die Speisekarte/Rechnung / einen Löffel / eine Gabel / ein Messer haben?*		Restaurant vocabulary: menu, saying you are full, asking for the bill
7.3 Wir gehen aus! (pp. 98–99) Find out details about entertainment	*Was läuft im Kino? Was für ein Film ist das? Das ist ein Krimi/Liebesfilm/Horrorfilm/Musical/Fußballspiel. Wann beginnt die Vorstellung/es? Wie viel/Was kostet der Eintritt?*		Questions students need to recognise (*Was für, Was heißt, Wann, Wie viel?*)
7.4 Geld! (pp. 100–101) Manage money	*Ich möchte englisches Geld wechseln. Ich möchte einen Zehneuroschein / einen Zwanzigeuroschein / zwei Zehneuroscheine / ein Zweieurostück / zwei Fünfeurostücke / einen Reisescheck.*		Difference between *Stück* and *Münze*
7.5 Was hast du gemacht? (pp. 102–103) Talk about activities in the past	*Ich habe ferngesehen/getanzt / Pizza/Spaghetti gegessen / Karten/Fußball/Computer gespielt / Hausaufgaben gemacht / Schuhe gekauft / einen Film gesehen. Ich bin ins Kino/Bett/Restaurant / in die Stadt gegangen. Ich bin nach Hamburg gefahren. gestern/ am Wochenende/ Samstag Abend*	Revision of perfect tense Time before place *Ich/Es war*	
7.6 Können Sie mir helfen? (pp. 104–105) Deal with a car breakdown	*Ich habe eine Panne. Der Motor ist nicht in Ordnung. Mein Auto/Motorrad ist kaputt / hat kein Benzin mehr. Die Bremsen/Lampen sind nicht in Ordnung. Können Sie mir bitte helfen / einen Mechaniker herschicken / mein Auto reparieren / die Polizei rufen? Mein Auto steht auf der …straße. Wo ist die nächste Tankstelle/ Reparaturwerkstatt?*	*Könnten Sie …?*	Useful phrases for calling emergency services
Lesen/Schreiben (pp. 174–175)			Reading and Writing skills

- The vocabulary and structures taught in Chapter 7 are summarised on the **Wörter** pages of the Student's Book, 106–107.
- Further Speaking practice on the language of the chapter is provided on **Sprechen** p. 122.
- Coursework pages relating to this chapter can be found on pp. 158–159 of the Student's Book.
- For a selection of assessment tasks for Chapters 7 and 8, please refer to the separate Assessment Pack for your chosen examination board: AQA, OCR or Edexcel.

Logo! 4 7 Freizeit und Urlaub

1 Imbiss und Café (pp. 94–95)

Students will learn how to:
- order a drink and a snack

Key language
Ich habe Hunger/Durst
Er/Sie isst ... und trinkt ...
Ich möchte/nehme ...
   Pommes frites mit Mayonnaise/Ketchup/Senf
   Kartoffelsalat
   ein Wiener Schnitzel
   eine Bratwurst/Bockwurst/Cola/Limonade
   ein halbes Hähnchen
   einen
Apfelsaft/Orangensaft
ein Stück Apfelkuchen/Erdbeertorte mit/ohne Sahne
eine Tasse Tee/Schokolade
ein Kännchen Kaffee mit Milch

Resources
- Cassette C Side A
- Workbook p. 49
- Sprechen p. 122, Rollenspiel 1

Start the spread by asking students to brainstorm as many German words for drinks and snacks as they can remember.

1a Was passt zusammen? (Reading)
Students write letters to link pictures of snacks with words.

Answers
1 k, 2 g, 3 i, 4 l, 5 c, 6 b, 7 d, 8 e, 9 f, 10 a, 11 h, 12 j

1b Hör zu. Wer bestellt was? (Listening)
Students listen to two teenagers deciding what to order, and note down letters to show they have understood. Make sure they realise they must write down four letters for Carla and five for Andreas.

Answers
Carla: g, c, e, j, **Andreas:** i, d, e, a, h

– Was willst du denn essen, Carla?
– Hmmm ... Was gibt's? Ich möchte eine Bratwurst.
– Mit Pommes frites?
– Ja bitte, und Ketchup.
– Bitte schön. Und möchten Sie etwas trinken?
– Ja bitte. Ich möchte eine Cola. Was möchtest du essen, Andreas?
– Ich möchte ein halbes Hähnchen.
– Ein halbes Hähnchen, jawohl. Und Pommes frites?
– Nein, ich nehme Kartoffelsalat.
– Mit Ketchup? Oder mit Mayonnaise?
– Mit Ketchup, und auch Senf, bitte.
– Möchten Sie etwas trinken?
– Ja bitte! Eine Limonade.

1c Schreib Sätze. (Writing)
Students now write out the information about Carla and Andreas, based on their answers to Exercise 1b.

Answers
1 Carla isst eine Bratwurst mit Pommes frites und Ketchup und sie trinkt eine Cola. 2 Andreas isst ein halbes Hähnchen mit Kartoffelsalat, Ketchup und Senf. Er trinkt eine Limonade.

2a Wie viel bezahlen diese Personen? (Reading)
Students read the menu from Ollis Imbiss and write down the prices paid for the items in the speech bubbles.

Answers
1 €4,25, 2 €3,30, 3 €3,–, 4 €2,95, 5 €1,50, 6 €1,50, 7 €1,70, 8 €4,69, 9 €2,85, 10 €2,90

2b Partnerarbeit. Bestellt die Sachen aus Übung 2a. (Speaking)
In pairs, students practise ordering the items illustrated in Exercise 2a. Make sure this exercise is done both ways round.

2c Du bist der Kellner / die Kellnerin. Schreib die Bestellungen auf. (Writing)
Now students write down the same orders as if they were a waiter or waitress.

Answers
1 Ein halbes Hähnchen mit Pommes frites, 2 Ein Hamburger mit Pommes frites, 3 Eine Bratwurst mit Pommes frites, 4 Eine Bockwurst mit Kartoffelsalat, 5 Pommes frites mit Ketchup, 6 Pommes frites mit Mayonnaise, 7 Pommes frites mit Ketchup und Mayonnaise, 8 Wiener Schnitzel und Pommes frites, 9 Eine Bratwurst und eine Cola, 10 Eine Bockwurst und eine Limonade

3 Hör zu und lies den Dialog. Wähle a, b oder c. (Listening)
Tell students about typical German, Swiss or Austrian cafés where elderly people like this like to meet in the afternoons for *Kaffee und Kuchen*. They can listen to the dialogue at the same time as reading it, or it can be used first as a pure listening. Students select answers from a choice of pictures.

Answers
1 c, 2 b, 3 b, 4 a

– Guten Tag, Frau Schlüter. Was nehmen Sie heute?
– Ich möchte ein Glas Tee.
– Möchten Sie auch Kuchen, Frau Schlüter?
– Ach ja, ich möchte ein Stück Apfelkuchen. Und Sie, Frau Meyer?
– Ich nehme eine Tasse Kaffee.
– Und möchten Sie auch Kuchen, Frau Meyer?
– Ja, ich möchte ein Stück Erdbeertorte mit Sahne. Fräulein!

4 Partnerarbeit. (Speaking)
Students practise ordering items based on pictures. The conversations must be done both ways round. Then students can improvise conversations of their own.

Further practice of the language and vocabulary of this unit is given on the following pages:
Sprechen: p. 122
Workbook: p. 49

Logo! 4 7 Freizeit und Urlaub

2 Im Restaurant (pp. 96–97)

Students will learn how to:
- go out for a meal

Key language
Was für Getränke/Suppen/
  Eis haben Sie?
Ich möchte …
  Hühnersuppe/
  Erbsensuppe/Lasagne/
  Fisch/Spaghetti/
  Bolognese/Pizza/
  Erdbeereis
ein Glas Weißwein/
  Rotwein/
  Mineralwasser/Cola
Kann ich bitte …
  die Speisekarte / die
  Rechnung / einen
  Löffel / eine Gabel /
  ein Messer / Salz und
  Pfeffer / das Brot
  haben?

Language skills
- saying you are full
- word for menu
- asking to pay

Resources
- Cassette C Side A
- Workboook p. 50
- Sprechen p. 122, Rollenspiel 2

Before starting this spread, ask students, in English, what sort of things they might want or need to say in a restaurant. How many of them can they say in German?

1 Wer sagt was? (Reading)
Make sure students understand the meanings of the expressions in the speech bubbles before they link the letters to the pictures to show that they have understood.

Answers
1 c, 2 d, 3 a, 4 g, 5 e, 6 b, 7 f

2 Hör zu. Wer möchte was? (1–10) (Listening)
Students listen to people ordering items in a restaurant and write down, in German, the items ordered. The words are provided on the page to copy.

Answers
1 Hühnersuppe, 2 Erbsensuppe, 3 Lasagne, 4 Fisch, 5 Spaghetti Bolognese, 6 Pizza, 7 Weißwein, 8 Mineralwasser, 9 Cola, 10 Erdbeereis

1 Ich nehme eine Hühnersuppe.
2 Ich möchte eine Erbsensuppe.
3 Als Hauptspeise möchte ich Lasagne.
4 Ich möchte Fisch.
5 Für mich bitte Spaghetti Bolognese.
6 Ich möchte Pizza.
7 Ich nehme ein Glas Weißwein.
8 Und ich möchte Mineralwasser.
9 Ich möchte Cola.
10 Als Nachtisch möchte ich Erdbeereis.

Tip box
How to ask for the menu and say you have had enough to eat.

3 Partnerarbeit. (Speaking)
In pairs, students construct restaurant conversations based on picture prompts. All dialogues should be done twice, so that each student practises both roles.

4 Hör zu. Wer sagt was? (1–4) (Listening)
Students listen to the tape and find out which character has which complaint. The names must be written down.

Answers
1 Andreas, 2 Carla, 3 Petra, 4 Gerd

1 Ich habe keine Gabel. Kann ich bitte eine Gabel haben?
2 Ich habe keinen Löffel! Kann ich bitte einen Löffel haben?
3 Ich habe kein Messer! Kann ich bitte ein Messer haben?
4 Wo ist das Salz? Wo ist der Pfeffer? Kann ich bitte Salz und Pfeffer haben?

Tip box: How to ask to pay in a restaurant
Add that you can also say *Kann ich bezahlen?* or *Ich möchte bezahlen*. It is less common to say *Die Rechnung bitte*, but the word *Rechnung* often crops up in this context in exams, so students need to be aware of it.

5 Stell Fragen. (Speaking)
Students practise using the expressions from the Key Language box, based on picture prompts.

6 Entwerfe eine Speisekarte für ein italienisches Restaurant ODER ein deutsches Restaurant. (Writing)
Students design a menu for an Italian or German restaurant. This is a good exercise for using ICT skills and can be done at home.

Further practice of the language and vocabulary of this unit is given on the following pages:
Sprechen: p. 122
Workbook: p. 50

3 Wir gehen aus! (pp. 98–99)

Students will learn how to:
- find out details about entertainment

Key language	Language skills
Was läuft im Kino?	• questions students need to recognise
Was für ein Film ist das?	
Das ist ein …	**Resources**
Krimi/Liebesfilm/ Horrorfilm/Musical/ Fußballspiel	• Cassette C Side A
	• Workbook p. 51
Wann beginnt es/die Vorstellung?	• Sprechen p. 122, Rollenspiel 3
Wie viel / Was kostet der Eintritt?	• Lesen/Schreiben A + B pp. 174–175

Before starting this spread, ask students how many German words they can remember for types of show or sporting activity.

1 Was passt zusammen? (Reading)
Students look at the pictures and link them to the adverts for various types of show.

Answers
1 c, 2 b, 3 e, 4 d, 5 a

2 Hör zu. Schreib die Formulare ab und füll sie aus. (Listening, Reading)
Students copy out the forms and fill in the information about the shows, based on what they hear on the tape. This can be done either as a pure listening activity or with students following the script in the book. The words to copy are provided on the page. The first form has been filled in for them.

Answers
1 Emma, Liebesfilm, 20 Uhr, € 4,– , 2 „Cats", Musical, 14.30, € 12,50, 3 Fußball, Berlin, 15 Uhr, € 22,50

1 – Hallo, hier das Appollo-Kino.
  – Guten Tag. Was läuft heute, bitte?
  – „Emma".
  – Was für ein Film ist das?
  – Das ist ein Liebesfilm.
  – Wann beginnt die Vorstellung?
  – Um 20 Uhr.
  – Und was kostet der Eintritt?
  – € 4,–.
  – Also, 20 Uhr, € 4,–. Danke schön!
2 – Königstheater, Guten Tag.
  – Guten Tag. Welches Stück läuft im Moment?
  – „Cats", von Andrew Lloyd Webber.
  – Was für ein Stück ist das?
  – Das ist ein Musical.
  – Wann beginnt das Stück?
  – Um 14.30.
  – Und was kostet der Eintritt?
  – € 12,50.
  – Also, 14.30 Uhr, € 12,50. Danke!
3 Guten Tag. Hier spricht der Telefondienst vom Fußballverein Bayern München. Unser nächstes Spiel ist am Samstag um 15 Uhr, gegen Hertha Berlin. Die Karten kosten € 22,50. Also, Samstag, 15 Uhr, gegen Berlin, € 22,50. Danke schön.

3 Beantworte die Fragen auf Deutsch. (Reading)
Students read adverts for various activities and answer questions in German. The answers are provided to choose from on the page.

Answers
1 a ein Horrorfilm, b Das Biest, c 18 Uhr, d 23 Uhr, e € 5,50
2 a ein Handballspiel, b 15 Uhr, c nichts
3 a 8 Uhr, b 18 Uhr, c € 1,75
4 a Romeo und Julia, b 19.30 Uhr, c € 11,00

Tip box
Questions which students need to be able to recognise (*Was für, Wie heißt, Wann, Wie viel*).

4a Partnerarbeit. (Speaking)
In pairs, students construct four dialogues based on various cues provided. These must be done both ways round.

4b Schreib die Dialoge auf. (Writing)
Finally, students write up all four of the dialogues practised in Exercise 4a.

Further practice of the language and vocabulary of this unit is given on the following pages:
Sprechen: p. 122
Lesen/Schreiben A + B: pp. 174–175
Workbook: p. 51

Logo! 4 7 Freizeit und Urlaub

4 Geld! (pp. 100–101)

Students will learn how to:
- change money

Key language	Language skills
Ich möchte …	• difference between *Stück* and *Münze*
englisches Geld wechseln	
einen Zehneuroschein	**Resources**
einen Zwanzigeuroschein	• Cassette C Side A
zwei Zehneuroscheine	• Workbook p. 52
ein Zweieurostück	• Sprechen p. 122, Rollenspiel 4
zwei Fünfeurostücke	
einen Reisescheck	

1 Hör zu und lies. Was passt zusammen?
(Listening, Reading)
Students study the photos of the notes and coins and link them to the words on the page by writing down letters.

Answers
1 f, 2 a, 3 d, 4 b, 5 g, 6 e, 7 c, 8 h

1 ein Zwanzigeuroschein
2 ein Eurostück
3 ein Zehncentstück
4 ein Zweieurostück
5 ein Fünfzigeuroschein
6 ein Fünfeurosschein
7 ein Fünfzigcentstück
8 ein Hunderteuroschein

Tip box
An explanation of the difference between *ein Stück* and *eine Münze*.

2 Hör zu und lies. Beantworte die Fragen.
(Listening, Reading)
This listening activity can be done as a pure listening with students not looking at the script, or can be done while looking at the script. They write down numbers in answer to the questions. The script lends itself to being read aloud in pairs and changing the sums of money involved.

Answers
1 60, 2 4, 3 5

– Guten Tag. Bitte schön?
– Ich möchte englisches Geld in Euro wechseln.
– Ja. Wie viel Pfund haben Sie?
– Sechzig Pfund.
– Moment …hundert Euro. Bitte schön, ein Fünfzigeuroschein, zwei Zwanzigeuroscheine und ein Zehneuroschein.

– Oh, kann ich für zehn Euro Kleingeld haben?
– Hier … ein Fünfeuroschein, ein Zweieurostück und drei Eurostücke.

3 Vervollständige die Sätze. (Writing)
Students fill in gaps in sentences and write them out, based on information cues provided. The endings to the sentences are also provided on the page.

Answers
1 David möchte englisches Geld in Euro wechseln.
2 Carla möchte für €100 Kleingeld haben. 3 Beate möchte für €50 Kleingeld haben. 4 Herr Müller möchte €400 in Pfund Sterling wechseln.

4 Hör zu und wähle die richtige Antwort.
(Listening)
Students listen to the tape and select from multi-choice answers.

Answers
1 fünfundzwanzig, 2 siebzig, 3 drei,
4 zwei Zweieurostücke

– Guten Tag. Bitte schön?
– Ich möchte englisches Geld in Euro wechseln.
– Selbstverständlich. Wie viel Pfund haben Sie?
– Fünfundzwanzig Pfund Sterling.
– Moment … fünfunddreißig Euro. Bitte schön, drei Zehneuroscheine und ein Fünfeuroschein.
– Oh, kann ich für fünf Euro Kleingeld haben?
– Hier … zwei Zweieurostücke und ein Eurostück.

5 Was sagen diese Personen? (Speaking)
Students work out what the people must be saying and say it out loud. This can be done round the class or in pairs.

Further practice of the language and vocabulary of this unit is given on the following pages:
Sprechen: p. 122
Workbook: p. 52

5 Was hast du gemacht?
(pp. 102–103)

Students will learn how to:
- talk about activities in the past

Key language
Ich habe …
  ferngesehen
  Musik gehört
  meine Hausaufgaben gemacht
  Pizza/Spaghetti gegessen
  getanzt
  Fußball/Karten/Computer gespielt
  einen Film gesehen
Ich bin …
  in die Stadt gegangen
  ins Kino/Bett/Restaurant gegangen
Ich bin nach Hamburg gefahren
Ich habe gestern/am Wochenende/am Samstag/am Abend Schuhe gekauft

Grammar points
- revision of perfect tense
- time before place

Resources
- Cassette C Side A
- Workbook p. 53
- Sprechen p. 122, Gespräch
- Kursarbeit pp. 158–159

Start the spread by asking students for as many contributions as possible using the perfect tense to say something they have done in the past.

1a Carlas Abend. Was passt zusammen? (Reading)
Students link speech bubbles to illustrations by writing down letters.

Answers
1 e, **2** a, **3** g, **4** b, **5** f, **6** d, **7** c, **8** h

1b Hör zu und ordne die Sätze. (1–8) (Listening)
Based on the same illustrations, students listen to the tape and write down letters to show the order in which the activities are mentioned. The script is not on the page, so the tape may need to be played a couple of times.

Answers
1 f, **2** h, **3** g, **4** e, **5** c, **6** b, **7** d, **8** a

> 1 Ich bin nach Hause gekommen.
> 2 Ich habe ferngesehen.
> 3 Ich habe Hausaufgaben gemacht.
> 4 Ich bin zu einer Party gegangen.
> 5 Ich habe eine Bratwurst gegessen.
> 6 Ich habe viel Bier getrunken.
> 7 Ich habe getanzt.
> 8 Ich bin um 12 Uhr ins Bett gegangen.

1c Schreib die Sätze in der richtigen Reihenfolge auf. (Listening)
Now students write out the answers to Exercise 1b in the correct order.

Answers
See tapescript for 1b.

Wiederholung: A reminder of the formation of the perfect tense (with *haben* and *sein*)
Tell students they will have to be careful about this when doing the speaking activity which follows.

2 Partnerarbeit. (Speaking)
Students ask and answer questions about pictures of activities in the perfect tense, using both *haben* and *sein* verbs. This exercise must be done both ways round.

3 Hör zu und ordne die Sätze. (1–7) (Listening)
Students listen to a description of a weekend away and note down letters to show the order in which things happened. This may have to be played a couple of times, as the script is not on the page.

Answers
1 f, **2** d, **3** g, **4** b, **5** c, **6** e, **7** a

> 1 Ich bin am Freitag mit dem Zug nach Trier gefahren.
> 2 Ich habe in der Jugendherberge gewohnt.
> 3 Ich bin am Samstag in den Bergen gewandert.
> 4 Ich bin am Abend in die Disco gegangen.
> 5 Ich habe am Sonntag Tischtennis gespielt.
> 6 Ich habe in einem Imbiss gegessen.
> 7 Ich bin am Nachmittag ins Kino gegangen.

Grammatik: Time comes before the place in a sentence
Practise this by giving students examples of items to put in the right order in sentences:
Teacher: in die Schule, gestern
Student: Ich bin gestern in die Schule gegangen.

4a Ein Interview. Partnerarbeit. (Speaking)
Students construct an extended dialogue in the perfect tense, based on picture prompts. This activity must be done both ways round.

4b Schreib das Interview (4a) auf. (Writing, Reading)
Now students write out the complete dialogue from Exercise 4a. Remind students how writing things out can help to reinforce them in their minds. Remind them again how vital it is for them to show they can talk about the past.

Logo! 4 7 Freizeit und Urlaub

Answers

Was hast du am Freitag gemacht? Ich habe am Freitag Karten gespielt.
Was hast du am Abend gemacht? Ich habe am Abend Pizza gegessen.
Was hast du am Samstag gemacht? Ich bin am Samstag nach Hamburg gefahren.
Was hast du am Sonntag gemacht? Ich bin am Sonntag ins Kino gegangen.

Wiederholung: A reminder that *war* means 'was'

This point can't be re-emphasised often enough. Just the occasional use of *war* can qualify as an attempt to use the past tense, thus gaining exam points.

5 Schreib Sätze. (Writing)

Students write simple sentences using *war* and based on picture prompts.

Answers

1 Das Hotel war gut. **2** Das Hotel war nicht gut. **3** Das Essen war gut. **4** Das Essen war nicht gut. **5** Das Wetter war gut. **6** Das Wetter war nicht gut.

Further practice of the language and vocabulary of this unit is given on the following pages:
Sprechen: p. 122
Workbook: p. 53

The activities of this unit form an ideal introduction to coursework preparation. For further information and guidelines about the preparation of cousework on this topic, please refer to **Coursework** spread pp. 158–159.

6 Können Sie mir helfen?
(pp. 104–105)

Students will learn how to:
- deal with a car breakdown

Key language
Ich habe eine Panne
Der Motor ist nicht in Ordnung
Mein Auto ist kaputt
Mein Motorrad hat kein Benzin mehr
Die Batterie ist leer
Die Lampen sind kaputt
Können Sie …
  mir bitte helfen?
  einen Mechaniker herschicken?
  mein Auto reparieren?
  die Polizei rufen?

Mein Auto steht auf der … straße
Wo ist die nächste Tankstelle/ Reparaturwerkstatt?

Grammar point
- *Könnten Sie …?*

Language skills
- Useful phrases in an emergency

Resources
- Cassette C Side A

Start the spread by asking students to contribute, in English, possible types of mechanical problem they might encounter while driving in Germany.

1 Hör zu. Wer hat welches Problem? (1–5)
(Listening)
Most of the vocabulary will be new to students, but it is listed in the Key Language box below. It is probably best to go over these expressions before playing the tape. Students then write down letters to link the problems on the tape to the pictures.

Answers
1 c, 2 d, 3 b, 4 a, 5 e

> 1 Hallo? Ich habe ein Problem. Mein Motorrad hat kein Benzin mehr.
> 2 Was? Ja, die Bremsen sind kaputt.
> 3 Hmmm – Der Motor ist nicht in Ordnung.
> 4 Die Lampen sind kaputt.
> 5 Ja, schrecklich, die Batterie ist leer.

2 Partnerarbeit. (Speaking)
Based on picture cues, students work in pairs to make short dialogues with an information gap element.

3 Verbinde die Satzteile. (Reading)
Students read the script of a telephone call in the speech bubble, then link up halves of sentences to form correct wholes, which should be written out.

Answers
1 Können Sie mir bitte helfen? 2 Der Motor ist nicht in Ordnung. 3 Mein Auto steht auf der Bundesstraße. 4 Können Sie einen Mechaniker herschicken? 5 Ich habe eine Panne.

4 Partnerarbeit. (Speaking)
Pair work activity in which students construct a conversation based on picture prompts.

Tip box: Phrases to learn for an emergency
Warn students that not only might these come in useful in real life, they could well crop up in the exam, too!

5 Partnerarbeit. (Speaking)
A final chance to practise the new expressions in pairs.

All the vocabulary and structures from this chapter are listed on the **Wörter** pages 106–107. These can be used for revision by covering up either the English or the German. Students can check here how much they remember from the chapter.

Assessment materials for Chapters 7 and 8 are available after Chapter 8.

Further speaking and grammar practice on the whole chapter is provided on pp. 54–55 of the **Workbook**.

Kursarbeit

7 Freizeit (pp. 158–159)

The coursework section in *Logo! 4 Grün* gives regular, guided practice in preparing for the coursework element of the GCSE examination. It is cross-referenced to relevant sections in the core units. Each double-page spread is linked to a GCSE theme, and always starts with a model text on that theme (at a higher level than that expected by the student). This text acts as a stimulus to give students ideas about what they might include in their own piece of work. Students are encouraged to look at the detail of the text through the structured reading activities. They are gradually guided to produce good German sentences in the various activities, through to the final task in which they are asked to produce an extended piece of writing.

The *Hilfe* column is a feature on all the spreads. It shows students language they might include and particular structures that will raise the level of their writing. It is important to remind students who are capable of achieving a grade at the upper end of the Foundation level that they should always include examples of two or three tenses in their writing.

This spread guides students to produce an extended piece of writing on the topic of hobbies.

1 Schreib die Sätze mit den richtigen Verben auf.

Students write out the sentences choosing the correct verbs from the three given.

Answers

1 geschrieben, 2 stehe, 3 gehe, 4 sehe, 5 spiele, 6 gewonnen, 7 kaufen, 8 gespielt, 9 gemacht, 10 bekommen

2 Du bist Karola. Schreib Sätze. Die Antworten sind grün.

Students answer the questions as if they were Carola. The answers are all in green in the text.

Answers

1 Ich habe jeden Tag viel gemacht. 2 Ich stehe um 6 Uhr auf. 3 Nach dem Frühstück gehe ich schwimmen. 4 Am Nachmittag höre ich Musik oder ich lese ein bisschen. 5 Am Abend sehe ich fern, telefoniere mit Freunden oder ich gehe ins Kino. 6 Das war fantastisch! 7 Ich bekomme jetzt 30 Mark Taschengeld pro Woche. 8 Ich möchte am Wochenende drei CDs kaufen. 9 Ich habe letze Woche in Lübeck Handball für die Schulmannschaft gespielt. 10 Ich habe zum Geburtstag ein Fahrrad von meinen Eltern bekommen.

3 Schreib einen Brief an deinen Brieffreund/an deine Brieffreundin.

Students should now be ready to write a letter to their penfriend using the prompts and the support in the *Hilfe* column.

Hilfe
Tips for students when writing a letter:
- beginnings and endings of letters
- include some examples of the perfect tense
- word order: when, how, where (to)

Workbook

p. 49

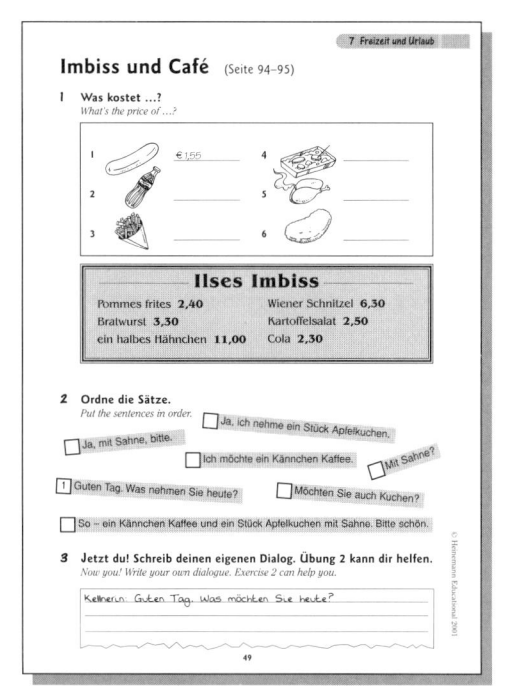

1
1 €3,30,
2 €2,30,
3 €2,40,
4 €2,50,
5 €11,00,
6 €6,30,

2 *Kellnerin:* Guten Tag. Was nehmen Sie heute?
Kundin: Ich möchte ein Kännchen Kaffee.
Kellnerin: Möchten Sie auch Kuchen?
Kundin: Ja, ich nehme ein Stück Apfelkuchen.
Kellnerin: Mit Sahne?
Kundin: Ja, mit Sahne, bitte.
Kellnerin: So – ein Kännchen Kaffee und ein Stück Apfelkuchen mit Sahne. Bitte schön.

3 Open-ended

p. 50

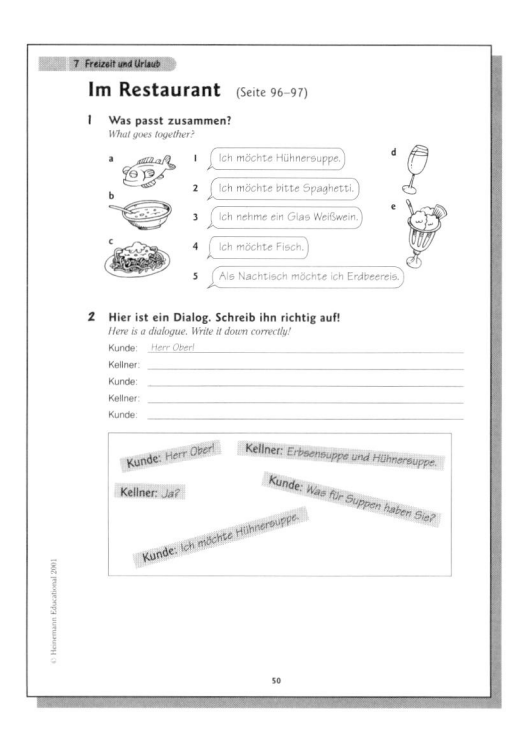

1 1 b, 2 c, 3 d, 4 a, 5 e

2
Kunde: Herr Ober!
Kellner: Ja?
Kunde: Was für Suppen haben Sie?
Kellner: Erbsensuppe und Hühnersuppe.
Kunde: Ich möchte Hühnersuppe.

p. 51

1 1 c, 2 d, 3 e, 4 a, 5 b
2 1 a, 2 c, 3 a, 4 b, 5 b, 6 c
3 1 falsch, 2 richtig, 3 falsch, 4 richtig, 5 falsch, 6 falsch

p. 52

1 Markus – 2, Beate – 3, Otto – 5, Max – 4, Wiebke – 1

2
A: Bitte schön.
B: Ich möchte amerikanisches Geld in Euro wechseln.
A: Wie viel Dollar haben Sie?
B: Fünfzig Dollar.
A: Moment … bitte schön, fünfzig Dollar Scheine. B: Danke schön.

3 Guten Tag. Bitte schön? Ich möchte amerikanisches Geld in Euro wechseln. Wie viel Dollar haben Sie? Hundert Dollar. Gern. Moment … Fünfundfünfzig Euro. Bitte schön – fünf Zehn-Euro-Scheine und ein Fünf-Euro-Schein
Oh, kann ich für zehn Euro Kleingeld haben? Hier – zwei fünf-Euro-Stücke.

96

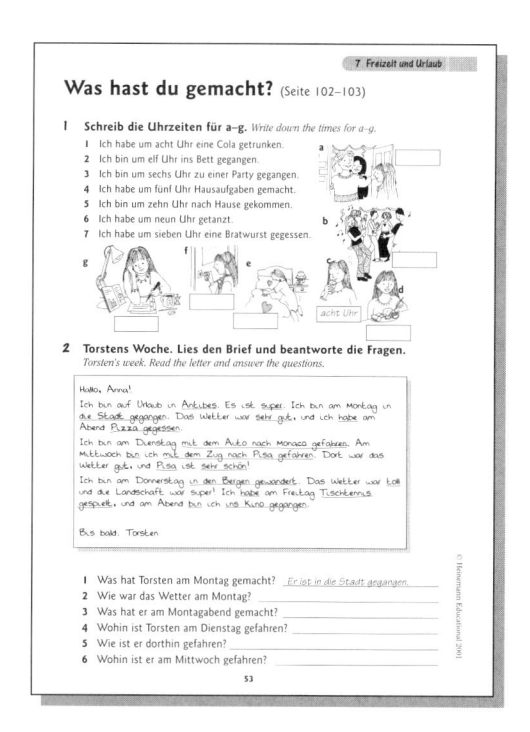

Logo! 4 7 Freizeit und Urlaub

p. 53

p. 54

1 **a** sechs Uhr, **b** neun Uhr, **c** acht Uhr, **d** sieben Uhr, **e** elf Uhr, **f** zehn Uhr, **g** fünf Uhr

2 **1** Er ist in die Stadt gegangen. **2** Das Wetter war sehr gut. **3** Er hat Pizza gegessen. **4** Er ist nach Monaco gefahren. **5** Er ist mit dem Auto dorthin gefahren. **6** Er ist nach Pisa gefahren.

p. 55

1 **1** Ich habe am Wochenende Fußball gespielt. **2** Ich bin gestern in die Stadt gegangen. **3** Ich habe am Montag Pizza gegessen. **4** Ich habe am Dienstag einen Film gesehen. **5** Ich bin am Wochenende ins Kino gegangen. **6** Ich habe gestern Schuhe gekauft.

2 Open-ended

97

8 Mein Leben zu Hause (pp. 108–121)

Topic area	Key language	Grammar	Language skills
8.1 Essen (pp. 108–109) Give information about eating at home	*Ich esse, du isst, er/sie isst. Ich trinke, du trinkst, er/sie trinkt. gern/lieber/am liebsten. Was isst/trinkst du zum Frühstück/Mittagessen/Abendessen? Toast/Brötchen/Salat/Käse/Butterbrot/Fisch/Fleisch/Kaffee/Tee/Wasser/Wein/Cola*	Present tense of first, second and third person of *essen* and *trinken gern/lieber/am liebsten*	
8.2 Mein Alltag (pp. 110–111) Talk about day-to-day activities	*Ich wache um … Uhr auf. Ich stehe um … Uhr auf. Ich dusche um … Uhr auf. Ich frühstücke um … Uhr. Ich putze mir um … Uhr die Zähne. Ich verlasse das Haus um … Uhr. Ich esse um … Uhr Abendbrot. Ich mache um … Uhr meine Hausaufgaben. Ich sehe um … Uhr fern. Ich gehe um … Uhr schlafen.*	Present tense verbs	Learning by heart
8.3 Hausarbeiten (pp. 112–113) Talk about household chores	*Ich wasche ab. Ich trockne ab. Ich saube Staub. Ich kaufe ein. Ich räume mein Zimmer auf. Ich decke den Tisch. Ich bügle. Ich muss (nicht) [+ infinitives]. Ich hasse Abtrocknen.*	Separable verbs *müssen* + infinitives	Difference between *Hausarbeit* and *Hausaufgaben Ich hasse …*
8.4 Aua! (pp. 114–115) Talk about illness and injury	*Ich habe Ohren/Bauch/Kopf/Hals/Rücken/Zahnschmerzen. Mein Bein/Fuß/Arm/Finger/Knie tut weh. Ich habe / Er hat Durchfall/Fieber/Schnupfen / eine Grippe / einen Sonnenbrand. Ich bin / Er ist müde/krank.*		Two ways of complaining about pain
8.5 Feste (pp. 116–117) Talk about festivals in Germany	*Ostern, der Osterhase, Ostereier, Weihnachten, die Bescherung, Heiligabend, Silvester, Neujahr, Fasching/Karneval. (Weihnachten) ist toll. Mein Lieblingsfest ist …*		Using *Lieblings-* to describe favourite things
8.6 So bleibt man fit! (pp. 118–119) Talk about health issues	*Was machst du, um fit zu bleiben? Ich gehe joggen / spiele Squash / esse viel Salat. Ich arbeite nicht viel mit dem Computer. Ich rauche nicht / trinke keinen Alkohol / sehe nicht viel fern. Was ist gesund und was ist nicht gesund? Sport/Joggen/Gemüse ist gesund. Rauchen/Trinken/Faulenzen ist ungesund. Pommes frites/Bonbons sind ungesund. Das stimmt (nicht). Das ist (nicht) wahr.*	*um … zu*	
Lesen/Schreiben (pp. 176–177)			Reading and Writing skills

- The vocabulary and structures taught in Chapter 8 are summarised on the **Wörter** pages of the Student's Book, 120–121.
- Further Speaking practice on the language of the chapter is provided on **Sprechen** p. 123.
- For a selection of assessment tasks for Chapters 7 and 8, please refer to the separate Assessment Pack for your chosen examination board: AQA, OCR or Edexcel.

Logo! 4 8 Mein Leben zu Hause

1 Essen (pp. 108–109)

Students will learn how to:
- give information about meals at home

Key language	Grammar points
Was isst/trinkst du zum Frühstück/ Mittagessen/ Abendessen? Ich esse Du isst Er/Sie isst Ich trinke Du trinkst Er/Sie trinkt gern/lieber/am liebsten Toast/Brötchen/Salat/ Käse/Butterbrot/Fisch/ Fleisch/Kaffee/Tee/ Wasser/Wein/Cola	• first, second and third person of *essen* and *trinken* • *gern, lieber, am liebsten* **Resources** • Cassette C Side A • Workbook p. 56 • Sprechen p. 123, Gespräch 1 • Lesen/Schreiben A p. 176

Before starting this unit, ask students to brainstorm any food vocabulary not already covered in the Eating Out sections, for example breakfast items. Can they remember the German names for the various meals?

1 Was passt zusammen? (Reading)
Students match the speech bubbles to the food pictures by writing down letters.

Answers
1 f, 2 g, 3 a, 4 c, 5 e, 6 h, 7 i, 8 b, 9 d, 10 j

2a Hör zu. Wer isst und trinkt was? (Listening)
Students listen to the tape and note down, using letters, what the three interviewees eat and drink. Make sure they realise that the pictures are the same as those in Exercise 1 and that they must give several answers for each person.

Answers
1 **Oliver:** f, j, a und h, 2 **Sabine:** d, c, und b,
3 **Robert:** i, e und g

 1 – Oliver, was isst du gern?
   – Ich frühstücke um 8 Uhr. Ich esse Cornflakes mit Milch, dann Toast mit Wurst und Käse und ich trinke Kaffee.
 2 – Sabine, was isst du gern?
   – Ich frühstücke nicht. Aber ich esse Mittagessen in der Kantine. Ich esse Salat und ein Butterbrot. Und ich trinke Wasser.
 3 – Gut, Sabine. Und du, Robert, isst du gesund?
   – Nein, mein Essen ist nicht sehr gesund! Zum Abendessen gehe ich gern ins Hamburger-Restaurant. Ich esse Hamburger mit Pommes und Ketchup. Und ich trinke Cola dazu. Lecker!
   – Ja, lecker, ... aber auch ungesund!

2b Jetzt schreib Sätze. Was essen und trinken Oliver, Sabine und Robert? (Writing)
Students now write out the answers to Exercise 2a, using full sentences.

Answers
1 Oliver isst Cornflakes, Toast mit Wurst und Käse. Er trinkt Kaffee.
2 Sabine isst Salat und ein Butterbrot. Sie trinkt Wasser.
3 Robert isst Hamburger mit Pommes und Ketchup. Er trinkt Cola.

Grammatik: The present tense
This shows the present tense of the first, second and third person forms of *essen* and *trinken*. Full paradigms and verb lists are not provided, only the forms which students need immediately. For full verb and tense information, refer to the Grammar Section.

Grammatik: Expressing preferences
Give students types of food and drink in threes, asking them to list them in order of preference.
Teacher: Brot, Wurst, Eis.
Student: Ich esse gern Brot, ich esse lieber Wurst aber ich esse am liebsten Eis.

3 Partnerarbeit. (Speaking)
Working in pairs, students practise stating preferences about food. Make sure the exercise is done both ways round.

4a Was isst und trinkt Olli gern? Schreib *ja* oder *nein*. (Reading)
This is a form which Olli Meyer has filled in before going on an exchange visit. Students work out what Olli does and doesn't like eating and write down *ja* or *nein*.

A photocopiable grid is available for this exercise. (p.139)

Answers
1 nein, 2 ja, 3 ja, 4 nein, 5 nein, 6 ja, 7 nein, 8 ja

4b Schreib das Formular ab und füll es FÜR DICH aus. (Writing)
Students copy out the form which Olli filled in (Exercise 4a) and fill it in for themselves.

5 Partnerarbeit. (Speaking)
Students practise talking about what they eat for various meals. The first one is done for them.

Further practice of the language and vocabulary of this unit is given on the following pages:
Sprechen: p. 123
Lesen/Schreiben A: p. 176
Workbook: p. 56

2 Mein Alltag (pp. 110–111)

Students will learn how to:
- talk about day-to-day activities

Key language	Ich gehe um … Uhr schlafen
Ich wache um … Uhr auf	
Ich stehe um … Uhr auf	**Grammar points**
Ich dusche um … Uhr	• present tense verbs
Ich frühstücke um … Uhr	**Language skills**
Ich putze mir um … Uhr die Zähne	• learning daily routine by heart
Ich verlasse das Haus um … Uhr	**Resources**
Ich esse um … Uhr Abendbrot	• Cassette C Side A
Ich mache um … Uhr meine Hausaufgaben	• Workbook pp. 57–58
Ich sehe um … Uhr fern	• Sprechen p. 123, Gespräch 2

Before starting the spread, make sure students are still confident about telling the time in German. Also ask them, in English, what items they would mention when describing a typical day's routine. Explain to students that the 24-hour clock is used more widely in Germany than in the UK. Both the 12-hour and the 24-hour clock are used on the spread.

1a Fatimas Tag. Was sagt Fatima? Trag die Sätze ins Heft ein. (Reading)
Make sure students understand exactly what to do in this simple reading/writing exercise. They identify what Fatima does at each of the numbered digital times and simply copy down the sentence.

Answers

1 Ich putze mir um acht Uhr die Zähne. 2 Ich gehe um 22.30 schlafen. 3 Ich sehe um 21 Uhr fern. 4 Ich stehe um 7.15 Uhr auf. 5 Ich verlasse das Haus um 8.15. 6 Ich wache um 7 Uhr auf. 7 Ich mache um 19 Uhr meine Hausaufgaben. 8 Ich dusche um 7.30 Uhr. 9 Ich esse um 18 Uhr Abendbrot. 10 Ich frühstücke um 7.45 Uhr.

1b Berndts Tag. Hör zu und notiere die Uhrzeit. (1–10) (Listening)
Students listen to Berndt describing his day and note down the times.

Answers

1 6.30, 2 6.45, 3 7.00, 4 7.15, 5 7.20, 6 7.30, 7 6.00, 8 7.00, 9 9.00, 10 11.00

1 Ich wache um sechs Uhr dreißig auf.
2 Ich stehe um Viertel vor sieben auf.
3 Ich dusche um sieben Uhr.
4 Ich frühstücke um Viertel nach sieben.
5 Ich putze mir um zwanzig nach sieben die Zähne.
6 Ich verlasse das Haus um halb acht.
7 Ich esse um sechs Uhr Abendbrot.
8 Ich mache um sieben meine Hausaufgaben.
9 Ich sehe um neun Uhr fern.
10 Ich gehe um elf Uhr schlafen.

2a Partnerarbeit. Gib Information über deinen Alltag. (Speaking)
In pairs, students practise questions and answers about daily routine. Make sure this is done both ways round.

2b Jetzt gib DEINE Antworten. (Speaking)
Students again practise questions and answers about daily routine, this time supplying the true information about themselves, in preparation for Exercise 2c.

Tip box
Advice to students to learn their daily routine by heart and the suggestion that they also record it on tape. This tip applies to many other topics in the book as well. Stress to students the importance of learning by heart NOW. They will then be much more likely to remember the language at a later date and use it in an exam.

2c Jetzt schreib die Informationen über DEINEN Alltag auf. Schreib 10 Sätze. (Writing)
Students now write out the information about their own daily routine. This can be done for homework. Encourage the more able to add in extra information.

Further practice of the language and vocabulary of this unit is given on the following pages:
Sprechen: p. 123
Workbook: pp. 57–58

Logo! 4 8 Mein Leben zu Hause

3 Hausarbeiten (pp. 112–113)

Students will learn how to:
- talk about jobs in the home

Key language	Grammar points
Was für Hausarbeiten machst du?	• separable verbs
Ich wasche ab	• *Ich muss (nicht)* + infinitive
Ich trockne ab	
Ich sauge Staub	**Language skills**
Ich kaufe ein	• meaning of *Hausarbeit* and *Hausaufgaben*
Ich räume den Zimmer auf	• *Ich hasse Abtrocknen*
Ich decke den Tisch	
Ich bügle	**Resources**
Ich muss (nicht) abwaschen	• Cassette C Side A
Ich hasse Abtrocknen	• Workbook p. 59
	• Sprechen p. 123, Rollenspiel 1

Start the unit by finding out, in English, what household chores students do. The results might be quite a shock! Explain that they are going to learn to talk about this topic in German.

1a Hör zu. Wer macht was? (1–7) (Listening)
Students look at the pictures and captions, then listen to the tape. They identify who does what by writing down letters.

Answers
1 g, 2 e, 3 b, 4 c, 5 a, 6 f, 7 d

1 – Rikki, was machst du denn zu Hause?
   – Ich bügle.
2 – Und du, Imke, was machst du?
   – Ich räume mein Zimmer auf.
3 – Machst du Hausarbeiten, Silke?
   – Ich trockne ab.
4 – Tommy, was für Hausarbeiten machst du denn?
   – Ich sauge Staub.
5 – Und du, Anni?
   – Ich wasche ab.
6 – Gabi, hilfst du deinen Eltern zu Hause?
   – Ja, schon. Ich decke den Tisch für das Mittagessen.
7 – Und zum Schluss noch Eduard. Was machst du?
   – Ich kaufe am Wochenende ein.

Tip box: *Hausarbeit* and *Hausaufgaben*
Although this seems obvious, it is often misunderstood in Speaking or Writing Tests and leads to students giving lengthy answers to the wrong question!

1b Jetzt schreib die Antworten auf. (Writing)
Students now write down the answers to Exercise 1a in the order in which they appeared.

Answers
1 Ich bügle. 2 Ich räume mein Zimmer auf. 3 Ich trockne ab. 4 Ich sauge Staub. 5 Ich wasche ab. 6 Ich decke den Tisch. 7 Ich kaufe ein.

2 Partnerarbeit. (Speaking)
Students conduct interviews, based on picture prompts, about what they do and don't do around the house.

Grammatik
An explanation of separable verbs, with examples from page 112.
How to say you must (or don't have to) do household tasks. This explanation is intended to help students avoid saying things like *Ich nicht abwaschen*. The concept is not easy and can be omitted for the least able.

3 Was muss Morten machen? Wähle die richtigen Bilder. (Reading)
Students look at the pictures and the note from Morten's mother. They write down letters to indicate the THREE things he has to do.

Answers
d, a, c

4 Partnerarbeit. (Speaking)
This is a pairwork activity in which students ask and answer questions about what they have to do and don't have to do around the house. Make sure students realise that *muss nicht* means 'don't have to' and not 'mustn't'. Otherwise it won't make much sense to them!

Tip box: How to say 'I hate' doing household tasks
This is useful because most teenagers hate housework and need to be able to say so.

5 Was für Hausarbeiten machst du? (Writing)
Students sum up this spread by writing down what they do in the way of chores. This needs to be marked, kept and learnt.

Further practice of the language and vocabulary of this unit is given on the following pages:
Sprechen: p. 123
Workbook: p. 59

4 Aua! (pp. 114–115)

Students will learn how to:
- talk about illness and injury

Key language	Ich bin/Er ist …
Ich habe Ohren/Bauch/ Kopf/Hals/Rücken/ Zahn…schmerzen	krank müde
Mein Arm/Bein/Fuß/ Finger/Knie / Meine Hand tut weh	**Language skills** • two different ways of complaining about pain
Ich habe/Er hat … Durchfall Fieber Schnupfen eine Grippe einen Sonnenbrand	**Resources** • Cassette C Side A • Workbook p. 60 • Sprechen p. 123, Rollenspiel 2

Start the spread by using mime to revise the German words for the parts of the body (before looking at the picture!).

1 Hör zu. Wer sagt was? (1–10) (Listening)
The sports teacher has a lot of malingerers! Students listen to the tape and look at the picture in order to identify who is who by writing down letters.

Answers
1 d, 2 i, 3 f, 4 h, 5 e, 6 b, 7 g, 8 j, 9 a, 10 c

> 1 Herr Klein, mein Bein tut weh!
> 2 Es tut mir Leid, Herr Klein, mein Finger tut weh!
> 3 Oh, Herr Klein, mein Knie tut weh!
> 4 Ich kann keinen Sport treiben. Mein Fuß tut weh.
> 5 Meine Hand tut weh, Herr Klein!
> 6 Ich habe Halsschmerzen!
> 7 Entschuldigen Sie, Herr Klein, ich habe Bauchschmerzen.
> 8 Aua, ich habe furchtbare Kopfschmerzen!
> 9 Ich habe schreckliche Ohrenschmerzen!
> 10 Ich kann keinen Sport machen. Ich habe Rückenschmerzen.

2 Lies den Brief. Wo tut es Timo weh? Schreib *ja* oder *nein*. (Reading)
Students read the letter that Timo has sent in to school and work out which ailments he has and hasn't got, by writing down *ja* or *nein*.

Answers
1 nein, 2 ja, 3 nein, 4 ja, 5 nein, 6 ja, 7 ja, 8 nein

Tip box
An explanation that in German (as in English) there are two ways of complaining about pain.
Students must understand that the expressions are not interchangeable. In other words, just as in English you would say 'My leg hurts' rather than 'I've got leg-ache', so in German you would say *Mein Bein tut weh* rather than *Ich habe Beinschmerzen*.

3 Partnerarbeit. Was sagen diese Personen? (Speaking)
Working in pairs, students use the picture prompts to make short dialogues with an information gap element to them.

4 Schreib an den Sportlehrer. Du bist SEHR, SEHR krank!! (Writing)
Students use their imagination to write a letter to the sports teacher, listing lots of reasons not to take part in the lesson.

5 Wer hat welches Problem? (Reading)
Students read the e-mail and work out who is who by referring to the pictures. They write down names.

Answers
1 Tanita, 2 Klaus, 3 Frank, 4 Susanne, 5 Frank, 6 Tanita

6 Partnerarbeit. (Speaking)
Students work in pairs to find out ailments as shown in the picture prompts.

> Further practice of the language and vocabulary of this unit is given on the following pages:
> Sprechen: p. 123
> Workbook: p. 60

Logo! 4 8 Mein Leben zu Hause

5 Feste (pp. 116–117)

Students will learn how to:
- talk about German festivals

Key language	Language skills
Ostern	• *Lieblings-*
der Osterhase	
Ostereier	**Resources**
Weihnachten	• Cassette C Side A
die Bescherung	• Workbook p. 61
Heiligabend	• Sprechen p. 123,
Silvester	Gespräch 3
Neujahr	• Lesen/Schreiben B
Fasching/Karneval	p. 177
(Weihnachten) ist (toll)	
Mein Lieblingsfest ist ...	

Before starting this spread, ask students what German vocabulary they remember about Christmas, Easter and Carnival. What other details do they remember about these festivals in Germany and how they differ from the UK?

1 (Reading)
A Finde die deutschen Wörter.
A longer reading task in which students are asked to find German equivalents of some English phrases.

Answers
1 Ostereier, 2 vielleicht, 3 die Eltern, 4 gesund, 5 Osterhase, 6 lustig, 7 wer weiß?

B Finde die deutschen Wörter.
Students find more German equivalents of English phrases.

Answers
1 Neujahr, 2 Weihnachten, 3 die Bescherung, 4 Silvester, 5 die Geschenke, 6 Großbritannien, 7 Heiligabend

C Finde die deutschen Wörter.
Explain to students that, although *Fasching* officially begins in November, the main celebrations are in February/March.

Answers
1 Köln, 2 Süddeutschland, 3 Fasching, 4 Rheinland, 5 am elften elften um elf Uhr elf!

D Wähle ein Fest und beschreib es auf Englisch!
A comprehension activity in which students select one (or more) of the festivals detailed and write down in English as much as they can about it.

2a Hör zu. Was ist dein Lieblingsfest? Schreib *Ostern*, *Karneval* oder *Weihnachten*. (Listening)
The people are being interviewed on a talk show about their favourite festival. Students write down each person's favourite.

Answers
1 Peter: Karneval, 2 Olaf: Weihnachten, 3 Susanne: Weihnachten, 4 Maike: Ostern, 5 Andrea: Karneval

1 – Guten Abend und herzlich willkommen bei „Jugend heute". Heute ist unser Thema „Was ist dein Lieblingsfest?" Na, Peter, was ist dein Lieblingsfest?
 – Mein Lieblingsfest ist Karneval! Ich komme aus Köln, da ist der Karneval wunderbar. Viel essen, viel trinken und viel feiern! Karneval macht Spaß!
2 – Danke. Und du, Olaf? Magst du auch Fasching?
 – Nein. Mein Lieblingsfest ist Weihnachten! Da gibt's viele Geschenke.
3 – Vielen Dank. Magst du auch Weihnachten, Susanne?
 – Natürlich! Ich finde Weihnachten toll! Weihnachten ist mein Lieblingsfest!
4 – Und du, Maike? Was meinst du?
 – Mein Lieblingsfest ist Ostern. Ich liebe Schokolade!
5 – Was meinst du, Andrea? Magst du auch Schokolade?
 – Nein! Schokolade, igitt! Ich mag Ostern nicht. Mein Lieblingsfest ist Karneval.

2b Was sagen diese Personen? Schreib *richtig* oder *falsch*. (Reading)
Students note down whether the statements (which refer to the listening items in Exercise 2a) are true or false.

Answers
1 richtig, 2 falsch, 3 falsch, 4 richtig, 5 falsch

3a Was passt zusammen? (Reading)
Students link up halves of sentences to prove they have understood the information. They write a letter with each number.

Answers
1 d, 2 g, 3 e, 4 f, 5 a, 6 h, 7 b, 8 c

3b Jetzt schreib die Sätze auf. (Writing)
Now they write out the answers to Exercise 3a in sentences.

Answers
1 Heiligabend ist am 24. Dezember. 2 Silvester ist am 31. Dezember. 3 Es gibt Geschenke bei der Bescherung. 4 Der Osterhase bringt die Ostereier. 5 Karneval beginnt am 11. November. 6 Köln ist in Süddeutschland. 7 Schokolade ist nicht gesund. 8 Der 1. Januar heißt Neujahr.

Tip box: Using *Lieblings-* to describe favourite things
Point out how flexible this structure is and how they can apply it to other topic areas.

4 Partnerarbeit. (Speaking)
Working in pairs, students construct brief dialogues about festivals. They can vary the content of what they say in any way they like.

Further practice of the language and vocabulary of this unit is given on the following pages:
Sprechen: p. 123
Lesen/Schreiben B: p. 177
Workbook: p. 61

Logo! 4 8 Mein Leben zu Hausea

6 So bleibt man fit! (pp. 118–119)

Students will learn how to:
- talk about health issues

Key language	Rauchen/Trinken/
Was machst du, um fit zu bleiben?	Faulenzen/Fernsehen ist ungesund
Ich gehe joggen/spiele Squash/esse viel Salat	Das stimmt (nicht)
Ich arbeite nicht viel mit dem Computer	Das ist (nicht) wahr
Ich rauche nicht	**Grammar points**
Ich trinke keinen Alkohol	• *um ... zu*
Ich sehe nicht viel fern	**Resources**
Was ist gesund und was ist nicht gesund?	• Cassette C Side A
Sport/Joggen/Gemüse ist gesund	

Start this spread by asking in English for contributions about ways to live healthily.

1 Hör zu. Wer macht was? (1–6) (Listening)
Students listen to the tape and write down a letter to identify which picture refers to which interviewee.

Answers
1 b, 2 c, 3 d, 4 e, 5 a, 6 f

> 1 – Otto, was machst du am Abend?
> – Ich sehe bis zehn Uhr fern.
> 2 – Sascha, siehst du auch viel fern?
> – Nee, ich gehe lieber zum Squash-Club.
> 3 – Bist du sportlich, Ali?
> – Nein, ich gehe aber gern in die Kneipe und trinke Bier.
> 4 – Hmmm ... gehst du auch oft in die Kneipe, Roland?
> – Nein, Alkohol trinke ich nicht, aber ich rauche ungefähr 20 Zigaretten pro Tag.
> 5 – Sylvia, rauchst du auch?
> – Nein! Rauchen ist dumm. Ich gehe jeden Abend joggen.
> 6 – Und jetzt noch Jutta. Joggst du auch?
> – Nein, ich habe keine Zeit. Ich arbeite oft am Computer.

2 Wer lebt gesund? Wer lebt ungesund? (Writing)
Students look at the pictures and write down sentences to show whether each person is healthy or unhealthy.

Answers
1 Lara lebt ungesund. 2 Mohammed lebt ungesund. 3 Carolin lebt gesund. 4 Marcel lebt gesund. 5 Felix lebt ungesund. 6 Wiebke lebt gesund.

3a Partnerarbeit. (Speaking)
In pairs, students use the picture prompts to make questions and answers.

3b Partnerarbeit. (Speaking)
An extension of Exercise 3a. Students look at pictures and decide what is healthy and what isn't.

4 Schreib deine Meinung über diese Sätze. (Writing)
Students write what they think about the five statements. As this is an area which students may not have covered before, make sure they use the glossary or a dictionary for any unfamiliar vocabulary. Draw attention to the expressions *Das stimmt / Das stimmt nicht / Das ist wahr / Das ist nicht wahr*, which will be useful in Speaking Tests.

5 Welche Artikel gibt es im *Fitness-Spezial*? Schreib *ja* oder *nein*. (Reading)
Students look at the contents list from a health magazine and say whether these topics are being covered by writing *ja* or *nein*.

Answers
1 nein, 2 ja, 3 ja, 4 ja, 5 ja, 6 ja

6 Was machst du, um fit zu bleiben? Schreib auf! (Writing)
Students use the picture prompts to write down ways of keeping fit.

Answers
1 Ich spiele Squash. 2 Ich trinke kein Bier. 3 Ich esse Gemüse. 4 Ich rauche nicht.

7 Bring die Anweisungen in die richtige Reihenfolge. (Reading, Writing)
A simple recipe in which students have to write out the directions in the correct order on the basis of the pictures.

Answers
Schälen Sie die Äpfel. Dann schneiden Sie die Eier und das Gemüse. Fügen Sie Salz und Pfeffer dazu. Mischen Sie die Zutaten. Gießen Sie zum Schluss Essig und Öl darüber. Stellen Sie den Salat in den Kühlschrank.

All the vocabulary and structures from this chapter are listed on the **Wörter** pages 120–121. These can be used for revision by covering up either the English or the German. Students can check here to see how much they remember from the chapter.

Assessment materials for Chapters 7 and 8 are available after Chapter 8.

Further grammar and speaking practice on the whole chapter is provided on pp. 62–63 of the **Workbook**.

Workbook

p. 56

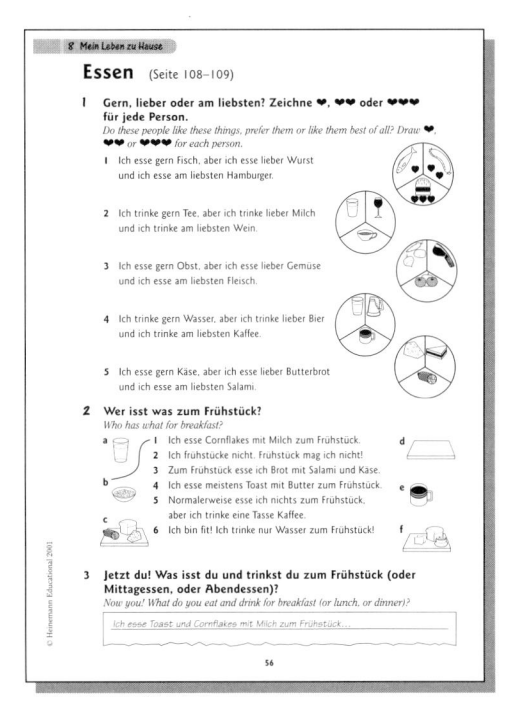

1
1 fish ♥ sausage ♥♥ hamburger ♥♥♥
2 tea ♥ milk ♥♥ wine ♥♥♥
3 fruit ♥ vegetables ♥♥ meat ♥♥♥
4 water ♥ beer ♥♥ coffee ♥♥♥
5 cheese ♥ sandwich ♥♥ salami ♥♥♥

2 1 b, **2** d, **3** c, **4** f, **5** e, **6** a

3 Open-ended. Overlook minor errors.

p. 57

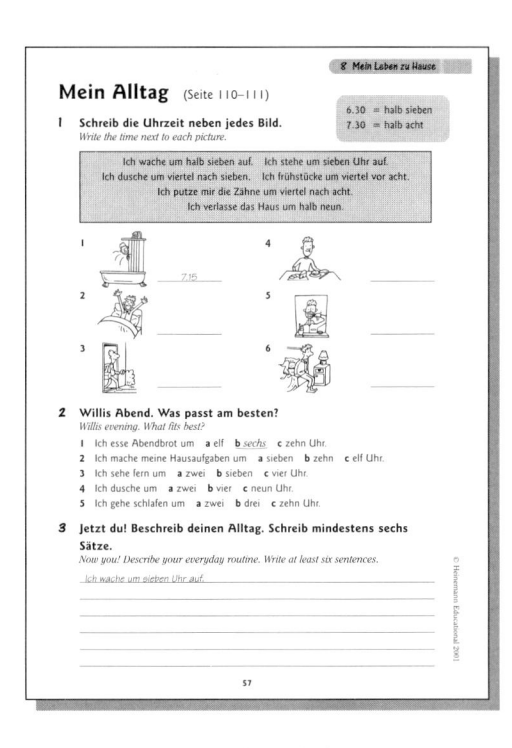

1 1 7.15, **2** 6.30, **3** 8.30, **4** 7.45, **5** 8.15, **6** 7.00

2 1 b, **2** a, **3** b, **4** c, **5** c

3 Open-ended. Overlook minor errors.

p. 58

1 1 Klimm, **2** Klimm, **3** Matthias, **4** Matthias, **5** Klimm, **6** Klimm, **7** Matthias

2 Open-ended. Overlook minor errors.

p. 59

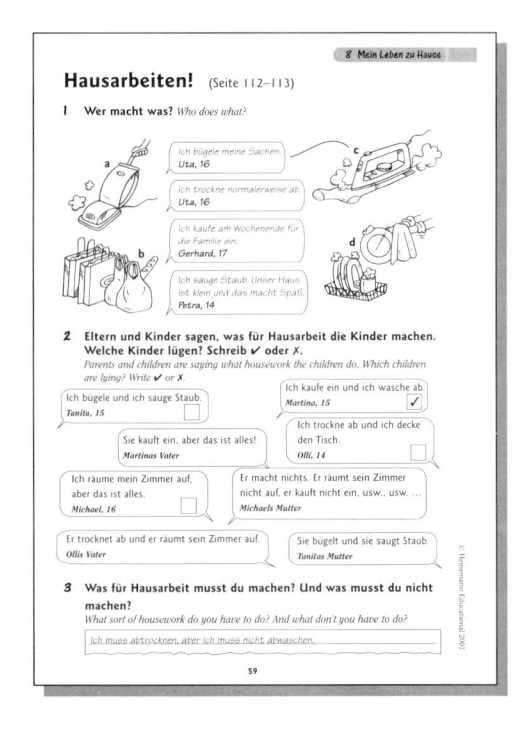

1 Uta – c Gerhard – b Petra – a Gabi – d

2 Olli, Martina, Michael

3 Open-ended. Overlook minor errors.

106

Logo! 4 8 Mein Leben zu Hausea

p. 60

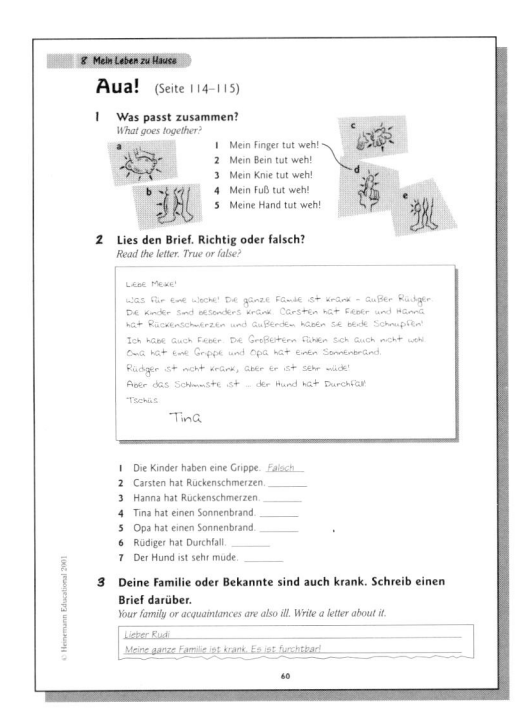

1 1 d, **2** b, **3** e, **4** a, **5** c
2 1 Falsch, **2** Falsch, **3** Richtig, **4** Falsch, **5** Richtig, **6** Falsch, **7** Falsch
3 Open-ended. Overlook minor errors.

p. 61

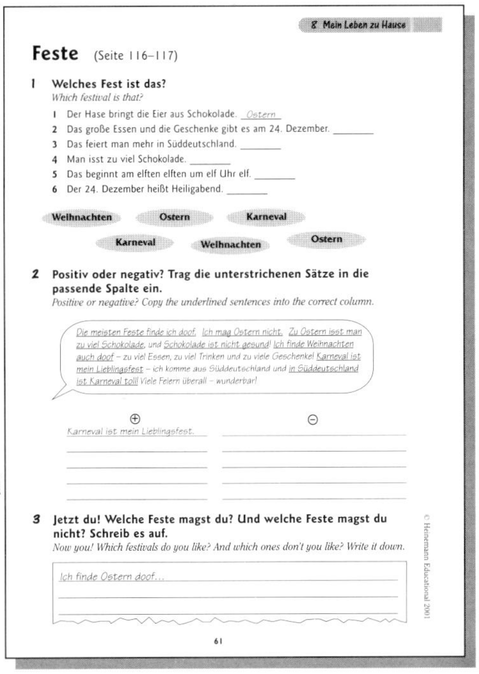

1 1 Ostern, 2 Weihnachten, 3 Karneval, 4 Ostern, 5 Karneval, 6 Weihnachten
2 ⊕ Karneval ist mein Lieblingsfest. In Süddeutschland ist Karneval toll.
⊖ Die meisten Feste finde ich doof. Ich mag Ostern nicht. Zu Ostern isst man zu viel Schokolade. Schokolade ist nicht gesund! Ich finde Weihnachten auch Schokolade. Schokolade ist nicht gesund! Ich finde Weihnachten auch doof.
3 Open-ended. Overlook minor errors.

p. 62

p. 63

1 1 Ich trinke gern Tee, aber ich trinke lieber Kaffee und ich trinke am liebsten Wein. **2** Ich esse gern Käse, aber ich esse lieber Salami und ich esse am liebsten Hamburger. **3** Ich esse gern Brot, aber ich esse lieber Pommes frites und ich esse am liebsten Chips.
2 Open-ended. Overlook minor errors.

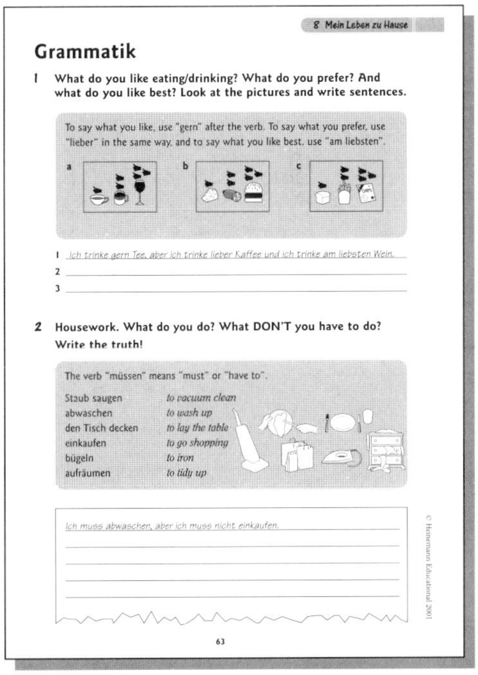

107

9 Die Arbeit (pp. 124–135)

Topic area	Key language	Grammar	Language skills
9.1 Was machst du? (pp. 124–125) Talk about jobs and where people work	*Ich bin / Er/Sie ist [jobs]. Mein Vater/Bruder/Onkel ist … . Ich arbeite / Er/Sie arbeitet in der Schule / bei der Polizei / im Krankenhaus / in Büro / zu Hause / in einem Büro/Restaurant/Geschäft*	Masculine and feminine forms of jobs No article needed with jobs Revision of first and third person of *sein* and *arbeiten*	Listening advice: not necessary to understand every word and listen for words similar to the English
9.2 Teilzeitjobs (pp. 126–127) Talk about part-time work	*Hast du einen Teilzeitjob? Nein, ich habe keinen Job. Ja, ich arbeite in einem Büro/Supermarkt / in einer Fabrik / als Babysitter. Ich arbeite am Samstag/ Wochenende / einmal/zweimal in der Woche / jeden Tag. Ich trage Zeitungen aus. Ich arbeite für … Stunden. Ich verdiene € … .*	*in einem / in einer* Frequency expressions	References to sections on expressing opinions and talking about spending money
9.3 Am Apparat (pp. 128–129) Make and understand phone calls	*Wie ist deine Telefonnummer? Kann ich bitte Frau/Herrn … sprechen? … ist nicht hier. Soll er/sie zurückrufen? Mein Name ist … Meine Telefonnummer ist … .*		How to say phone numbers including codes. How to answer the phone.
9.4 Das Betriebspraktikum (pp. 130–131) Talk about work experience	*Ich war bei der Firma … Ich habe in einer Fabrik/ Schule / in einem Geschäft gearbeitet. Ich bit mit dem … gefahren. Der Tag hat um … Uhr begonnen. Der Tag war um … Uhr zu Ende. Ich habe die Arbeit langweilig/interessant/schwer/leicht gefunden.*	Reminder of the perfect tense (with *haben* and *sein*) plus *war* and *hatte*	Advice about talking or writing about work experience.
9.5 Pläne für die Zukunft (pp. 132–133) Talk about career plans	*Ich will (Arzt) werden. Ich will auf die Uni(versität) / zur Hochschule gehen/studieren / eine Lehre machen / in … arbeiten / reisen. Ich möchte in einem Büro / in einer Schule arbeiten. Ich möchte heiraten/Kinder haben.*	Talking about the future: *ich will …, ich möchte, ich werde …*	Giving more detailed answers.
Lesen/Schreiben (pp. 178–179)			Reading and Writing skills

- The vocabulary and structures taught in Module 9 are summarised on the **Wörter** pages of the Student's Book, 134–135.
- Further Speaking practice on the language of the chapter is provided on **Sprechen** p. 150.
- Coursework pages relating to this chapter can be found on pp. 160–161 of the Student's Book.
- For a selection of assessment tasks for Module 9, please refer to the separate Assessment Pack for your chosen examination board: AQA, OCR or Edexcel.

Logo! 4 9 Die Arbeit

1 Was machst du? (pp. 124–125)

Students will learn how to:
- talk about jobs

Key language
Ich bin ...
Mein Vater/Meine Mutter ist ...
 Arzt/Ärztin
 Beamter/Beamtin
 Hausmann/Hausfrau
 Kellner/Kellnerin
 Krankenpfleger/ Krankenschwester
 Lehrer/Lehrerin
 Mechaniker/ Mechanikerin
 Polizist/Polizistin
 Schüler/Schülerin
 Sekretär/Sekretärin
 Verkäufer/Verkäuferin
 Zahnarzt/Zahnärztin
 arbeitslos
Er/Sie arbeitet ...
 in der Schule / bei der Polizei / in einem Büro / im Krankenhaus / in einem Geschäft / in einem Restaurant / zu Hause

Grammar points
- masculine and feminine forms of job titles
- no article necessary with jobs
- first and third person of *sein* and *arbeiten*

Language skills
- Listening advice: understanding every word is not necessary; listen for words similar to the English equivalent

Resources
- Cassette C Side B
- Workbook p. 64

Introduce this spread by asking students how many German words for types of job they can remember. Flashcards and OHP transparencies from earlier in the course can be used. Can students remember how to describe their parents' jobs?

1a Was passt zusammen? (Reading)
Students practise the job titles by writing letters to link the titles to the illustrations.

Answers
1 h, 2 j, 3 d, 4 g, 5 f, 6 i, 7 a, 8 b, 9 e, 10 c

1b Schreib Sätze. (Writing)
Now students write out the answers to Exercise 1a in sentences.

Answers
1 Er ist Kellner. 2 Sie ist Ärtzin. 3 Sie ist Hausfrau. 4 Er ist Krankenpfleger. 5 Er ist Lehrer. 6 Er ist Mechaniker. 7 Er ist Polizist. 8 Sie ist Sekretärin. 9 Sie ist Verkäuferin. 10 Er ist Zahnarzt.

Tip box: Advice on listening skills
Remind students that they don't need to understand every word. They should listen for words which are similar to their English equivalents. This is practised in Exercise 2.

2 Hör zu. Was für ein Beruf ist das? (1–10) (Listening)
Warn students that they won't just hear the words for the jobs. The people will say things which will give clues as to what they do. They write down numbers from Exercise 1b, or write down the words if they have time.

Answers
1 4 (Krankenpfleger), 2 1 (Kellner), 3 8 (Sekretärin), 4 10 (Zahnarzt), 5 7 (Polizist), 6 9 (Verkäuferin), 7 6 (Mechaniker), 8 5 (Lehrer), 9 2 (Ärztin), 10 3 (Hausfrau)

1 Guten Tag! Mein Name ist Martin Krüger und ich arbeite im Krankenhaus.
2 Ich arbeite in einem Restaurant.
3 Hallo! Ich bin Brigitte und ich arbeite in einem Büro.
4 – Aua! Ich habe Zahnschmerzen!
 – Kommen Sie herein!
5 Ich arbeite bei der Polizei.
6 Ich arbeite in einem Kaufhaus und verkaufe Sachen.
7 Ich arbeite in einer Werkstatt und repariere Autos.
8 Ich arbeite in einer Realschule und unterrichte Mathematik.
9 Du hast Fieber. Du musst im Bett bleiben.
10 Ich arbeite auch, aber ich arbeite zu Hause.

Grammatik: No article before a job/profession
Ask students to find examples and sentences on the page.

3 Partnerarbeit. (Speaking)
In pairs, students conduct short interviews about jobs, based on the picture prompts. Make sure they don't insert definite articles and, above all, make sure they get the gender of the person right. It sounds awful if they say something like *Meine Schwester ist Lehrer*.

Wiederholung: The present tense
A reminder of the first and third person of *sein* and *arbeiten*. Only the parts immediately needed by students are included. Further verb details are contained in the Grammar section.

4 Wer arbeitet wo? (Writing)
Students complete and write out sentences about where people work, based on the Key Language box.

Answers

> 1 Eine Krankenschwester arbeitet im Krankenhaus.
> 2 Eine Sekretärin arbeitet in einem Büro. 3 Ein Kellner arbeitet in einem Restaurant. 4 Eine Hausfrau arbeitet zu Hause. 5 Ein Polizist arbeitet bei der Polizei. 6 Eine Lehrerin arbeitet in der Schule.

5 Jetzt du. Wer macht was in deiner Familie?
(Writing)
Students should write as much as they can about their family members' jobs. Refer them back to Chapter 1 for details of other family members (step-parents, etc.). This material must be marked, kept and learnt.

Tip box
Advice to students about how to talk about more unusual jobs – either to ask the teacher, or to make up a different job!

Further practice of the language and vocabulary of this unit is given on the following pages:
Workbook: p. 64

Logo! 4 9 Die Arbeit

2 Teilzeitjobs (pp. 126–127)

Students will learn how to:
- talk about part-time work

Key language
Hast du einen Teilzeitjob?
Nein, ich habe keinen Job.
Ja, ich arbeite …
   in einem Büro/ Supermarkt /
   in einer Fabrik /
   als Babysitter
Ich arbeite …
   am Samstag/ Wochenende
   einmal/zweimal in der Woche
   jeden Tag
Ich trage Zeitungen aus

Ich arbeite für … Stunden
Ich verdiene € …

Grammar points
- *in einem / in einer*
- Frequency expressions

Language skills
- expressing opinions
- spending money

Resources
- Cassette C Side B
- Workbook p. 65
- Lesen/Schreiben A p. 178

Start this spread by conducting a class poll about which students have part-time jobs. How many of them can already say in German what they do, how long they work and how much they earn?

1 Wie viel Prozent sagen …? (Reading)
Students look at the pie chart and the pictures and write down a percentage number to show how many people in this poll do what in the way of part-time jobs.

Answers
1 e 5%, 2 d 17%, 3 a 23%, 4 b 15%, 5 c 30%, 6 f 10%

2 Hör zu. Wann macht man das? (1–6) (Listening)
Students listen to the tape in which people say when and how long they work. They note down the letters referring to the appropriate symbols.

Answers
1 e, 2 d, 3 c, 4 f, 5 b, 6 a

1 – Hast du einen Teilzeitjob, Felix?
   – Ja, ich arbeite am Samstag in einem Büro.
2 – Und du, Ines, hast du auch einen Job?
   – Ja, ich arbeite am Wochenende in einem Supermarkt.
3 – Wie ist es mit dir, Katharina?
   – Ich habe auch einen Job. Ich arbeite zweimal in der Woche in einer Fabrik.
4 – Arbeitest du auch, Lars?
   – Nein, ich habe keine Zeit. Ich muss so viele Hausaufgaben machen.
5 – Und du, Björn?
   – Ich arbeite dreimal in der Woche als Babysitter.
6 – Und du, Wiebke? Machst du auch Babysitting?
   – Ich? Nee, ich trage Zeitungen aus.
   – So, wie oft?
   – Jeden Tag!

3a Partnerarbeit. (Speaking)
Working in pairs, students conduct short interviews based on the picture prompts. There is an information gap element and the first one is done for them.

3b Jetzt schreib die Sätze auf. (Writing)
Now students write out sentences based on the information in Exercise 3a.

Answers
1 Ich arbeite am Wochenende im Supermarkt. 2 Ich arbeite am Sonntag als Babysitter. 3 Ich trage jeden Tag Zeitungen aus. 4 Ich arbeite zweimal in der Woche in einer Fabrik. 5 Ich arbeite einmal in der Woche in einem Büro.

4 Hör zu und kalkuliere. Wie viel verdienen diese Personen? (Listening)
Students listen to the tape and note down how much each person earns. The amounts to select from are printed to the right.

Answers
1 Katharina: € 48,–, 2 Ines: € 56,–, 3 Felix: € 30,– 4 Lars: € 0, 5 Björn: € 45,–, 6 Wiebke: € 15,–

1 – Wie viel verdienst du, Katharina?
   – Ich arbeite sechs Stunden in einer Fabrik. Ich bekomme nur € 8,– die Stunde.
2 – Ines?
   – Ich arbeite acht Stunden und ich bekomme € 7,– die Stunde.
3 – Und du, Felix?
   – Ich bekomme € 5,– die Stunde und ich arbeite sechs Stunden.
4 – Lars?
   – Für meine Hausaufgaben verdiene ich nichts!
5 – Wie viel bekommst du als Babysitter, Björn?
   – Nicht viel. € 5,– die Stunde. Aber ich arbeite neun Stunden.
6 – Und Wiebke?
   – Ich verdiene nur € 15,– in der Woche.

5 Wer sagt was? Schreib *Frank* oder *Sonja*. (Reading)
Students read the statements and work out who is saying what. They write down the names.

Answers
1 Sonja, 2 Frank, 3 Frank, 4 Sonja, 5 Frank, 6 Sonja

6 Partnerarbeit. (Speaking)
A pair work activity in which students construct brief dialogues based on the information in the speech bubbles.

7 Und du? Hast du einen Job? (Writing)
Students write down information about their own part-time jobs. If they don't have one and want to be truthful, they can say *Ich habe leider keinen Job*. Draw their attention to the adjacent **Tip Box** about opinions and spending money. This material must be marked, kept and learnt.

Tip box
References for students to look up, for help to express opinions and to talk about spending money.

Further practice of the language and vocabulary of this unit is given on the following pages:
Lesen/Schreiben A: p. 178
Workbook: p. 65

Logo! 4 9 Die Arbeit

3 Am Apparat (pp. 128–129)

Students will learn how to:
- make and understand phone calls

Key language	Language skills
Wie ist deine Telefonnummer?	• phone numbers including codes
Kann ich bitte Frau/Herrn … sprechen?	• answering the phone
… ist nicht hier	**Resources**
Soll er/sie zurückrufen?	• Cassette C Side B
Mein Name ist …	• Workbook p. 66
Meine Telefonnummer ist …	• Sprechen p. 150, Rollenspiel 1 + 2

Before starting this unit, explain that it is an exam-specific topic which may well contain much unfamiliar vocabulary.

Tip box: German phone numbers said in groups of two
Make sure they have plenty of practice in this area, which foxes even people who have spoken German for years. Point out how important it is to note down phone numbers accurately.

1 Hör zu. Wer hat welche Telefonnummer? (1–10) (Listening)
Students listen to the phone numbers on the tape as often as they need in order to write down the letters beside the correct numbers.

Answers
1 f, 2 c, 3 h, 4 a, 5 j, 6 d, 7 g, 8 i, 9 b, 10 e

1 Meine Telefonnummer ist	62–41–94–21.
2 Meine Telefonnummer ist	28–42–93–76.
3 Meine Telefonnummer ist	71–45–20–72.
4 Meine Telefonnummer ist	88–23–19–12.
5 Meine Telefonnummer ist	44–43–28–11.
6 Meine Telefonnummer ist	98–89–42–24.
7 Meine Telefonnummer ist	73–62–39–49.
8 Meine Telefonnummer ist	31–24–63–82.
9 Meine Telefonnummer ist	15–16–12–99.
10 Meine Telefonnummer ist	21–41–38–90.

Tip box
This gives advice on how to give the dialling code, ie **not** in groups of two.

2 Partnerarbeit. (Speaking)
This is a pair work activity with an information gap element. It can be tackled in any order they like.

Tip box: Advice to practise numbers regularly
One fun way to do this is to imagine they have just met the boy/girl of their dreams who is pulling out of the station on a train. At the last moment, he/she calls out his/her phone number. The partner has one chance only to note it down.

3 Partnerarbeit. Jetzt erfindet Telefonnummern. (Speaking)
This time the students make up the numbers themselves. Point out the tip about writing them down. This avoids disputes about who is responsible for any wrong answers!

4 Im Büro. Hör zu und lies. Finde die Wörter oder Ausdrücke. (Listening, Reading)
Students listen and read, noting down the German versions of the English expressions in the exercise. These are highlighted in the text.

Answers
1 zurückrufen, 2 ausrichten, 3 sprechen, 4 Telefonnummer, 5 in Ordnung

– Meyer.
– Guten Tag. Kann ich bitte Herrn Schulz sprechen?
– Herr Schulz ist nicht hier. Kann ich etwas ausrichten?
– Ja. Mein Name ist Richter. R-I-C-H-T-E-R. Meine Telefonnummer ist 49–32–66–14. Herr Schulz soll mich bitte zurückrufen.
– Danke, Herr Richter. Geht in Ordnung.

Tip box: How to answer the phone in German
Remind students just to say a surname, not say 'Hallo' or give the number.

5a Partnerarbeit. (Speaking)
Students now practise the new expressions in short guided dialogues. They can choose whether to say *Herr* or *Frau*. Point out that in the question they must say *Herrn* (but don't go into grammatical detail).

5b Schreib die Gespräche (5a) auf. (Writing)
Finally, students write out the conversations from Exercise 5a.

6 Finde die deutschen Ausdrücke. (Reading)
Students match the English and German instructions for using a public telephone.

Answers
1 f, 2 e, 3 d, 4 c, 5 a, 6 b

Further practice of the language and vocabulary of this unit is given on the following pages:
Sprechen: p. 150
Workbook: p. 66

4 Das Betriebspraktikum
(pp. 130–131)

Students will learn how to:
- talk about work experience

Key language
Ich war bei der Firma …
Ich habe …
  in einer Fabrik/Schule /
  in einem Geschäft
  gearbeitet
Ich bit mit dem …
  gefahren
Der Tag hat um … Uhr
  begonnen
Der Tag war um … Uhr
  zu Ende
Ich habe die Arbeit …
  langweilig/interessant/
  schwer/leicht
  gefunden

Grammar points
- revision of perfect tense (*haben* and *sein*)
- *war* and *hatte*

Language skills
- advice about talking/writing about work experience

Resources
- Cassette C, Side B
- Workbook p. 67
- Sprechen p. 150, Gespräch 1
- Lesen/Schreiben B p. 179
- Kursarbeit pp. 160–161

Introduce the spread by pointing out that work experience is a topic which they might well need in Speaking or Writing Tests, particularly also Coursework or as a presentation in the Speaking Test.

1 Lies das Interview und wähle die richtige Antwort. (Reading)
Students read this magazine interview (not on tape) and choose from multiple-choice answers. More able students should write full sentence answers.

Answers
1 Gottlieb, 2 in einer Fabrik, 3 mit dem Bus, 4 20 Minuten, 5 8 Uhr, 6 5 Uhr

2 Hör zu. Welche Wörter fehlen? Schreib Martinas Text ab und trag die Wörter ein. (Listening, Writing)
Students first copy out Martina's report, leaving gaps to be filled in. Then they listen to the interview as many times as necessary in order to copy the words into the correct gaps. This is a pure listening exercise.

Answers
Mein Betriebspraktikum war in einer **Schule**. Das war ein **Gymnasium**. Ich bin mit dem **Rad** gefahren. Die Fahrt hat **fünfzehn** Minuten gedauert. Der Arbeitstag hat um **Viertel vor acht** begonnen und war um **ein** Uhr zu Ende. Ich habe die Arbeit **ziemlich schwer** gefunden.

– Wo hast du dein Betriebspraktikum gemacht, Martina?
– Ich habe in einer Schule gearbeitet.
– Was für eine Schule war das?
– Das war ein Gymnasium.
– So? Und wie bist du hingefahren?
– Mit dem Rad.
– Wie lange hat die Fahrt gedauert?
– Fünfzehn Minuten.
– Wann hat der Arbeitstag begonnen?
– Um Viertel vor acht.
– Und wann war der Tag zu Ende?
– Um 1 Uhr.
– Wie hast du die Arbeit gefunden?
– Ziemlich schwer!

Wiederholung: The perfect tense
A reminder of the perfect tense (with *haben* und *sein*) as well as *war* and *hatte*. It won't hurt to repeat yet again how vital it is for students to include a few past tense items if they wish to achieve a good grade.

3 Partnerarbeit. Mach mit deinem Partner / deiner Partnerin Interviews. (Speaking)
A detailed pair work activity about work experience. Students use the information provided to construct two further interviews as well as the one provided.

4a Schreib die Antworten aus Übung 3 in ganzen Sätzen auf. (Writing)
Now they write out all the information from Exercise 3. This is a challenging task requiring full sentences. It can be done as homework, or classwork with the teacher providing guidance.

Answers
1 Ich war bei der Firma Krüger. Ich habe in einem Geschäft gearbeitet. Ich bin mit dem Auto gefahren. Der Arbeitstag hat um 7.30 Uhr begonnen. Der Tag war um 4.30 Uhr zu Ende. Ich habe die Arbeit ziemlich interessant gefunden.
2 Ich war bei der Firma Grimm. Ich habe in einem Supermarkt gearbeitet. Ich bin mit dem Rad gefahren. Der Arbeitstag hat um 7.00 begonnen. Der Tag war um 4.00 Uhr zu Ende. Ich habe die Arbeit gut/leicht/interessant gefunden.
3 Ich war bei der Firma Hasemann. Ich habe in einem Büro gearbeitet. Ich bin mit dem Zug gefahren. Der Arbeitstag hat um 8.30 Uhr begonnen. Der Tag war um 6.00 Uhr zu Ende. Ich habe die Arbeit schwer/langweilig gefunden.

4b Jetzt du. Wie war dein Betriebspraktikum? Schreib sechs Sätze über dein Betriebspraktikum. (Writing)
Students use the sentences practised in Exercise 4a to write detailed information about their own work experience. This must be marked, kept and learnt.

Further practice of the language and vocabulary of this unit is given on the following pages:
Sprechen: p. 150
Lesen/Schreiben B: p. 179
Workbook: p. 67

The activities of this unit form an ideal introduction to coursework preparation. For further information and guidelines about the preparation of coursework, please refer to the **Coursework** spread pp. 160–161.

5 Pläne für die Zukunft
(pp. 132–133)

Students will learn how to:
- talk about career plans

> **Key language**
> Ich will (Arzt) werden
> Ich will ...
>   auf die Uni(versität) gehen
>   zur Hochschule gehen
>   studieren
>   eine Lehre machen
>   in ... arbeiten
>   reisen/heiraten/ Kinder haben
> Ich möchte ...
>   in einem Büro/in einer Schule arbeiten
>
> **Grammar points**
> - three ways to express future plans (*ich will, ich möchte, ich werde*)
>
> **Language skills**
> - Giving more detailed answers
>
> **Resources**
> - Cassette C Side B
> - Workbook p. 68
> - Sprechen p. 150, Gespräch 2

Start this spread by asking students, in English, about their plans for what to do after leaving school. Also remind them about the marks to be gained by talking about the future in their exam, and that the Present tense is usually enough.

1 Hör zu und lies die Gespräche. Beantworte die Fragen mit *ja* oder *nein*. (Listening, Reading)
This can be tackled either as a pure listening activity with students just listening to the tape, or they can read the dialogues at the same time. They simply answer *ja* or *nein* to the questions.

Answers
1 a ja, b nein, 2 a nein, b nein, 3 a ja, b nein

1 – Was willst du machen, wenn du 18 bist, Margret?
  – Ich will auf die Uni gehen.
  – Was willst du studieren?
  – Medizin.
  – Was für einen Beruf willst du haben?
  – Ich will Ärztin werden.
2 – Und du, Jana? Willst du studieren?
  – Nein, ich will mir eine Stelle suchen.
  – Was für einen Beruf willst du denn haben?
  – Ich will Programmiererin werden.
3 – Was willst du denn machen, Adrian?
  – Ich will eine Lehre machen.
  – Was für eine Lehre?
  – Eine Lehre als Mechaniker.

2 Hör zu. Wer will was werden? Wähle das richtige Bild. (1–8) (Listening)
Students listen to the tape and identify the jobs mentioned. They write down the letters which relate to the pictures.

Answers
1 f, 2 h, 3 g, 4 a, 5 e, 6 b, 7 c, 8 d

1 Ich will Polizistin werden.
2 Ich will Zahnärztin werden.
3 Ich will Sekretärin werden.
4 Ich will Programmierer werden.
5 Ich will Krankenschwester werden.
6 Ich will Verkäufer werden.
7 Ich will Mechaniker werden.
8 Ich will Lehrerin werden.

Grammatik: The future tense
Three ways of expressing future plans: using *Ich will ...*, *Ich möchte ...* and *Ich werde*.
Teachers can decide whether to omit this explanation. At least make sure that students realise that they can say *Ich will ...* but only meaning 'I want to ...' and not 'I will ...'.

3 Partnerarbeit. (Speaking)
Students conduct short dialogues with an information gap element.

4 Wer will was machen? Schreib *Dieter*, *Anja* oder *Birte*. (Reading)
Students read the speech bubbles and answer the questions by writing down names. More able students can write full sentence answers.

Answers
1 Birte, 2 Birte, 3 Anja, 4 Dieter, 5 Dieter, 6 Anja

Tip box
Remind students that they should always add in extra details if they can. Look at and point out the differences in the three answers given.

5 Was willst du werden? (Writing)
Students first write down sentences based on the information in the speech bubbles, then, with the help of the adjacent tip box, their own plans.

Answers
1 Ich will an der Technischen Hochschule Informatik studieren. Dann möchte ich als Programmierer arbeiten.
2 Ich will an der Universität Medizin studieren. Dann möchte ich als Ärztin arbeiten.

> Further practice of the language and vocabulary of this unit is given on the following pages:
> Sprechen: p. 150
> Workbook: p. 68

Logo! 4 9 Die Arbeit

All the vocabulary and structures from this chapter are listed on the **Wörter** pages 134–135. These can be used for revision by covering up either the English or the German. Students can check here to see how much they remember from the chapter.

Assessment materials for Chapters 9 and 10 are available after Chapter 10.

Further speaking and grammar practice on the whole chapter is provided on pp. 69–70 of the **Workbook**.

Kursarbeit

9 Betriebspraktikum

(pp. 160–161)

The coursework section in *Logo! 4 Grün* gives regular, guided practice in preparing for the coursework element of the GCSE examination. It is cross-referenced to relevant sections in the core units. Each double-page spread is linked to a GCSE theme, and always starts with a model text on that theme (at a higher level than that expected by the student). This text acts as a stimulus to give students ideas about what they might include in their own piece of work. Students are encouraged to look at the detail of the text through the structured reading activities. They are gradually guided to produce good German sentences in the various activities, through to the final task in which they are asked to produce an extended piece of writing.

The *Hilfe* column is a feature on all the spreads. It shows students language they might include and particular structures that will raise the level of their writing. It is important to remind students who are capable of achieving a grade at the upper end of the Foundation level that they should always include examples of two or three tenses in their writing.

This spread guides students to produce an extended piece of writing on the topic of work experience.

1 Du bist Nils. Welches Bild passt zu welchem Tag?

Students look at the pictures and note the correct day for each one.

Answers

1 Dienstag, 2 Freitag, 3 Mittwoch, 4 Montag, 5 Donnerstag, 6 Freitag

2 Du bist Nils. Beantworte die Fragen.

Students answer the questions as if they were Nils. Parts of the answers are given for students to complete.

Answers

1 Mein Wecker **hat** um **halb** sieben **geklingelt**. 2 Ich bin um **halb sieben** aufgestanden. 3 Ich bin **mit dem** Bus zum **Sportgeschäft** gekommen. 4 Das Sportgeschäft **liegt** in der Nähe vom **Rathaus** in der **Fußgängerzone**. 5 Die Arbeit **hat** um **8** Uhr begonnen. 6 Mein erster Tag war **sehr gut**. 7 Am Mittwoch Nachmittag **habe** ich mit dem **Computer** gearbeitet. 8 Es **hat** geregnet.

3 Schreib ein Tagebuch über dein Betriebspraktikum. Diese Fragen helfen dir.

Students should now be ready to write about their own work experience, using the questions and prompts below and the support in the *Hilfe* column.

Hilfe

Tips for students when writing about their work experience:
- adapt the expressions underlined in blue
- include a form with details of your work experience
- include some opinions

Workbook

p. 64

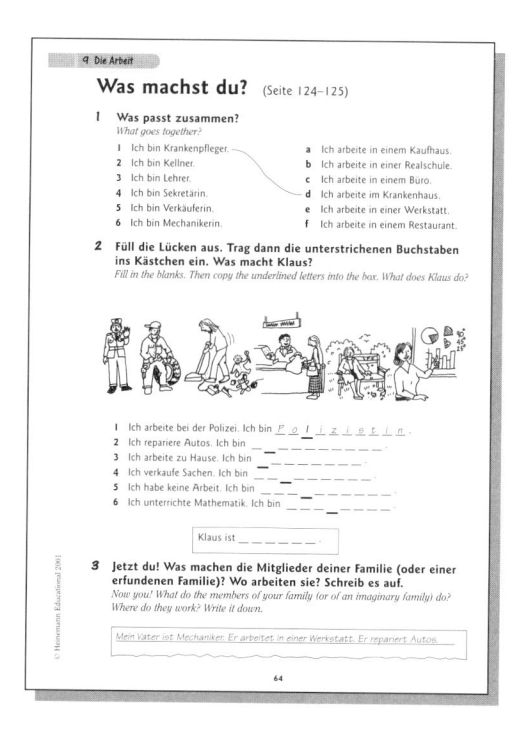

1 1 d, 2 f, 3 b, 4 c, 5 a, 6 e
2 a Po**l**izistin, b M**e**chaniker, c **H**ausfrau, d Ve**r**käufer, e a**r**beitslos, f Leh**r**erin.
Klaus ist Lehrer.
3 Open-ended. Overlook minor errors.

p. 65

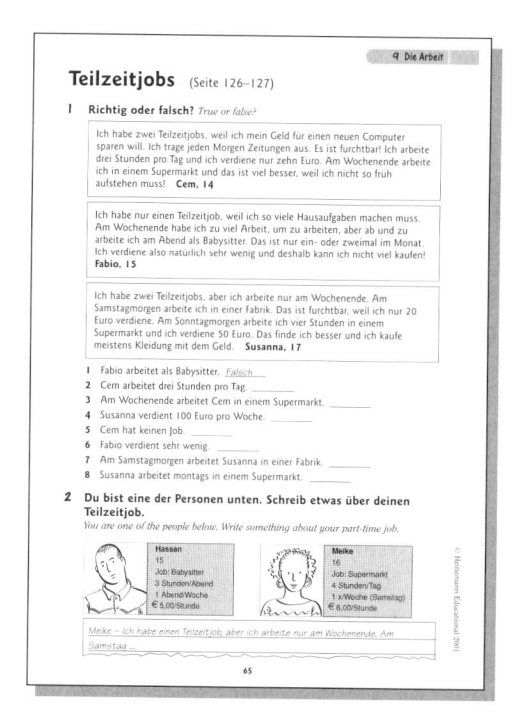

1 1 Daniel, 2 Anna, 3 Hugo, 4 Olli, 5 Fahim, 6 Meike
2 1 Richtig, 2 Richtig, 3 Richtig, 4 Falsch, 5 Falsch, 6 Richtig, 7 Richtig, 8 Falsch
3 Open-ended. Overlook minor errors.

p. 66

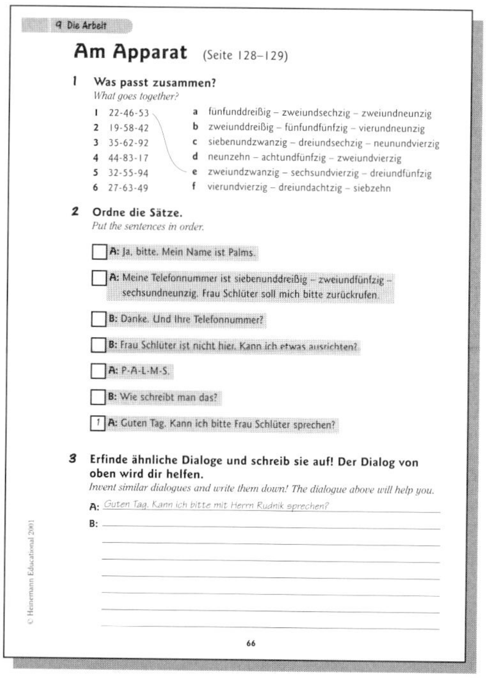

1 1 e, 2 d, 3 a, 4 f, 5 b, 6 c
2 A: Guten Tag. Kann ich bitte Frau Schlüter sprechen?
B: Frau Schlüter ist nicht hier. Kann ich etwas ausrichten?
A: Ja, bitte. Mein Name ist Palms.
B: Wie schreibt man das?
A: P-A-L-M-S.
B: Danke. Und Ihre Telefonnummer?
A: Meine Telefonnummer ist siebenunddreißig – zweiundfünfzig – sechsundneunzig. Frau Schlüter soll mich bitte zurückrufen.
3 Open-ended. Overlook minor errors.

p. 67

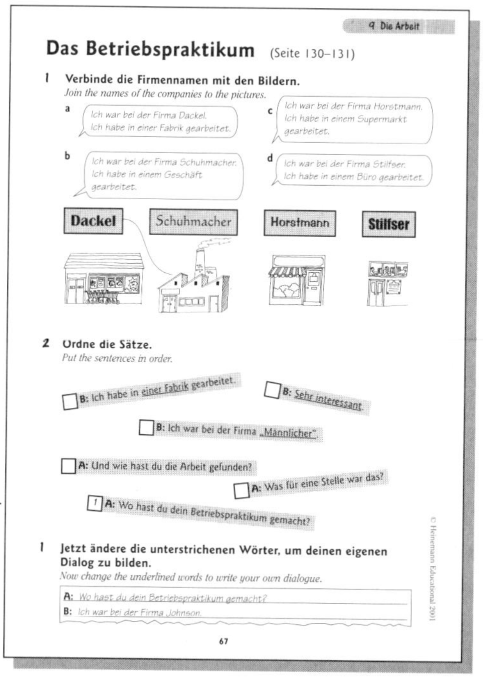

1 Dackel –
Schuhmacher –
Horstmann –
Stilfser
2 A: Wo hast du dein Betriebspraktikum gemacht?
B: Ich war bei der Firma Männlicher.
A: Was für eine Stelle war das?
B: Ich habe in einer Fabrik gearbeitet.
A: Und wie hast du die Arbeit gefunden?
B: Sehr interessant.
3 Open-ended. Overlook minor errors.

p. 68

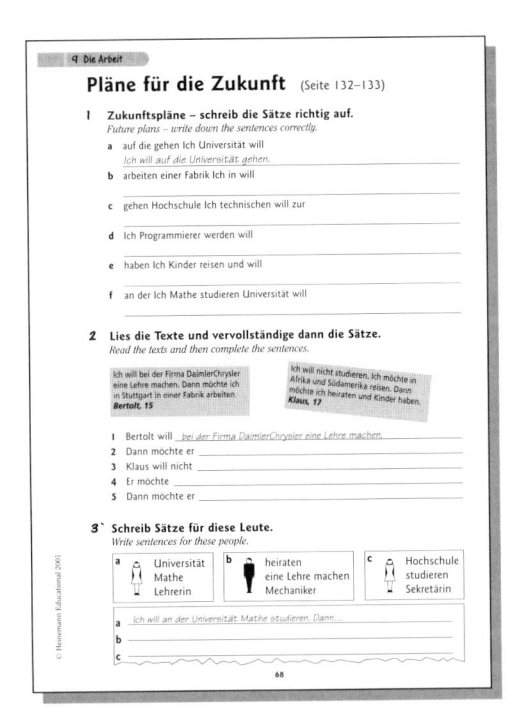

p. 69

1 a Ich will auf die Universität gehen. b Ich will in einer Fabrik arbeiten. c Ich will zur technischen Hochschule gehen. d Ich will Programmierer werden. e Ich will reisen und Kinder haben. f Ich will an der Universität Mathe studieren.

2 1 Bertolt will bei der Firma DaimlerChrysler eine Lehre machen. 2 Dann möchte er in Stuttgart in einer Fabrik arbeiten. 3 Klaus will nicht studieren. 4 Er möchte in Afrika und Südamerika reisen. 5 Dann möchte er heiraten und Kinder haben.

3 Open-ended. As long the essential information is given in correct German, any variations are possible.

p. 70

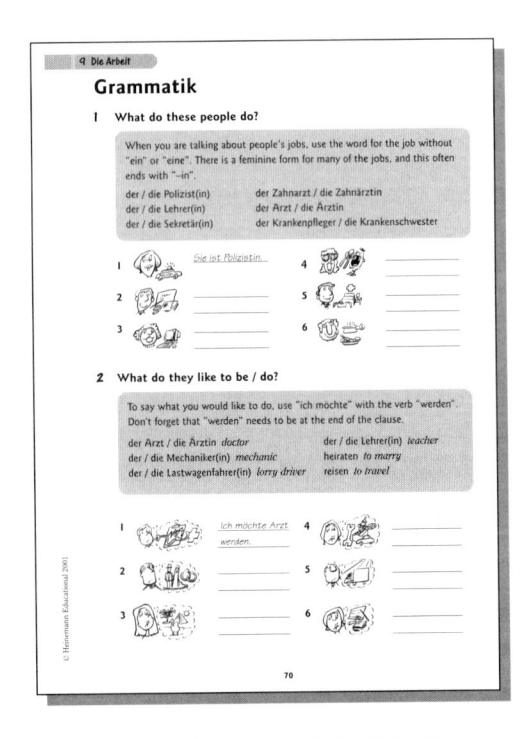

1 1 Sie ist Polizistin. 2 Er ist Lehrer. 3 Sie ist Sekretärin. 4 Sie ist Zahnärztin. 5 Er ist Krankenpfleger. 6 Er ist Hausmann.

2 1 Ich möchte Arzt werden. 2 Ich möchte heiraten. 3 Ich möchte reisen. 4 Ich möchte Mechanikerin werden. 5 Ich möchte Lastwagenfahrer werden. 6 Ich möchte Lehrerin werden.

10 Teenies! (pp. 136–147)

Topic area	Key language	Grammar	Language skills
10.1 Bist du doof? (pp. 136–137) Describe people and pets	Ich bin / Er/Sie ist oft/manchmal/sehr/ziemlich faul/doof/freundlich/streng/nett/la unisch/lustig/fleißig/intelligent/laut/ruhig. Er/Sie ist größer/kleiner/jünger (usw.) als ich. Ich habe eine Katze / einen Hund / ein Kaninchen usw. Er/Sie ist süß/niedlich/unartig/nübsch.	Making comparisons	Feminine forms of *Hund* and *Katze*
10.2 Was für ein Haus hast du? (pp. 138–139) Talk about where you live	Ich wohne in einem Reihenhaus/Wohnblock/Bungalow/Doppelhaus/ in einer Wohnung / auf einem Bauernhof. Ich wohne in der Stadtmitte / in einem Dorf / am Stadtrand / auf dem Land / in der Nähe von …	in einem / in einer / in der / am, etc.	
10.3 Das ist ungesund! (pp 140–141) Talk about healthy and unhealthy lifestyles	Ich trinke Bier/Wein/Alkohol. Ich rauche (nicht). Ich nehme keine Drogen. Man sollte Sport treiben / gesund essen / zu Fuß gehen. Man sollte nicht rauchen / viel Auto fahren / viele Hamburger essen.	Man sollte … with infinitive at the end of sentence	Adjectives and their opposites Adapting text in the Writing Test
10.4 Rettet die Umwelt! (pp. 142–143) Talk about the environment	der Abfall/Lärm/Verkehr; die Abgase/Luft/Umwelt/Fußgängerzone/Verkehrsmittel, atmen, obdachlos; gut/schlecht für die Umwelt	Wir müssen … and Wir können … with the infinitive at the end of the sentence	Advice to guess hard words by looking at illustrations and the context
10.5 Problemseite (pp. 144–145) Talk about teenage problems	Ich war betrunken. Ich möchte lieber nach … fahren. Was kann ich tun? Hilf mir bitte! Meine Kleidung ist nicht modern und modisch. Ich kann nicht gut verstehen. Meine Noten sind nicht sehr gut.		More extended reading
Lesen/Schreiben (pp. 180–181)			Reading and Writing skills

- The vocabulary and structures taught in Chapter 10 are summarised on the **Wörter** page of the Student's Book, 146.
- Further Speaking practice on the language of the chapter is provided on **Sprechen** pp. 150–151.
- For a selection of assessment tasks for Chapters 9 and 10, please refer to the separate Assessment Pack for your chosen examination board: AQA, OCR or Edexcel

1 Bist du doof? (pp. 136–137)

Students will learn how to:
- talk about personalities and pets

Key language
Ich bin …
Er/Sie ist …
 oft/manchmal/sehr/
 ziemlich faul/doof/
 freundlich/ruhig/
 intelligent/launisch/
 lustig/laut/fleißig/
 streng/nett
Er/Sie ist …
 größer/kleiner/dicker/
 jünger/älter/schlanker/
 intelligenter als ich
Ich habe …
 eine Katze/einen
 Hund/einen
 Wellensittich/ein
 Kaninchen/ ein
 Meerschweinchen

Er/Sie ist …
 süß/niedlich/unartig/
 hübsch

Grammar points
- making comparisons

Language skills
- feminine of *Hund* and *Katze*

Resources
- Cassette C Side B
- Workbook pp. 71–72
- Sprechen p. 151, Rollenspiel 3a + 3b

Start the spread by asking students to suggest, in English, personality traits which members of their family might have and how many of the expressions they know in German. Also revise the German names for pets.

1a Was passt zusammen? (Reading)
Students match words describing personality to the correct pictures.

Answers
1 d, 2 e, 3 h, 4 i, 5 b, 6 j, 7 g, 8 c, 9 a, 10 f

1b Hör zu und schreib a, b, c, usw. (1–10) (Listening)
This is a pure listening activity and many of the words may be unfamiliar. First ask students to use the glossary or dictionaries to find out the meanings. They then listen to the tape and match the statements to the pictures by writing down letters.

Answers
1 i, 2 e, 3 d, 4 f, 5 g, 6 c, 7 h, 8 j, 9 b, 10 a

 1 Mein Vater ist sehr intelligent.
 2 Mein Bruder nervt mich. Er ist so laut!
 3 Ich mag meinen Onkel. Er ist lustig.
 4 Meine Oma ist schön ruhig.
 5 Meine Schwester ist unheimlich faul.
 6 Ich mag meine Freundin, aber manchmal ist sie launisch.
 7 Julia ist sooo fleißig!
 8 Herr Müller ist sehr streng.
 9 Meine Katze ist freundlich.
 10 Du bist doof!

2 Partnerarbeit. (Speaking)
A simple pair work activity in which students ask and answer questions based on picture prompts. Make sure it is done both ways round.

Grammatik: Comparisons
Using the comparative to compare people. Point out the added umlaut where appropriate and practise on people and things in the classroom.

3 Was sagen diese Personen? Schreib es auf. (Writing)
Students write down comparative descriptions based on pictures and the information in the Grammar Box. Make sure they say …*er als ich*, not *als mich*.

Answers
1 Er ist größer als ich. 2 Sie ist kleiner als ich. 3 Er ist älter als ich. 4 Er/Sie ist jünger als ich. 5 Er ist doofer als ich. 6 Sie ist schlimmer als ich.

Tip box: *Hündin* and *Kater*
A seemingly insignificant matter, this can get many a Speaking Test off to an inauspicious start because it sounds so peculiar if students get it wrong.

4 Hör zu. Wer hat welches Tier? (1–7) (Listening)
A straightforward listening activity in which students write down letters to show they have understood which animal picture is being talked about.

Answers
1 c, 2 e, 3 d, 4 f, 5 g, 6 b, 7 a

 1 Ich habe eine Katze. Sie ist niedlich.
 2 Mein Kaninchen ist freundlich.
 3 Ich habe einen Wellensittich.
 4 Ich habe eine Hündin. Sie ist unartig.
 5 Mein Kater ist süß.
 6 Ich habe ein Meerschweinchen. Es ist braun.
 7 Mein Hund ist doof.

5 Lies Jessicas Homepage und dann mach eine Homepage für dich. (Writing)
Based on the home page provided, students write down their own details, including information about pets, character and comparisons. This paragraph must be marked, kept and learnt.

Further practice of the language and vocabulary of this unit is given on the following pages:
Sprechen: p. 151
Workbook: pp. 71–72

Logo! 4 10 Teenies!

2 Was für ein Haus hast du?
(pp. 138–139)

Students will learn how to:
- talk about where they live

Key language	Grammar points
Ich wohne …	*in einem / in einer / in der / am*, etc.
in einem Einfamilien-/ Doppel-/Reihenhaus/ Bungalow/Wohnblock	
in einer Wohnung	**Resources**
auf einem Bauernhof	• Cassette C Side B
Ich wohne …	• Workbook p. 73
in der Stadtmitte	• Sprechen p. 151, Gespräch 2
in einem Dorf	
am Stadtrand	
auf dem Land	
in der Nähe von	

Start the spread by seeing how much vocabulary about different types of housing students can remember from earlier in the course.

1 Hör zu. Wer wohnt wo? Schreib zwei Buchstaben für jede Person. (1–6) (Listening)
After studying the photos and the words, students listen to the tape and note down letters to show they have understood who lives where. Make sure they realise they have to write down two letters for each dialogue.

Answers
1 b h, 2 g a, 3 e i, 4 c j, 5 h d, 6 f h

1 – Wo wohnst du, Peter?
  – Ich wohne in einer Wohnung.
  – In der Stadtmitte?
  – Nein, am Stadtrand.
2 – Und du, Sylvia?
  – Ich wohne auf dem Land.
  – Wo denn?
  – Auf einem Bauernhof.
3 – Hallo, Ayse, wo wohnst du?
  – Ich? Ich wohne in einem Bungalow.
  – Wo denn?
  – In einem Dorf.
4 – Wie ist es mit dir, Jürgen?
  – Ich wohne in einem Reihenhaus.
  – Am Stadtrand?
  – Nein, in der Stadtmitte.
5 – Und Vanessa, wo wohnst du denn?
  – Ich wohne am Stadtrand.
  – In einem Bungalow?
  – Nein, in einem Wohnblock.
6 – Wo wohnst du, Rüdiger?
  – In einem Doppelhaus.
  – In Hamburg?
  – Ja, am Stadtrand.

2 Partnerarbeit. (Speaking)
Students work in pairs with questions and answers based on picture prompts. The exercise must be done both ways round.

3 Lies die Briefe und beantworte die Fragen. (Reading)
Students read the two letters and answer the questions with a name.

Answers
1 Manja, 2 Dennis, 3 Dennis, 4 Manja, 5 Dennis, 6 Manja, 7 Dennis, 8 Manja

4 Schreib eine Antwort auf Manjas E-Mail. (Writing)
Students reply briefly to the printed e-mail. More able students should be encouraged to add in as much extra information as they can.

Further practice of the language and vocabulary of this unit is given on the following pages:
Sprechen: p. 151
Workbook: p. 73

3 Das ist ungesund (pp. 140–141)

Students will learn how to:
- talk about health matters

Key language
Ich trinke
Bier/Wein/Alkohol
Ich rauche (nicht)
Ich nehme keine Drogen
Man sollte ...
   Sport treiben
   gesund essen
   zu Fuß gehen
Man sollte nicht ...
   rauchen
   viel Auto fahren
   viele Hamburger essen

Grammar points
- *man sollte* + infinitive

Language skills
- adjectives and their opposites
- adapting text in the writing exam

Resources
- Cassette C Side B
- Workbook p. 74
- Sprechen p. 150, Gespräch 1
- Lesen/Schreiben A p. 180

If you dare, start the spread by introducing some of the key language and asking students to confess whether they drink or smoke.

1 Was passt zusammen? (Reading)
Students match sentences to pictures by writing down letters.

Answers
1 f, 2 a, 3 b, 4 d, 5 e, 6 c

2 Hör zu und beantworte die Fragen mit *ja* oder *nein*. (Listening)
Students listen to three interviews with young German speakers with differing health habits. The questions are to be answered with *ja* or *nein*.

Answers
1 ja, 2 ja, 3 nein, 4 nein, 5 ja, 6 nein, 7 nein, 8 nein, 9 nein

- Heute haben wir ein kompliziertes Thema: Drogen, Alkohol und Tabak. Wer raucht? Wer trinkt? Und wer nimmt Drogen? Hallo, wie heißt du?
- Ich heiße Werner.
- Rauchst du, Werner?
- Ich rauche 20 Zigaretten pro Tag. Leider!
- Hmm. Und trinkst du Alkohol?
- Ja, aber nur Bier.
- Und nimmst du Drogen, Werner?
- Nein, natürlich nicht.
- Danke.
- Und du, wie heißt du?
- Hallo, ich bin die Sonja.
- Und wie ist es mit dir?
- Also, ich rauche keinen Tabak, aber ich trinke manchmal ein Glas Wein.
- Nimmst du auch Drogen?
- Nein, gar nicht.
- Und du, wie heißt du?
- Mein Name ist Udo.
- Na, Udo? Nimmst du Drogen?
- Nein, nie. Mein Bruder hat Heroin genommen. Er war sehr krank, das war furchtbar.
- Trinkst du Alkohol?
- Nein. Ich trinke nicht, ich rauche nicht und ich nehme keine Drogen. Ich bin Sportler.

Tip box: Adjectives and their opposites
Allow students to study them for a moment, then make controversial statements and ask them to contradict them:
Teacher: Ein Jaguar ist billig!
       Rauchen ist gesund!
       EastEnders ist schlecht! usw.

3a Lies die Zigarettenwerbung. Das stimmt alles nicht! Schreib die Wahrheit. (Writing)
Students should write out a full list of truthful sentences to contradict the mis-information in this spoof cigarette advert.

Answers
1 Rauchen ist **schlecht** für die Gesundheit! 2 Tabak ist **schrecklich** für Sportler! 3 Zigaretten sind **schlecht** für die Umwelt! 4 Mädchen finden Rauchen **furchtbar**! 5 Tabak ist **schlecht** für die Lungen! 6 Zigaretten riechen **schlecht**! 7 Rauchen ist **teuer**! 8 Rauchen ist **schlechter** als essen!

Tip box: Adapting texts in the Writing Test
Emphasise that writing tasks are often not as daunting as they seem because the printed prompt can help a lot with constructing an answer.

3b Jetzt mach ein Poster gegen Zigaretten, Alkohol oder Drogen. (Writing)
Students design a poster against smoking, drinking or drugs. This activity has potential as an ICT task.

Grammatik: *Man sollte*
The infinitive goes to the end of the sentence after this phrase.

4a Ein gesundes Leben. Was sollte man machen? Was sollte man <u>nicht</u> machen? (Writing)
A simple writing exercise in which students complete sentences beginning *Man sollte* ... .

Answers
1 Man sollte viel Sport treiben. **2** Man sollte nicht rauchen. **3** Man sollte gesund essen. **4** Mann sollte nicht viel Auto fahren. **5** Man sollte oft zu Fuß gehen. **6** Man sollte nicht viele Hamburger essen.

4b Partnerarbeit. (Speaking)
The questions from Exercise 4a are re-used as the basis for a speaking task in which students construct short dialogues in pairs.

Further practice of the language and vocabulary of this unit is given on the following pages:
Sprechen: p. 150
Lesen/Schreiben A: p. 180
Workbook: p. 74

4 Rettet die Umwelt!
(pp. 142–143)

Students will learn how to:
- talk about the environment

Key language	Grammar points
der Abfall	• *wir müssen..., wir können* + infinitive
der Lärm	
der Verkehr	
die Luft	**Language skills**
die Umwelt	• guessing words from context and illustrations
die Fußgängerzone	
die Abgase	
das Verkehrsmittel	**Resources**
atmen	• Cassette C Side B
obdachlos	• Workbook p. 75
gut/schlecht für die Umwelt	• Lesen/Schreiben B p. 181

Start the spread by warning students that it contains much new exam-specific vocabulary. Ask them in English what kinds of words would be useful when talking about the environment.

1 Hör zu und lies den Text. Finde diese Ausdrücke im Text. Wie heißen sie auf Englisch? (Listening, Reading)

This is a hard and dense text but it is helped by being both on tape and on the page. First ask students to look up any unknown words in the glossary or a dictionary. They then read and listen to the news item and write down the English equivalents for the German words.

Answers

1 traffic, 2 environment, 3 litter, 4 pedestrian precinct, 5 exhaust fumes, 6 noise, 7 homeless, 8 air, 9 breathe, 10 transport

– Guten Tag, meine Damen und Herren. Hier spricht Jürgen Schiller aus Wurmhausen. Hier ist es sehr laut! Es gibt sehr viel Verkehr. Autos, Motorräder und Busse fahren durch die Stadt. Es ist furchtbar, es gibt viel zu viel Lärm. Das ist ein großes Problem.
Hier gibt es auch sehr viel Abfall. Die jungen Leute essen im Hamburger-Restaurant und werfen das Papier einfach auf die Straße. Hier auf der Straße liegt auch ein junger Mann. Er ist obdachlos. Und die Luft ist sehr schlecht. Hier kann man nicht gut atmen. Die Autos produzieren viele Abgase. Das ist alles schlecht für die Umwelt.
Was können wir tun? Wir müssen
– eine Fußgängerzone bauen.
– öffentliche Verkehrsmittel einführen.
– Abfall mit nach Hause nehmen.

Tip box
Advice to students to guess the meaning of words by using illustrations and the context. This advice can be used to help with Exercises 1 and 2.

2 Welcher Satz passt zu welchem Bild? (Reading)

Students match pictures to sentences by writing down letters. More able students should write out the sentences.

Answers

1 d, 2 f, 3 b, 4 a, 5 e, 6 c

Grammatik: *Wir müssen* ... and *Wir können* ... + infinitive at the end of the sentence

Inform students that the only exception to this is when a small child says *Ich muss!* (meaning 'I need to go to the toilet.').

3a Lies den Text in Übung 1 nochmal. Wähle die richtige Antwort. (Reading)

Students re-read the text in Exercise 1 and choose from multi-choice answers.

Answers

1 a, 2 b, 3 c, 4 b

3b Schreib die Sätze in 3a auf. (Writing)

Now students write out the answers to Exercise 3a in full sentences.

Answers

1 Die Autos sind laut. 2 Der Abfall auf der Straße kommt vom Hamburger-Restaurant. 3 Der junge Mann ist obdachlos. 4 Die Abgase kommen von den Autos.

4 Schau die Bilder an and schreib entweder *Gut für die Umwelt* oder *Schlecht für die Umwelt*. (Writing)

Students write down in German whether the illustrated activities are good or bad for the environment.

Answers

1 Gut für die Umwelt. 2 Schlecht für die Umwelt. 3 Schlecht für die Umwelt. 4 Schlecht für die Umwelt. 5 Gut für die Umwelt.

Further practice of the language and vocabulary of this unit is given on the following pages:
Lesen/Schreiben B: p. 181
Workbook: p. 75

Logo! 4 10 Teenies!

5 Problemseite (pp. 144–145)

Students will learn how to:
- deal with teenage problems

Key language
Ich habe zu viel getrunken
Ich möchte lieber nach ... fahren
Was kann ich tun?
Was soll ich tun?
Hilf mir bitte!
Meine Klamotten sind nicht modern und modisch
Meine Kleidung ist billig
Ich kann nicht gut verstehen
Meine Noten sind nicht sehr gut

Language skills
- coping with more extended reading

Resources
- Cassette C Side B
- Sprechen p. 151

Further practice of the language and vocabulary of this unit is given on the following pages:
Speaking: p. 151

All the vocabulary and structures from this chapter are listed on the **Wörter** page 146. These can be used for revision by covering up either the English or the German. Students can check here to see how much they remember from the chapter.

Assessment materials for Chapters 9 and 10 are available after Chapter 10.

Further speaking and grammar practice on the whole chapter is provided on pp. 76–77 of the **Workbook**.

Everyone likes a problem page, so this spread is intended as a fairly light ending to the book, with plenty of reading practice.

1 Lies die Briefe und die Antworten. Welcher Brief passt zu welcher Antwort? (Reading)
Students read the letters and the answers and decide which goes with which. They write down letters.

Answers
1 C, 2 D, 3 F, 4 A, 5 E, 6 B

2 Wer hat welches Problem? Schreib *Joschke, Stefanie, Lydia, Ines, Björn* oder *Samira*. (Reading)
Students read sentences and match them to the letters by writing down names of the correspondents.

Answers
1 Björn, 2 Samira, 3 Stefanie, 4 Ines, 5 Stefanie, 6 Lydia, 7 Joschke, 8 Samira, 9 Joschke, 10 Lydia

3 Schreib den Brief ab und füll die Lücken aus. (Writing)
Students copy the letter and fill in the gaps with the words provided. More able students can then be asked to invent and write a problem letter of their own.

Answers
Liebe Karin, ich habe ein **Problem**. Mein **Deutschbuch** heißt **LOGO**. Es ist zu **schwer**. Ich habe keine Lust, meine **Hausaufgaben** zu machen. Aber meine **Deutschlehrerin** sagt, ich muss sie machen. Was soll ich **tun**? Elton (15)

Prüfungstipps (pp. 148–149)

The spread on pages 148–149 contains a selection of tips to help students to get a high mark in their exam. These tips home in on the typical errors they are likely to make and the kinds of trap that students sometimes fall into in exams. They need to be studied carefully, as they could make the difference between a good grade and a very good one.

Workbook

p. 71

1 1 d, 2 f, 3 e, 4 b, 5 a, 6 c
2 1 a, 2 b, 3 a, 4 b, 5 b

p. 72

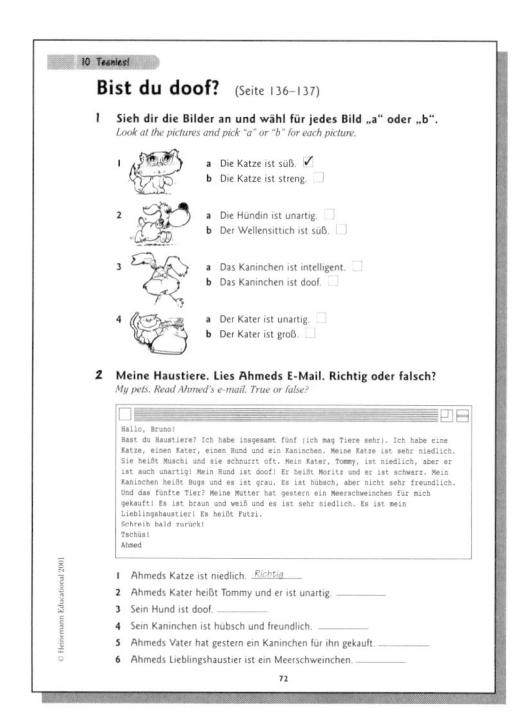

1 1 a, 2 a, 3 b, 4 a
2 1 Richtig, 2 Richtig, 3 Richtig, 4 Falsch, 5 Falsch, 6 Richtig

p. 73

1 1 d, g, 2 a, j, 3 b, i, 4 c, h, 5 e, f
2 Liebe(r) Brieffreund(in)
Hi! Ich heiße <u>München</u> und ich wohne auf einem <u>Fahrrad</u> in der Nähe von <u>Christina</u>. Ich habe viele Haustiere und ich wohne gern auf dem Land. Das ist <u>langweilig</u> und <u>nicht interessant</u>. Ich habe eine Katze, Mitzi, und sie ist sehr unartig. Ich habe auch drei <u>Fernseher</u> – Flopsy, Mopsy und Cottontail. Flopsy ist grau und niedlich, Mopsy ist braun und doof und Cottontail ist <u>grün</u> und süß. Ich möchte einen Hund haben, aber meine Mutter sagt <u>ja</u>. Das ist unfair!
Und du? Wo wohnst du? Hast du Haustiere?
Schreib mir bald! Christina
3 Open-ended – the errors can be changed in any way that makes sense.

p. 74

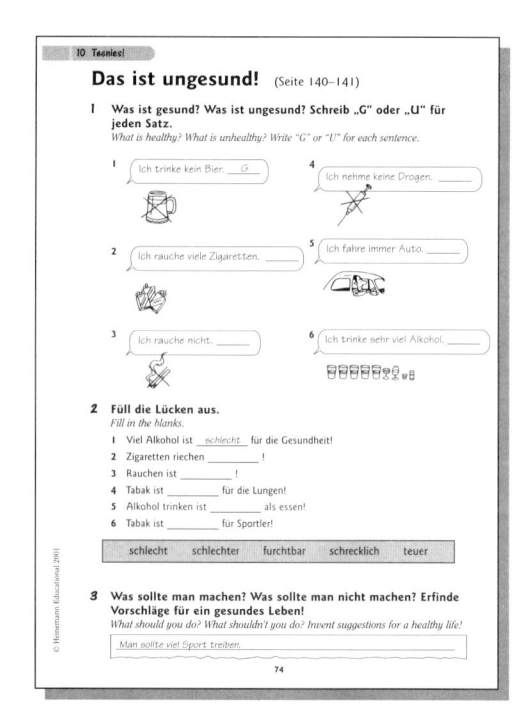

1 1 G, 2 U, 3 G, 4 G, 5 U, 6 U
2 1 schlecht, 2 schlecht/schrecklich/furchtbar, 3 teuer, 4 schlecht, 5 schlechter, 6 schrecklich
3 Open-ended

128

p. 75

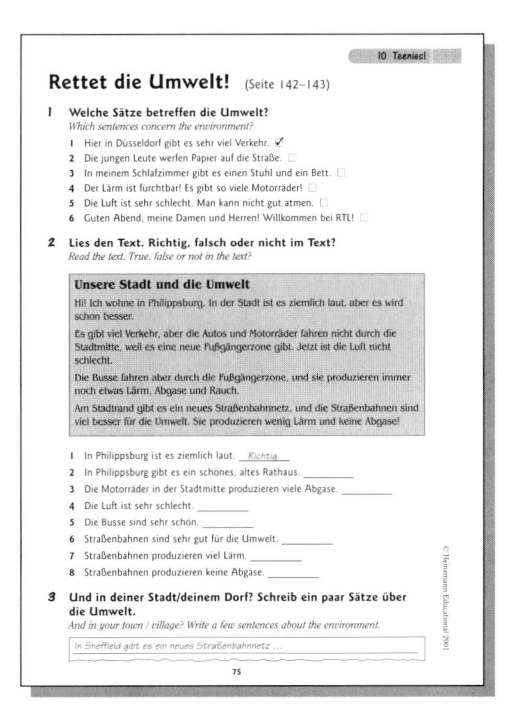

1 1, 2, 4, 5
2 **1** Richtig, **2** Nicht im Text, **3** Falsch, **4** Falsch, **5** Nicht im Text, **6** Richtig, **7** Falsch, **8** Richtig
3 Open-ended

p. 76

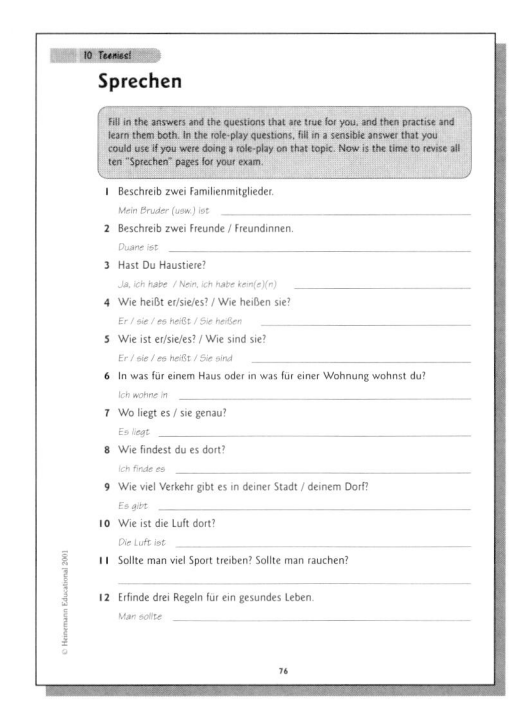

p. 77

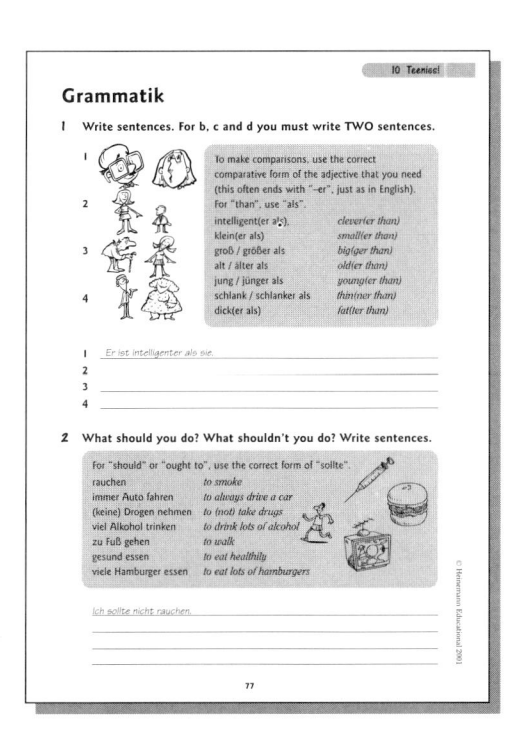

1 **1** Er ist intelligenter als sie. **2** Er ist kleiner als sie. Sie ist größer als er. **3** Er ist älter als sie. Sie ist jünger als er. **4** Er ist schlanker als sie. Sie ist dicker als er.
2 Ich sollte nicht rauchen. Ich sollte nicht immer Auto fahren. Ich sollte keine Drogen nehmen. Ich sollte nicht viel Alkohol trinken. Ich sollte oft zu Fuß gehen. Ich sollte gesund essen. Ich sollte nicht viele Hamburger essen.

Lesen/Schreiben

These pages are designed to give students extra practice in reading and structured writing. There are two pages relating to each chapter: A and B. The A page is at a slightly easier level than the B page for each chapter. You may wish students to work on the page more appropriate to their level or to work through both pages.

The intention is to give students a variety of types of authentic texts to work on. Sometimes they relate closely to the relevant chapter of the Student's Book, sometimes the link is more general. This is deliberate, to avoid the impression of all the language tasks being too tightly controlled and over-prescriptive. Teachers may feel it is useful to work with students on the exercises, but it should also be possible for most students to work independently on them. The most apppropriate time to use each page is indicated within the relevant teaching notes.

They are *not* designed as GCSE tests but rather as ways of developing the skills of reading and writing. With that in mind teachers *might* still allow some judicious use of dictionaries. The writing tasks are based on the language of the reading texts *and the reading tasks*. It is important that students understand this – once they have done all the reading tasks they should be able to re-use in the writing tasks much of the language they have encountered.

Chapter 1
A Ferienhaus in Österreich
(p. 162)

This page is best used after pp. 12–13 of the Student's Book.

1a Lies die Sätze. Richtig oder falsch? (Reading)
Students read the sentences and say whether they are true or false.

Answers
1 falsch, 2 richtig, 3 richtig, 4 falsch, 5 falsch

1b Geht das? ✔ Geht das nicht? ✗ (Reading)
Students read the sentences and put a tick or cross for each depending on whether the accommodation in the text above would suit them or not.

Answers
Die Familie Robinson – Das geht: 1, 5; Das geht nicht: 2, 3, 4 Anna und Steve – Das geht: 6, 7, 8, 9. Haus besser für Anna und Steve.

2 Kannst du die Wohnung für einen Artikel in einer Zeitschrift besser beschreiben? Schreib den Text ab und füll die Lücken aus. (Writing)
Students write out the text, completing the gaps with the words listed below.

Answers
Diese **Wohnung** liegt in einem schönen Ferienhaus. Es hat zwei **Zimmer** und ist ungefähr **dreißig** Quadratkilometer groß. Es gibt ein **Schlafzimmer** und ein **Wohnzimmer**. Man kann im Wohnzimmer **fernsehen** und **essen** (und auch **schlafen**). Die **Küche** ist ganz **klein** – es gibt nur einen 2-Platten-**Herd**. Im Badezimmer gibt es ein **WC** und eine **Dusche**. Es gibt eine schöne **Terrasse** aber keinen **Garten**.

B Familienbrief (p. 163)

This page is best used after pp. 10–11 of the Student's Book.

1a Sieh das Foto an. Wer ist das? (Reading)
Students look at the photo and say who each person is by reading the text.

Answers
1 Tante Christina, 2 Onkel Manfred, 3 Richard, 4 Vater, 5 Jürgen, 6 Mutter,

1b Wie heißen sie? (Reading)
Students read the sentences and say who each is describing.

Answers
1 Richard, 2 Claudias Onkel, 3 Claudias Vater, 4 Tante Christina, 5 Richard, 6 Jürgen, 7 Schwester Sandra, 8 Claudia

2a Beschreib eine Familie! Schreib den Text ab und füll die Lücken aus. (Writing)
Students write out the text completing the gaps with the words below.

Answers
Mutter, Brüder, Schwester, Mann, Vater/Onkel, Vater/Onkel

2b Finde ein Foto von einer Gruppe. Beschreib die Personen (das kann DEINE Familie sein). (Writing)
Students bring in a photo and describe the people using the text as a model.

Chapter 2
A Ein Zeugnis (p. 164)

This page is best used after pp. 20–21 of the Student's Book.

1a Lies Bettinas Zeugnis. Welche Noten hat Bettina? Füll die Lücken aus. (Reading)
Students read the texts and write out what grade (1–6) would be given for each subject from the report.

Logo! 4 Lesen/Schreiben

Answers
Deutsch: 2, Französisch: 2, Sport: 2, Geschichte: 2, Textilgestaltung: 3, Mathematik: 3, Kunst: 4, Erdkunde: 2, Politik: 2, Biologie: 3, Englisch: 1, Musik: 3, Physik: 5, Chemie: 3

1b Richtig oder falsch? (Reading)
Students read the sentences and say whether they are true or false.

Answers
1 falsch, 2 falsch, 3 richtig, 4 falsch, 5 richtig

2 Schreib ein Zeugnis für einen Freund oder eine Freundin. (Writing)
Students write their own report for one of their friends using the language on the page as support.

B Die Schule in Deutschland
(p. 165)

This page is best used after pp. 24–25 of the Student's Book.

1a Was passt zusammen? (Reading)
Students read the speech bubbles and then match the figures with the correct word.

Answers
1 d, 2 e, 3 f, 4 a, 5 b, 6 c

1b Wähle die richtige Antwort. (Reading)
Students choose the correct alternative from the multi-choice options.

Answers
1 kürzer, 2 am Samstag, 3 um 8.50, 4 Man darf, 5 nicht verboten, 6 im Februar und Juni

2 Schreib den Text ab und füll die Lücken aus. (Writing)
Students copy the text and complete the gaps.

Chapter 3
A Aktivitäten in Annweiler
(p. 166)

The two pages for Chapter 3 are best used after pages pp. 36–37 of the Student's Book.

1a Was kann man in Annweiler machen? Schreib *Ja* oder *Nein*. (Reading)
Students write *ja* or *nein* depending on whether the activities listed are available in Annweiler.

Answers
1 Ja, 2 Nein, 3 Ja, 4 Ja, 5 Nein, 6 Ja, 7 Nein, 8 Ja, 9 Nein, 10 Nein

1b Was kann man klicken? (Reading)
Students read the sentences and say where you should click on the web page to find more information.

Answers
1 Fußball-Camp, 2 Wanderungen, 3 Minigolf, 4 Mountainbike, 5 Bustouristik/Auto mieten, 6 Freizeitbad

2 Kannst du eine Internetseite auf Deutsch für eine Stadt oder ein Dorf in Großbritannien entwerfen? (Siehe oben „Aktivitäten in Annweiler".) (Writing)
Students write their own web page for somewhere they know in Britain, using the language on the page as support. They then write sentences describing what you can do there.

B Unterhaltung (p. 167)

1a Was kannst du empfehlen? Schreib *Stomp*, *Internetcafé* oder *Stadtbad*. (Reading)
For each sentence, students choose the most suitable place from the three listed above.

Answers
1 Internetcafé, 2 Stadtbad, 3 Internetcafé, 4 Internetcafé, 5 Stomp

1b Ist das offen oder geschlossen? (Reading)
Students read the sentences and then say whether the places will be open or closed.

Answers
1 geschlossen, 2 offen, 3 geschlossen, 4 geschlossen

1c Wo waren sie? Im Stadtbad? Bei „Stomp"? Im Internetcafé? (Reading)
Students read the comments and say where the people were.

Answers
1 bei „Stomp", 2 im Stadtbad, 3 im Internetcafé, 4 bei „Stomp"

2 Schreib den Text ab und füll die Lücken aus. (Writing)
Students write out the text, completing the gaps with the words below.

Answers
zwei, Amerika, Freibad, schwimmen, fantastisch, nachmittags, geschlossen, Theater, Musik

Chapter 4
A Jugendgästehäuser in Berlin (p. 168)

This page is best used after pp. 56–57 of the Student's Book.

1a Du möchtest Ferien in Berlin machen. Wo kannst du billig wohnen? Schreib *Das stimmt* oder *Das stimmt nicht*. (Reading)
Students read the sentences and say whether they are correct or not.

Answers
1 Das stimmt, 2 Das stimmt nicht, 3 Das stimmt, 4 Das stimmt nicht, 5 Das stimmt nicht

1b Was für eine Nummer ist das? Schreib *eine Adresse*, *eine Telefonnummer* oder *eine Busnummer*. (Reading)
Students read the number and then say whether the number applies to an address, a telephone number or a bus number.

Answers
1 eine Telefonnumer (261 10 27), 2 Eine Telefonnummer (312 94 10), 3 eine Busnummer (129), 4 eine Adresse (24), 5 eine Telefonnumer (803 20 34)

2 Schreib den Text ab und füll die Lücken aus. (Reading)
Students write out the text completing the gaps.

Answers
Danke, E-Mail, Platz, Zentrum, Nummer, drei

B Rundreisen (p. 169)

This page is best used after pp. 154–155 of the Student's Book.

1a Wähle die richtige Antwort. (Reading)
Students choose the correct answer from the two alternatives.

Answers
1 im Süden, 2 neun Tage, 3 in München, 4 mit dem Bus, 5 in Stuttgart, 6 alte

1b Was kann man da sehen? Schreib Notizen. (Reading)
Students note what they could see in each of the places listed.

Answers
1 den Hafen, 2 den Dom, 3 die Altstadt, 4 den Zug, 5 die Residenz, 6 die Burg

2 Du arbeitest für eine Reisegesellschaft in Großbritannien. Mach eine Broschüre für eine Ferienreise für deutsche Touristen. (Writing)
Students write a similar brochure for a tour in Britain and write a few sentences about it using the language in the text and in Activity 1.

Chapter 5
A Was gibt es in Deutschland zu sehen? (p. 170)

This page is best used after pp. 64–65 of the Student's Book.

1a Welches Foto ist das? (Reading)
Students name the places pictured in each photo.

Answers
1 Dresden, 2 die Alpen, 3 Köln, 4 Neuschwanstein, 5 Koblenz, 6 Tannenbäume, 7 Hamburg

1b Wo ist das? Schreib *richtig* oder *falsch*. (Reading)
Students say whether each sentence is true or false.

Answers
1 richtig, 2 falsch, 3 falsch, 4 richtig, 5 richtig, 6 falsch

2 Was gibt es zu sehen? Schreib den Text ab und füll die Lücken aus. (Writing)
Students write out the text, completing the gaps.

Answers
Hamburg, Schiffe, Berge, Alpen, Koblenz, Fluss, Köln, Dom, Schwarzwald, Wälder

B Was gibt es in Berlin zu sehen? (p. 171)

This page is best used after pp. 66–67 of the Student's Book.

1a London und Berlin – Partner? Kannst du "Partner-Sehenswürdigkeiten" in Berlin finden? (Reading)
Students list the equivalent German place for the English places listed.

Answers
1 d, 2 j, 3 h, 4 a, 5 j, 6 b, 7 f, 8 e

1b Wie heißt das in Berlin? (Reading)
Students name the place to match each sentence.

Answers
1 das Schauspiel, 2 das Olympiastadion, 3 Unten den Linden, 4 der Berliner Dom, 5 die Siegesäule

1c Wie alt? Wie hoch? (Reading)
Students read the numbers and say to which place each refers.

Answers
1 das Berliner Tor, 2 das Olympiastadion, 3 das Reichstagsgebäude, 4 der Fernsehturm, 5 die Siegesäule

2 Hiptarade für deutsche Touristen. Schreib eine Liste von fünf Sehenswürdigkeiten in einer Großstadt in Großbritannien (aber nicht in London!). (Writing)
Students write a Hitparade of sites for German tourists and try to write something about each one.

Chapter 6
A Produkte (p. 172)
This page is best used after pp. 80–81 of the Student's Book.

1a Du möchtest etwas kaufen. Welche Kategorie musst du klicken? (Reading)
Students say which categorie or food they should click on to buy each of the items in the text.

Answers
Karamelgebäck = Kekse; Marsriegel = Schokolade; Wrigleys = Kaugummi; Pringles = Chips; Bärchen = Bonbons; Walnusskerne = Nüsse; Pulmoll Husten = Pastillen

1b Welches Produkt ist das? (Reading)
Students say which item matches each of the prices.

Answers
1 Pringles, 2 Bärchen, 3 Pulmoll Husten, 4 Walnusskerne, 5 Marsriegel, 6 Karamelgebäck

2 Lies die Produktkategorien. Was isst du gern? Was isst dein Freund / deine Freundin gern? (Reading)
Students complete the sentences for themselves and for a friend.

3 Schreib eine Liste von SECHS britischen Produkten. Hilf deutschen Touristen – beschreib die Produkte! (Writing)
Students write a list of six British products and say something about each one.

B Sonderangebote im Kauhof! (p. 173)
This page is best used after pp. 80–81 of the Student's Book.

1a Lies die Sonderangebote. Was passt zusammen? (Reading)
Students match the pictures and the items.

Answers
1 d, 2 e, 3 f, 4 a, 5 i, 6 c, 7 h, 8 b, 9 g

1b Sonja hat eine lange Weihnachtsliste. Was kannst du empfehlen? (Reading)
Students read the sentences and choose an item for each person.

Answers
1 a, 2 e, 3 d, 4 c, 5 i, 6 f, 7 b, 8 g

2 Was hat Dirk gekauft? (Reading)
Students read the prices and say which item goes with each one.

Answers
1 Schulbuch, 2 Bauern-Chrysanthemen, 3 Kinder-Moonboots, 4 Kerze im Glas

3 Du hast 40 Euro. Wie viele Geschenke kaufst du? Was kaufst du? (Writing)
Students say what they would buy from the list with 40 euros.

Chapter 7
A Möchtest du ins Kino gehen? (p. 174)
These pages are best used after pp. 98–99 of the Student's Book.

1a Woher kommt der Film? (Reading)
Students name the film from the sentences.

Answers
1 Taxi, Taxi, 2 Nur noch 60 Sekunden, 3 Im Juli, 4 Hennen Rennen

1b Geht das? Schreib *Ja* oder *Nein*. (Reading)
Students say whether each of the people in the sentences is able to watch the films listed.

Answers
1 Nein, 2 Ja, 3 Ja, 4 Nein

1c Welcher Film ist das? (Reading)
Students name the film from the sentences.

Answers
1 Hennen Rennen, 2 Im Juli, 3 Nur noch 60 Sekunden, 4 Taxi, Taxi

2 Was ist dein Lieblingsfilm? Schreib einen Bericht. (Writing)
Students write about their favourite film using the gapped text.

B Freizeit in Deutschland
(p. 175)

This page is best used after pp. 108-109 of the Student's Book.

1a In welcher Stadt findet das statt? (Reading)
Students name the town for each sentence.

Answers
1 in Nürnberg, 2 in München, 3 in Hamburg, 4 in Osnabrück

1b Was würdest du empfehlen? (Reading)
Students name the event for each sentence.

Answers
1 Musical – Cats, 2 FC Bayern München, 3 Altstadtfest, 4 OSNArena

1c Wie lange dauert das? (Reading)
Students name the event for each length of time.

Answers
1 12 Tage, 2 OSNArena, 3 Musical – Cats, 4 FC Bayern München

1d Was findet da statt? (Reading)
Students name the event for each place.

Answers
1 das Fußballspiel, 2 Cats, 3 Altstadtfest, 4 OSNArena

2 Was möchtest du in Deutschland sehen? Wähle ZWEI aus: Altstadtfest, OSNArena, FC. (Writing)
Students write about two things they would like to see in Germany.

Chapter 8
A Rezepte der Woche (p. 176)

This page is best used after pp. 108–109 of the Student's Book.

1a Wie viel? Was passt zusammen? (Reading)
Students match the quantity and the item.

Answers
1 e, 2 f, 3 d, 4 b, 5 c, 6 g, 7 a

1b Richtig oder falsch? (Reading)
Students say whether each sentence is true or false.

Answers
1 falsch, 2 richtig, 3 falsch, 4 richtig, 5 falsch

2a Trudi beschreibt, wie sie Kartoffelrösti macht. Füll die Lücken aus. (Writing)
Students complete the instructions with the missing words.

Answers
1 Kartoffeln, 2 Mischung, 3 heiß, 4 alles, 5 die, 6 Öl

2b Jetzt schreib die Sätze in der richtigen Reihenfolge auf. (Writing)
Students write out the completed sentences from 2a in the correct order.

Answers
Zuerst schäle ich die Kartoffeln. Dann reibe ich die Kartoffeln. Ich mische alles zusammen. Ich erhitze das Öl. Dann brate ich die Mischung. Und ich serviere das heiß.

B Silvesterabend (p. 177)

This page is best used after pp. 116–117 of the Student's Book.

1a Lies den Text. Wann haben sie das gemacht? (Reading)
Students read the text and match the two parts of each sentence.

Answers
1 d, 2 c, 3 e, 4 a, 5 b

1b Richtig oder falsch? (Reading)
Students say whether each sentence is true or false.

Answers
1 falsch, 2 richtig, 3 falsch, 4 falsch, 5 falsch, 6 richtig

2a Was hast Thomas am Silvesterabend gemacht? Füll die Lücken aus. (Writing)
Students write out the text, completing the gaps with the words given.

Answers
Abendessen, Käse-Fondue, Weißwein, zehn, sind, Marktplatz, zwölf, "Frohes Neues Jahr", haben, bis, zwei

2b Und was hast du gemacht? Schreib ein paar Sätze. (Writing)
Students write a few sentences about what they did, using the text in 2a as a model.

Chapter 9
A Jobanzeigen (p. 178)

This page is best used after pp. 126–127 of the Student's Book.

1a Was kannst du empfehlen? (Reading)
Students choose jobs to suit each person.

Answers
Maria: a, b, d Stefan: c, e, f

1b Wer spricht? (Reading)
Students say who is speaking in each sentence.

Answers
1 b, 2 e, 3 d, 4 a, 5 f, 6 c

1c An welchem Tag? (Reading)
Students say which job matches each sentence.

Answers
1 d, 2 b, 3 f, 4 c, 5 e, 6 a

2a Was möchtest DU machen? (Writing)
Students say which of the jobs they would like to do and write a few details.

2b Und was möchtest du nicht machen? (Writing)
Students say which of the jobs they would not like to do and write a few details.

B Österreich (p. 179)

This page is best used after pp. 130–131 of the Student's Book.

1a Wo war Sven und wann? (Reading)
Students match the times and the places.

Answers
1 d, 2 g, 3 b, 4 f, 5 a, 6 c, 7 e

1b Schreib *Ja* oder *Nein*. (Reading)
Students read the sentences and write yes or no for each.

Answers
1 Ja, 2 Nein, 3 Nein, 4 Nein, 5 Ja, 6 Nein, 7 Ja

Tip box
Advice to students to use their knowledge of the German school system to help them fill in the text.

2a Was macht Sven normalerweise zu Hause in Österreich? Schreib den Text ins Heft ein und füll die Lücken aus. (Writing)
Students write out the text, completing the gaps.

2b Hast du ein Betriebspraktikum gemacht? Wo warst du und wann? Mach eine Tabelle. (Writing)
Students write out a grid detailing their own work experience.

Chapter 10
A Teenager (p. 180)

This page is best used after pp. 140–141 of the Student's Book.

1a Aber sie haben auch Probleme! Wer ist das? (Reading)
Students name the person for each sentence.

Answers
1 Stefan, 2 Maria, 3 Nicole, 4 Jörg, 5 Martin

1b Faule Ausreden! Wer sagt das? (Reading)
Students name the person for each sentence.

Answers
1 Maria, 2 Martin, 3 Stefan, 4 Jörg, 5 Nicole

2 Schreib Sätze für diese junge Leute. Ersetze den Text oben. (Writing)

Students write out sentences for the pictures given using those in the text above as support.

Answers

1 Ich rauche vier Zigaretten pro Tag. 2 Ich esse jeden Tag einen Hamburger. 3 Ich spiele jeden Abend von 20 Uhr bis 1.00 morgens am Computer. 4 Ich sehe um 18.00 bis 23.00 Uhr fern. 5 Ich trinke am Samstag und Sonntag viel Bier.

B Bist du umweltfreundlich?

(p. 181)

This page is best used after pp. 142–143 of the Student's Book.

1a Warum? Was passt zusammen? (Reading)

Students match each of the sentences to one of the statements in the text.

Answers

1 d, 2 f, 3 g, 4 c, 5 b, 6 a

1b Was schlagen die Leute vor? (Reading)

Students match each of the sentences to one of the statements in the text.

Answers

1 g, 2 f, 3 a, 4 b, 5 e

2a Was kannst du machen? Schreib DREI Sätze. (Writing)

Students write three sentences about what they can do for the environment.

2b Und was ist unpraktisch? Was kannst du nicht machen? Schreib DREI Sätze. (Writing)

Students write three sentences about what they cannot do.

Solutions to *Grammatik* exercises
(Student's Book pp. 182–195)

1. **1** Der, **2** Die, **3** Der, **4** Der, **5** Das
2. **1** Ein, **2** Eine, **3** Ein, **4** Ein, **5** Ein
3. **1** die, **2** das, **3** den, **4** die, **5** die
4. **1** eine, **2** ein, **3** eine, **4** eine, **5** einen
5. **1** neue, **2** alte, **3** grünen, **4** schwarze, **5** rote
6. **1** alter, **2** kleines, **3** englischer, **4** junges, **5** deutsche
7. **1** meine, **2** Meine, **3** mein, **4** Mein, **5** meine, **6** Mein
8. **1** Er, **2** Es, **3** Sie, **4** Er, **5** Sie, **6** Es
9. **1** gehen, **2** finden, **3** trinken, **4** komme, **5** liegt, **6** Schwimmen, **7** Gehst, **8** singt, **9** Kommt, **10** macht
10. **1** Wir steigen am Hauptbahnhof aus. **2** Der Zug fährt um 9 Uhr ab. **3** Wir stehen sehr früh auf. **4** Er sieht jeden Abend fern. **5** Der Film fängt um 18 Uhr an. **6** Ich ziehe einen Pulli an.
11. **1** Ich will/muss heute Abend fernsehen. **2** Ich will/muss meine Hausaufgaben machen. **3** Ich will/muss Radio hören. **4** Ich will/muss in die Disco gehen. **5** Ich will/muss zu Hause bleiben. **6** Ich will/muss Tischtennis spielen.
12. **1** Ich muss in die Stadt gehen. **2** Wir wollen zu Hause bleiben. **3** Du musst deine Hausaufgaben machen. **4** Ich kann nicht ins Kino gehen. **5** Sie dürfen hier nicht rauchen. **6** Sie möchte eine Cola trinken. **7** Er will Tennis spielen. **8** Ihr könnt morgen zu mir kommen. **9** Wir dürfen unsere Hefte nicht vergessen. **10** Möchtest du ein neues T-Shirt kaufen?
13. **1** Ich mache heute Abend meine Hausaufgaben. **2** Ich gehe nächste Woche ins Theater. **3** Wir fahren nächstes Jahr nach Amerika. **4** Meine Freundin kommt nächsten Monat zu Besuch. **5** Er bleibt in den Sommerferien in Köln. **6** Sie feiert Ende Mai ihren Geburtstag.
14. **1** gelesen, **2** gegessen, **3** gesehen **4** gekauft, **5** gespielt
15. **1** Ich habe eine Cola getrunken. **2** Ihr habt eure Hausaufgaben gemacht. **3** Sie hat eine neues Computerspiel gekauft. **4** Wir haben Fußball gespielt. **5** Er hat immer Radio gehört. **6** Du hast die Zeitung gelesen. **7** Ich habe bis 11 Uhr geschlafen. **8** Sie haben ihre Mutter gesehen. **9** Wir haben keinen Kuchen gegessen. **10** Hast du eine Postkarte geschrieben?
16. **1** Ich bin, **2** Ich bin, **3** Ich habe, **4** Ich bin, **5** Ich bin, **6** Ich habe
17. **1** Ich bin ins Kino gegangen. **2** Wann ist er nach Hause gekommen? **3** Sie sind mit dem Zug nach London gefahren. **4** Sie sind jeden Tag im See geschwommen. **5** Wir sind nach Rom geflogen. **6** Ich bin den ganzen Tag im Bett geblieben. **7** Du bist schnell zum Supermarkt gelaufen. **8** Mein Hund ist gestorben. **9** Bist du zur Schule gegangen? **10** Der Bus ist vom Bahnhof abgefahren.
18. **1** das, **2** den, **3** die, **4** das, **5** die
19. **1** dem, **2** der, **3** dem, **4** dem, **5** dem
20. **1** dem, **2** den, **3** dem, **4** die, **5** den
21. **1** Spielst du gut Tennis? **2** Bleibt dein Freund zu Hause? **3** Kommt das Mädchen aus Griechenland? **4** Läuft sein Bruder gern Ski? **5** Gehen sie auf die Party? **6** Trinkt er Kaffee ohne Milch?
22. **1** Ich mache heute Abend meine Hausaufgaben. **2** Sie geht jeden Tag ins Schwimmbad. **3** Er arbeitet samstags in einer Drogerie. **4** Sie spielen am Sonntag gegen Stuttgart. **5** Wir haben vor drei Wochen einen neuen Wagen gekauft.
23. **1** Heute Abend mache ich meine Hausaufgaben. **2** Jeden Tag geht sie ins Schwimmbad. **3** Samstags arbeitet er in einer Drogerie. **4** Am Sonntag spielen sie gegen Stuttgart. **5** Vor drei Wochen haben wir einen neuen Wagen gekauft.
24. **1** Wir gehen am Freitag zusammen ins Theater. **2** Sie wohnt seit drei Jahren mit ihrer Schwester in Dortmund. **3** Ich fahre jeden Tag mit der Bahn zur Schule. **4** Er bleibt bis November bei seiner Tante in Hamburg.
25. **1** Ich bin immer sehr müde, weil ich spät ins Bett gehe. **2** Sie geht gern zur Schule, weil der Unterricht immer interessant ist. **3** Er hört gern Musik, wenn er allein ist. **4** Ich esse gern Pizza, wenn ich in die Stadt gehe. **5** Jürgen hat Kopfschmerzen, weil er zu viel Bier getrunken hat.

Photocopiable grids for use with Logo! 4 Grün Student's Book

Kapitel 1
Page 8, 2a

Name:
Wohnort:
Geschwister:

Name:
Wohnort:
Geschwister:

Kapitel 2
Page 21, 3a

	Mathe	Biologie	Deutsch	Französisch	Englisch
Felix					
Fatima					

Kapitel 3
Page 42, 1b

	Sendung	Typ	Uhrzeit
Gabi			
Hans			
Mutti			
Vati			

Kapitel 6
Page 82, 2

	Kleidungsstück	Größe	Farbe	Preis
1				
2				
3				
4				

Kapitel 6
Page 84, 1b

	Name	Wie viel Geld?	Kauft
1	Ines	€	
2	Roland	€ ..	
3	Anni	€ ..	
4	Sven	€ ..	
5	Paul	€ ..	

Kapitel 8
Page 109, 4a

Englandaustausch: Anmeldeformular

Name: _____ Klasse: _____

Was isst du gern? _____

Was isst du nicht gern? _____

Was trinkst du gern? _____

Was trinkst du nicht gern? _____